The International
GUIDE TO
FLY-TYING
MATERIALS

(and where to buy them)

Also published by Merlin Unwin Books
58 Broad Street, Ludlow,
Shropshire SY8 1DA, U.K.
Direct mail orders: 01584 877456

TROUT & SALMON FLIES OF IRELAND
Peter O'Reilly £20 Hb

TROUT & SALMON FLIES OF WALES
Moc Morgan £20 Hb

TROUT & SALMON RIVERS OF IRELAND
an angler's guide, 3rd edition
Peter O'Reilly £16.95 Hb

THE DRY FLY
Progress since Halford
Conrad Voss Bark £20 Hb

CONFESSIONS OF A SHOOTING, FISHING MAN
Lawrence Catlow £17.99 Hb

THE PURSUIT OF WILD TROUT
Mike Weaver £16.95 Hb

A HISTORY OF FLYFISHING
Conrad Voss Bark £25 Hb/£12.95 Pb

OLIVER EDWARDS' FLYTYERS MASTERCLASS
a step-by-step guide to tying 20 essential fly patterns
Oliver Edwards £19.99 Hb (or spiral-bound, direct mail only)

AN ANGLER FOR ALL SEASONS
the best of H.T.Sheringham £16.95 Hb

THE ONE THAT GOT AWAY
tales of days when fish triumphed over anglers
Jeremy Paxman, George Melly, David Steel, et al £16.95 Hb

THE HABIT OF RIVERS
reflections on trout streams and flyfishing
Ted Leeson £16.95 Hb

A PASSION FOR ANGLING
the companion to the TV series
Chris Yates, Bob James, Hugh Miles £16.99 Hb

A FAR FROM COMPLEAT ANGLER
Tom Fort £16.99 Hb

CHALKSTREAM CHRONICLE
living out the flyfisher's fantasy
Neil Patterson £17.99 Hb

THE RIVER WITHIN
a life of fly fishing
W. B. Currie £16.95 Hb

THE SECRET CARP
Chris Yates £9.95 Pb

The International
GUIDE TO
FLY-TYING
MATERIALS

(and where to buy them)

Barry Ord Clarke
& Robert Spaight

Photographs by Barry Ord Clarke

MERLIN UNWIN BOOKS

First published in Great Britain by Merlin Unwin Books, 1996
ISBN 1873674418X

Published by
Merlin Unwin Books
58 Broad Street, Ludlow
Shropshire SY8 1GQ
U.K.

Tel: 01584 877456 Fax: 01584 877457

British Library Cataloguing-in-Publication Data:
A catalogue record of this book is available from the British Library.

Designed and typeset in Times by Merlin Unwin Books
Printed in Great Britain by Bath Press.

Contents

Introduction   7

NATURAL MATERIALS   9

Natural Materials & CITES   9
Feathers   11
Hairs & Furs   27
Deer Hair   37
Hackles   43

DUBBINGS   51

MANMADE MATERIALS   67

Backs   68
Beads, Bubbles & Bullets   69
Bodies   70
Body Wrappings   71
Chenilles   76
Eggs   78
Eyes   78
Fibres   81
Foams   83
Legs   85
Optics   86
Pipings   89
Spooled Materials   91
Tails   91

Tubings 92

Wings 93

THREADS, TINSELS & FLOSSES 103

CEMENTS, EPOXIES & VARNISHES 115

DYES, PAINTS & PENS 120

TOOLS 123

VICES 129

ACCESSORIES 133

HOOKS 137

Directory of Listed Suppliers 149

Directory of Other Retail Suppliers 156

Behind-the-Scenes companies 164

List of Hookmakers 168

Magazines 173

Select Bibliography 175

Acknowledgements 177

Index 179

Introduction

IT IS 500 YEARS since the publication of *The Treatyse of Fysshynge with an Angle*, the book which contained the first reference in written English to fishing flies and the materials used to make them. Its author, Dame Juliana Berners, had she dropped in on, for example, the Fly Fair in Holland (May 1996), would have been truly amazed at what the modern flydresser has to choose from. The vast majority of materials would have been totally unknown to her - would have been unheard of even by our grandfathers. That alone is a warning to anyone who tries to produce a guide on what is available at any fixed point in time in flydressing history. Any attempt must be in the nature of a momentary snapshot.

This book was born out of the authors' own frustrations. So often the home tyer is confronted by a pattern in a magazine that calls for materials not in one's possession. Growing internationalism has brought to light many more materials from all parts of the globe, but for the tyer at the desk these are often not readily obtainable. A guide should 'lead, conduct, or direct' and the fruits of the authors' own wanderings have been distilled into this volume in the hope that others will be able to use the book to learn about and acquire international materials without the frustration of not knowing where to turn. Our hope is that this will be a 'working' reference book, by the tyer's side at the bench.

By the very nature of the explosion in flytying materials worldwide, the contents of this guide book are not exhaustive, but we have tried to select the best of what is traditional and what is new and important. We believe the contents are a fairly representative picture of the modern scene.

With the growth of saltwater flyfishing, a new frontier is opening up, offering new challenges to the tyer and new materials to experiment with. The philosophy that 'everything is tyable until proved otherwise' continues to remain true!

The present situation concerning materials is quite complex in some areas. For example, some man-made materials appear under different marketing names even though they may be identical or similar. The situation is rather like generic drugs in the pharmaceutical industry. Furthermore, while some manufacturers supply direct to the consumer, others do not; some suppliers have mail order catalogues, while others have no catalogue but will supply by mail on request. We have therefore included a Directory of 'Behind the Scenes' companies (see page 164), as well as the Directory of Suppliers (see page 149), so that the searching tyer can go back to 'home base' to be directed to the retail supplier nearest to him, should this be necessary when he cannot find his favourite 'brand name'. As the book is representative and not exhaustive, some suppliers' names familiar to people on their home patch are sure to be missing.

It is our intention to periodically update the contents of this book and we would therefore welcome further suggestions as to the inclusion of materials, sources and suppliers. It is fair to assume that if a supplier carries a particular manufacturer's product (which is highlighted in a particular entry) then that supplier should have ready access to other products produced by that same manufacturer - even if they are not specifically listed in the text.

Our primary purpose has been simply to help tyers to find suppliers. However, we hope that the global scope of this book may also help the travelling angler and tyer to find local supplies of materials when abroad. To this end, we have included an appendix of Magazines (page 173) which, of course, always carry many advertisements of local suppliers. The Directory of Other Retail Suppliers (see page 156) around the world - those not mentioned in the main text - has been included to supplement the geographical scope. Throughout the book we have endeavoured to deal alphabetically with items in each section.

Many, many other flytying materials exist than are recorded in this book but, if every one of them was written down, the result would be more, not less, confusing. So here is our current international picture, fixed for a moment in time. May your flies be bright and your hackles tight as you soldier on, as we have done, in pursuit of that elusive material you need to get your fly *just right*.

BARRY ORD CLARKE

ROBERT SPAIGHT

23 July 1996

Natural Materials

INDIVIDUAL COUNTRIES have varying laws and views about what are threatened species in their own neck of the woods. There are also supra-national agreements such as within the European Union. Tyers must, therefore, be aware of their own country's laws and those of any country they may be visiting. Ignorance will be no defence to having 'a find' removed at a point of emigration or immigration, and the consequences for you may be considerably more serious than confiscation.

CITES

In addition to the local laws which prevail in all countries, there exists the United Nations Convention on International Trade in Endangered Species (CITES) which came into force in 1975 and forbids unlicensed trade in more than 34,000 animals, birds and plants. One hundred and thirty two countries have signed up to CITES, and there is also a Convention on Migratory Species. Trade is legitimate only if permits are issued. These may be issued, for example, if an animal was bred and died in captivity, or if a specimen was antique. However, for an animal listed under Appendix One of CITES all movement is forbidden except between scientific institutions.

Thus, the tyer should be cautious about purchases of what appear to be rare or exotic fauna. However, such materials are available under the proper permits and, if in doubt, the tyer should ask to see the suppliers' permit.

Today, in any event, there are many adequate substitutes on offer, whether natural or man-made, and the development of the world of dyes and waterproof pens means that material of quite humble origin can be made to take on a very much more glamorous look. These substitutes are also often significantly cheaper than the original.

The Worldwide Fund for Nature has a monitoring arm for CITES called Traffic. The sentence of imprisonment for two years received by Dutchman Nicolaas Peters at Chester Crown Court in England in 1996 stands as a salutory warning to those seeking to evade the regulations and laws.

The tyer should always consider the five 'C's applicable to the business of buying flytying materials: Caution, Certificate, Conscience, Conservation, Cost.

RABIES AND ROADKILLS

Those fortunate enough to live in countries free of rabies really never consider the horror of this virus. However, with international travel on the increase, caution should be exercised even if the temptation to pick up a roadkill is overwhelming.

The rabies virus lives in saliva and nerve and brain tissue, and is usually transmitted by a bite. However, the virus can live on even after the death of the animal. It survives only a few hours in warm weather, but this period may run into days. If frozen, it can survive for two weeks and is able to become active again when the animal is thawed out.

For those determined to collect from roadkills, a pair of rubber gloves should be part of the kit at all times. Clorox kills the virus on contact, so drench the animal in this before setting about removing its skin. If it has gone into the freezer, it should be left untouched for at least a month.

Apart from the above general observations, tyers wanting to pick up roadkills in areas where rabies is endemic would be well advised to take advice from the local veterinary practitioner before even contemplating collecting materials.

Feathers

IN CASES where a species is protected or under threat the feathers offered by dealers are usually commercially accepted substitutes for the original feather. If you are not able to personally inspect the product before purchase you will need to look carefully at what is being offered in a catalogue. Cost is often a clue as to whether the feather is a legitimate substitute or not and you are reminded that it is strictly illegal in most countries to buy the feathers of birds which are on the endangered list (see Cites, page 9).

BLACKBIRD

Generally used for the wings of up-winged flies, such as Greenwell's Glory (hen), Iron Blue (cock). The usual substitute is natural or dyed starling.

AUS Alpine; *JAP* Sawada; *UK* Watercraft, Slater, Niche, Saville, Walker, McHardy; *US* E.A.T.

BUSTARD

Great

The British population of the great bustard was wiped out by indiscriminate shooting in the last century. 'Speckled' bustard wing quill slips are specified in several classic salmon fly patterns (eg. Gordon, Silver Grey). Substitutes commonly used include speckled wing quills from the oak turkey and saddle feathers from the peahen. The natural colour ranges from cinnamon to dark brown and almost black.

JAP Sawada; *NL* Kelson; *UK* Slater, Lathkill.

Florican

Florican wing quill slips are specified in many traditional mixed wing Atlantic salmon flies. An acceptable substitute is silver pheasant tail dyed tan, or the long speckled wing quills from a peacock. The natural colour of Florican wing quill is a sandy brown, barred with darker brown. Genuine Florican can be obtained, from time to time, in very limited amounts from some sources.

JAP Sawada; *UK* Saville, Slater, Lathkill; *US* E.A.T, Hunter.

CAPERCAILLIE

Regarded by some in the 19th century as the best feather for the March Brown when taken from the wing of a hen bird. Also used for Black Alders.

JAP Sawada; *US* Marriott.

CHATTERER, BLUE

Substitutes are usually offered for this feather. Kingfisher is a favoured one. At one time, Blue Chatterer was a substitute for Kingfisher.

JAP Sawada; *UK* Slater; *US* Hunter, Marriott, MM.

CHICKABOU

A genetic chicken marabou soft hackle substitute, which is similar to but shorter and finer than the familiar turkey marabou substitute. Available in dyed colours over both white and grizzle. The latter produces an attractive banding effect that lends itself to imitative fry patterns (eg. perch fry). The fluffy feathers come from the underparts of the chicken between the thighs and have many applications for mobile nymph and streamer patterns. Sold as single 'capes' that include the soft hackles from the bird's flanks (Matuka hackles) along with the 'marabou' type fluffy plumage. To promote the material, the packages contain a colour chart and full tying instructions for several fly patterns developed by

LEFT: Common Pheasant: back patch (top left), two tail sections (top right) and Ring-neck skin (below)

Henry Hoffman.

US Hunter, Whitetail.

CONDOR

Condors (several species of giant New World vulture) number amongst the world's most endangered birds. The closest substitutes are primary wing quills from peacocks or geese, which can be stripped to obtain the desired effect for the bodies of such flies as Ginger Quill. If using stripped peacock herl, be sure to select your herl from just under the eye of the peacock tail feather, the quills here are always much stronger, and are easily stripped if soaked in household bleach and then washed. Dyed herl can be stripped using a pencil eraser.

Retailers supply a substitute in a variety of dyed colours.

JAP Sawada; *UK* Sportfish, Saville, Niche, Walker, Slater, Rooksbury, McHardy, Watercraft

COOT

The wing quills from the coot can be used to wing the blue-winged olive. It can also be used as a substitute for Golden Plover, and Moorhen.

UK Sportfish, Slater, Lathkill, McHardy, Watercraft; *US* E.A.T., Fly & Field, Blue Ribbon

COQ DE LEON

These are spade hackles harvested from the roosters of rare breeds of domestic fowl, that originate from the Leon region of Northern Spain. The feathers have remarkable colourations and, in the traditional Spanish patterns in which they are used, are not wound onto the hook as normal. Instead, bunches of the fibres are bound on to the hook, then splayed with the tying thread to obtain the radial hackle effect. The plumage also makes very realistic speckled caddis wings. The feathers are not easy to obtain, and recent disease in the breeds has further exacerbated the problem. Local Spanish tackle shops are the best place to look for these. In their finest form the feathers have a stiffness and glasslike translucency and come from birds bred at high altitude on chalky soil. Quality is also affected by the time at which they are harvested from the birds. The feathers come in two types. Indio (grey) are solid and plain coloured, Pardo (brown) are mottled. The traditional names given to the feathers are:

INDIO: negrisco (black), palometas (white), rubion (natural red), palteado (silver grey), acerade (ash grey), avellandado (brownish grey), perla (pearl grey), claro (light grey), oscura (dark grey).

PARDO: flor de Escoba (dark background with reddish brown spots), sarrioso (light brown background with pale russet brown flecks), corzuna (fallow deer background with pale russet brown flecks), aconchado (conch shell), langareto (mottled in distinct yellow lines), encendido (flushed with red), medio (medium shaded and stippled), oscura (dark shade), crudo (immature, indistinct mottling).

CAN Howard's Hackle are now breeding these; *UK* Angling Pursuits; *US* Fly & Field, Kaufmann, MM.

CRANE

Very probably when this bird is named in early tying books the heron is meant. The crane has always been a very rare visitor to Britain. In Herefordshire the heron was called the 'crane'. Common crane feathers are large and cinnamon coloured - perfect for Dee strip wings. The shoulder feathers are naturally a deep jet black and some 2" in length. The flank hackles, ranging from black to very dark grey in colours denser than heron, have been described as 'spey hackle par excellence'. The crown of the common crane makes a lovely quill body of yellowish tan colour.

NL Nelson.

CROW

Carrion

The primaries of crows (and other large black corvids) are frequently used for the wing cases of beetle patterns and nymphs as well as for some wet fly patterns (Butcher, Watson's Fancy, Kingsmill). The natural colour is black, with iridescent blue or green sheen. Sold as paired wings, wing quills and tail feathers.

UK Sportfish, Saville, Sparton, Niche, Walker, Slater, Lathkill, McHardy, Watercraft; *US* E.A.T.; *JAP* Sawada.

Indian

Also known as Red Ruffed Fruit Crow. The prized feathers of this now protected bird, are no longer available. The classic Atlantic salmon fly dresser used the small orange-yellow, red-tipped breast feathers for tails, cheeks and veiling on some of the more exotic salmon flies. Many substitutes do not incorporate the yellow colouring. The small white neck feathers from the ring-necked pheasant can be dyed to an acceptable substitute.

GER Brinkhoff; *JAP* Sawada; *UK* Slater, Sportfish, Saville, Sparton, Slater, Lathkill, McHardy, Watercraft; *US* E.A.T., Hunter, Marriott, MM.

CUL DE CANARD (CDC)

These feathers come from the area surrounding the 'preen gland' on the rumps of ducks and geese. The earthily descriptive French name is now used almost universally. The individual feathers have a fluffy soft appearance, but the central spine has a degree of stiffness and even the barbs hold a shape - unlike marabou, by comparison. The outstanding feature of CDC is that the plumage is completely impregnated with natural waterproofing oils (secreted by the preen gland). This, combined with the structure of the feather, makes it very hydrophobic, to the extent that almost unsinkable dry flies can be made.

CDC has been popular in continental Europe for many years, but has gained a following in N. America only relatively recently. Most commonly used in the natural smoky grey shades or natural white. Dyed colours are available, but there is a view that the dying process reduces the natural waterproofing. Quality of these feathers as offered can be variable.

AUS Alpine; *GER* Brinkhoff; *JAP* Sawada; *NL* Kelson; *UK* Sportfish, Niche, Walker, Slater, Lathkill, Rooksbury, McHardy, Norris; *US* Orvis, Blue Ribbon, E.A.T., Kaufmann, Cabela, Gorilla, Hunter, Marriott, Hook & Hackle, MM; *INT* Orvis.

CUL DE CYGNE

A larger and therefore easier to work with feather than CDC - from the Swan.

NL Kelson.

DeLEON BLUE DUN TURKEY FEATHERS

Hard to find feathers that are highly regarded for realistic speckled caddis wings. These have lovely mottling and, being stiff and straight, make good tails.

US Marriott.

DOTTEREL

The feathers from the shoulder and back are a pale brown dun (coffee and milk colour with plenty of milk), with a fine rim of of yellow round the edge of the feather, so that every fibre is tipped with a yellow point. G.E.M.Skues regarded them as 'perhaps the mostly highly prized of all feathers of the fly dresser - the model of a honey dun'. Highly mobile in water they form the basis of patterns such as the Dotterel and Yellow and Dotterel and Orange. Substitutes are in use today, and the honey dun feather under a Starling's wing, the Golden Plover's shoulder and neck hackles, and the Curlew's shoulder hackle have been used over the years.

UK Slater.

DUCK

White

Wing quills (like goose and swan) are used - in the natural state - for the wings of such traditional patterns as Coachman and Parmachene Belle. They also dye readily for use in fancy wet flies and as substitute for unobtainable plumages (eg. ibis). Sold as paired wings or packs of matching quills. Generally widely available.

AUS Alpine; *UK* Saville, Walker, Slater, McHardy; *US* Gorilla, Hunter, Marriott, MM.

Casarca

Wing feathers are used for larger Butcher flies and small

salmon flies. The Flank feathers are a substitute for Lemon Wood Duck.

NL Kelson.

Gadwall

Now a more common species in North America, this medium sized duck is a somewhat drab coloured bird. However its flank has distinct bar marked feathers used for veilings and wings - a little like teal but darker.

US Hunter, Marriott, MM.

Lemon Wood

UK Watercraft, Saville, Slater, Angling Pursuits; *US* E.A.T., Cabela, Marriott, Hunter, Hook & Hackle.

Mallard

This duck provides the flytyer with a host of materials, used in many patterns. The blue speculum feathers are used for wings in the Butcher series of wet flies (those with the white tip for Heckham Peckam, McGinty, etc.), while the grey flight feathers are used in many of the larger traditional dry and wet flies requiring grey feather slip wings. The bronze (brown) barred shoulder plumage features in countless traditional wet and salmon flies (Mallard & Claret, Connemara Black, Thunder & Lightning, Blue Charm). The silver-grey, barred flank plumage is also used - both natural and dyed - for many wet and dry fly wings (Hornberg, Missionary, Mayflies). Mallard also provide many other feathers than can be used in fly dressing, though these - apart from 'cul de canard' - are not generally available commercially. Tyers who are wildfowlers themselves, or who are acquainted with shooters will be able to experiment with the entire plumage of this most useful duck.

Sold as paired wings; matched wing quills; matched blue speculum feathers; selected and sized bronze shoulder feathers. The grey flank feathers usually come in unsorted bulk packs.

Widely available from fly tying retailers.

GER Brinkhoff; *JAP* Sawada; *UK* Sportfish, Saville, Sparton, Niche, Walker, Slater, Lathkill, Rooksbury, McHardy, Norris, Watercraft; *US* E.A.T., Kaufmann, Cabela, Hunter, Marriott, Blue Ribbon, Montana Master; *INT* Orvis.

Mandarin

The pretty little oriental mandarin duck produces flank feathers that are very similar in coloration (both 'lemon' and black/white barred) to those of the Wood duck or Carolina (see below).

NL Kelson; *UK* McHardy.

Muscovey

UK Slater.

Pygmy

The buff coloured breast feathers are useful as eyes on streamers or cheeks of salmon flies.

NL Kelson.

Rouen

Breast feathers are used for winging floating mayflies.

UK Slater.

Teal (see page 24)

Tree

The breast feather is black with a brown tip, with others cinammon. The flank has a buff centre and cinammon edges and is used in Matuka-style flies.

NL Kelson.

Wood Duck or Carolina

Also known as the 'Summer Duck'. It is not cheap, but the barred 'lemon' plumage is used for the wings on some of the best known classic American dry flies. Wood duck also produces the distinctly marked flank feathers, with barred black and white tips, that are used for the veilings and wings of many Atlantic Salmon flies. Similar feathers are also obtained from the mandarin duck. The mottled breast feathers are also used for wings and shoulders in some dressings. The description 'wood duck' usually refers to the barred flank plumage. The term 'summer duck' is now rather dated. Quite a good substitute for 'lemon' wood duck can be achieved by skilful dyeing of mallard plumage taken from where the 'silver' flank feathers are just starting to shade into the 'bronze' shoulder plumage. Some substitutes offered for sale are less than successful.

AUS Alpine; *JAP* Sawada; *UK* Sportfish, Saville, Niche, Walker, Slater, Watercraft; *US* E.A.T., Cabela, Hunter, Marriott, MM; *INT* Orvis.

EMU

Much like Ostrich herl but the barbules are much longer and will make excellent thoraxes on stonefly nymphs or breathing gills on damselfly nymphs. Also has applications for minnow and streamer patterns. Usually available in black, natural tan/grey and olive.

NL Kelson; *US* Marriott, E.A.T; *UK* Anglian.

FLAMINGO

Light pink feathers with dark red tips.

JAP Sawada; *NL* Kelson.

Turkey biot quills, dyed in a range of colours.

GALLENA (see Guinea Fowl, page 16)

GOOSE

Shoulder feathers
From white domestic geese, these dye readily. Used extensively in traditional 'built wing' salmon flies, dyed goose is the accepted substitute for swan. The smaller shoulder feathers, dyed scarlet, are a good substitute for Ibis, used in wet fly tails (eg. Butcher, Alexandra, etc.). The larger primary and secondary wing quills are also used for salmon and wet fly wings and are stronger and rather easier to use than the equivalent plumage from ducks. Widely available and usually sold in matching pairs of wing quills, in most popular colours.

AUS Alpine; *JAP* Sawada; *UK* Sportfish, Saville, Sparton, Niche, Walker, Slater, Lathkill, Rooksbury, McHardy, Watercraft; *US* E.A.T., Kaufmann, Cabela, Gorilla, Hunter, Fly & Field, Marriott, Montana Master.

Biot
This is the name given to the short, stiff, blade-like barbs found on the leading edges of the major flight feathers of geese. Normally supplied in strips, removed from the quill, biot is used extensively for tails, wings, legs and antennae in many patterns (eg. dragonfly nymphs, stone fly nymphs, the Prince nymph, etc.). Often supplied in packs of mixed colour dyed strips. A useful tip for home dyeing is to bend the biot strip into a circle and staple the ends together, before immersing in the dye bath. This causes the individual barbs to flare out radially, allowing the dye to penetrate properly between them.
Widely available in many dyed colours.

AUS Alpine; *JAP* Sawada; *UK* Sportfish, Saville, Sparton, Niche, Walker, Rooksbury, McHardy, Watercraft; *US* E.A.T., Kaufmann, Cabela, Marriott, Whitetail; *INT* Orvis.

Canada
Canada geese have established themselves ferally throughout Britain to nuisance proportions. The fly fisher will often find moulted plumage on the banks of stillwaters in high summer. The brownish grey wing quills provide biot and herl for various drab nymph and dry fly patterns.

UK Slater.

Egyptian
Contains extremely large pale yellow-brown feathers, with black barrings - not unlike a very large lemon wood duck

UK Slater; *US* E.A.T.

Malaga
Flank feathers are very light brown with a darker bar.

NL Kelson

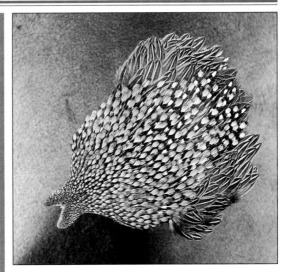

ABOVE: Jungle Cock cape

Maned
Similar to Silver Mallard, but much larger. Colours the same as Zebra Goose.

UK Saville.

Zebra
The broad barring make these feathers ideal for Perch fry, and the extra large feathers can be used for winging salmon flies. Colours: natural, red, orange, hot orange, yellow, teal blue, olive, brown claret, purple.

UK Saville.

GROUSE

Blue
Dorsal plumage is black and greenish tan with fine black tip markings.

US Blue Ribbon.

Red
The famous sporting bird of heather moorland, red grouse provide the speckled tail and wing quills used for the grouse winged series of wet flies (Grouse & Claret, etc.) and for various dark sedge (caddis) patterns. The body plumage provides dark speckled hackles for a number of traditional wet fly (spiders, eg. Poult Bloa) and nymph patterns. Few other feathers give such a good impression of larval insect legs. Usually supplied as paired wings or packets of tail feathers or body plumage.

AUS Alpine; *JAP* Sawada; *UK* Sportfish, Saville, Sparton, Niche, Walker, Slater, Lathkill, Rooksbury, McHardy, Norris, Watercraft; *US* E.A.T., Kaufmann, Hunter, Fly & Field, Blue Ribbon, Marriott, Hook & Hackle.

Ruffed
Plumage is black, cream, tan, green and brown. The distinctive fan-shaped tail has barring in alternating

bands of black, brown and buff. Used for soft hackled and wet flies, nymph legs and caddis wings.

US Blue Ribbon, Marriott, E.A.T.

Sage

Variegated black and grey plumage. Tails are black with tan markings and can be used for nymph and small dry fly bodies.

US Marriott.

Sharptail

Coloured cream, brown and white they are lighter than ruffed birds.

US E.A.T., Blue Ribbon, Marriott, MM.

GUINEA FOWL

Common (also known as Gallena)

Guinea fowl plumage is characteristically dark grey to black with white spots. It is used extensively in traditional salmon patterns (Dusty Miller, Jock Scott, Mar Lodge, Thunder & Lightning). Dyed blue guinea fowl is often given as a substitute for jay, while other dyed colours are becoming popular for Atlantic salmon and seatrout flies. Guinea fowl wing and tail quills are similarly marked with white spots and are also popular for winging smaller salmon and seatrout flies. Sold as packs of plumage, body skins, and paired wing quills.

AUS Alpine; JAP Sawada; UK Sportfish, Saville, Sparton, Niche, Walker, Slater, Lathkill, Rooksbury, McHardy, Norris, Watercraft
US E.A.T, Hunter, Marriott, MM.

Vulturine

This East African guinea fowl is the source of the strikingly striped plumage, used by Arthur Ransome for his famous Elver fly and described in his book *Mainly About Fishing*. The Elver feathers are long and form a mantle hanging down from the bird's neck. They have a well defined chalky white stripe along the centre stem. Outside this central stripe, the fibres are a dark grey, but are nevertheless quite translucent. The outer edges of the feather are fringed with an almost luminous cobalt blue. The bird also has intense cobalt blue plumage on its breast, which Ransome used for the collar hackle of the Elver. The purple-edged wing secondary feathers produce a really striking wing in a salmon or seatrout fly. The pad feathers from a grey jungle cock (*G. sonnerrati*) make acceptable substitutes for the Elver feather, if coloured with blue and black water proof markers.

JAP Sawada; *NL* Kelson; *UK* Saville, Slater; *US* E.A.T.

HEN (Domestic)

The wing quills of domestic poultry fowl are used widely in fly dressing. In particular the cinnamon brown primaries from certain varieties are used for winging the Cinnamon & Gold and various sedge (caddis) patterns.

Dyed duck is sometimes offered as a substitute, which some may find easier to use as the fibres stay 'married' rather better. Sold in paired wing quills.

JAP Sawada; *UK* Walker, Watercraft

HERON

The grey heron is now widely protected, though quite common in Britain. The major flight feathers provide smoky blue grey herl for various dry fly (eg. Kite's Imperial) and nymph patterns. The heron's long fibred body hackles were the characteristic component of the traditional 'Spey' and 'Dee' patterns, for which substitutes are now used (see: Blue Pheasant and Spey Hackle). A similar hackle effect can be obtained by bleaching goose shoulder feathers.

JAP Sawada; *UK* Slater, McHardy, Norris.

IBIS, SCARLET

Dyed duck or goose quills are now the accepted substitutes for plumage from this strictly protected bird.

JAP Sawada; *NL* Kelson (Flamingo feathers dyed in the correct colour as a substitute); *UK* Sportfish, Saville, Sparton, Niche, Walker, Slater, Norris, Watercraft.

JACKDAW

Smaller and not as stiff as crow, the wing quills are used in winging wet flies. The grey scalp of the jackdaw provides 'iron blue' hackles for a number of traditional trout and grayling spider patterns. Sold as paired wings and whole scalp.

JAP Sawada; *UK* Sportfish, Saville, Niche, Walker, Lathkill, McHardy, Watercraft; *US* E.A.T., Fly & Field, Blue Ribbon

JAY

The lesser wing coverts of the Eurasian jay (cf. N. American blue jay) provide the barred cobalt blue feathers used in many traditional trout, seatrout and salmon patterns of the British Isles (eg. Connemara Black, Invicta, Thunder & Lightning). The blue fibres are usually employed tied in as a beard hackle, but wings can be made from slips or the whole feathers (eg. matuka styles). Kingsmill Moore employed this feather as a soft head hackle in many of his Bumble patterns. Dyed blue guinea fowl is the usually accepted substitute for large sizes. Jay is usually sold as matched pairs of whole wings or in packets of the blue covert feathers.

JAP Sawada; *UK* Sportfish, Saville, Sparton, Niche, Walker, Slater, Lathkill, Rooksbury, McHardy, Norris, Watercraft; *US* E.A.T., Fly & Field, Blue Ribbon; *NL* Nelson.

JUNGLE COCK (Grey)

The cock bird of this wild chicken from India provides

the extraordinary 'enamelled' eye feathers (sometimes called nail feathers), that feature in the cheeks and wings of so many traditional salmon fly patterns.

The bird is now strictly protected and banned from importation into the UK and US, but feathers are available from domestically reared stock. Mostly used in salmon flies, the enamel 'nail' feathers are also found in several trout and seatrout patterns (eg. Dunkeld). Jungle cock which is specially reared for flytying commands a fierce price and £100 for a top grade cape cannot be such a distant prospect. Jungle cock is sold in various grades: in full and half capes and in packets of 10 feathers of matched size (small, medium or large). A professional pack of 200 feathers ordered to size can be obtained from Saville's.

Many substitutes have come onto the market over the years. Most involve painting a replica onto some other kind of feather, while another approach is to print a photographic reproduction of real jungle cock onto flexible plastic sheet, (which can then be cut out and tied in). Most substitutes fall far short of the genuine article and many discerning flytyers dispense with the feather entirely, rather than employ a poor substitute.

The Norwegian hookmaker, Mustad, has recently introduced a hand-painted feather substitute for jungle cock that appears to be the best facsimile of the real thing yet to come on to the market. This is available in packets of six matched pairs in sizes small, medium and large. Jungle cock shoulder 'pads' also provide a useful striped feather that makes a useful substitute (dyed blue) for small vulturine guinea fowl 'elver' feathers. Some noted fly dressers use this feather for the tails and legs of small imitative trout flies.

GER Brinkhoff; *JAP* Sawada;*UK* Saville, Sportfish, Walker, Slater, Lathkill, McHardy, Watercraft; *US* E.A.T., Kaufmann, Cabela, Hunter, Fly & Field, Hook & Hackle, MM.

KINGFISHER

Protected in the UK, the plumage of the European kingfisher is unobtainable. In China, however, kingfishers are apparently common and regarded as pests around fish farms, where they are culled. The intensely blue waxlike back feathers of the Chinese kingfisher are used for the cheeks of Atlantic salmon flies, while slips from the blue tail feather are used (almost uniquely) in the tail of the famous Scottish loch pattern, the Kingfisher Butcher. Kingfisher is the accepted substitute for Blue Chatterer. Sold as complete skins.

JAP Sawada; *UK* Saville; *US* Hunter.

LANDRAIL

Specified in a number of old patterns such as the Cowdung, Pink Wickham and Silver Sedge and by Kingsmill Moore for the Magenta and Gold Bumble,

with the pink-cinnamon wing feather being the shoulder hackle.

JAP Sawada; *UK* Saville, Slater, Watercraft, Walker; *US* E.A.T.

MACAW (various species)

The tail feathers from the blue and gold (more rarely the scarlet) macaw are used for the 'horns' of several traditional, fully dressed Atlantic salmon flies. The side tail feathers provide a longer fibre than the centre tail and can be used for dressing the larger hook sizes. Wing feathers are also used by some fly dressers for seatrout flies. The centre and side tail is normally sold in 1 inch sections (enough for about 20 salmon flies). Wing quills are sold in matched pairs.

JAP Sawada; *NL* Kelson; *UK* Saville, Slater, Lathkill; *US* E.A.T, MM.

MAGPIE

The iridescent green/black tail and wing feathers are used for beetle backs and legs and as an alternative to duck speculum (mallard or teal) in the wings of traditional wet flies (e.g., Butchers, etc.). Sold as paired wings, or paired tail feathers.

JAP Sawada; *UK* Sportfish, Saville, Sparton, Niche, Walker, Slater, Lathkill, Rooksbury, McHardy, Watercraft; *US* E.A.T., Blue Ribbon

MARABOU

Fluffy plumes that originally came from the African Marabou Stork. These birds have been strictly protected for many years and an acceptable substitute comes from thighs of the domesticated turkey. Turkey marabou is a favourite material for winging lures, streamers and saltwater patterns. The individual fibres are very soft and mobile, producing a sinuous lively action underwater. Marabou is also used extensively in imitative patterns such as dragon and damsel fly nymphs, leeches, etc. Turkey marabou is one of the most useful and cheap materials for sub-surface flies. It is widely available in a huge range of dyed colours. Dyed, mottled and barred (grizzle) marabou is now available. Obtainable from most shops.

AUS Alpine; *GER* Brinkhoff; *JAP* Sawada; *UK* Sportfish, Saville, Sparton, Niche, Walker, Slater, Lathkill, Rooksbury, McHardy, Norris, Watercraft; *US* E.A.T., Kaufmann, Cabela, Gorilla, Hunter, Marriott, MM; *INT* Orvis.

MINAH

Hackles have a blueish sheen over natural black feather 1-1^1/2" long.

NL Kelson.

MCGINTY QUILL

Small, naturally iridescent blue quill, sold in packets of 6 lefts and 6 rights.
US Wapsi (for local suppliers).

MOORHEN (Waterhen)

The wings have masses of tiny little covert feathers that are excellent for 'soft hackled' flies, such as traditional North of England spiders (e.g. Waterhen Bloa). The wing and tail quills provide the 'blae' (dark grey) wing for Iron Blue Duns, etc. The natural colour or moorhen is a more-or-less uniform dark slaty grey. Sold as paired wings and matched wing quills.

UK Sportfish, Saville, Sparton, Niche, Walker, Slater, Lathkill, McHardy, Watercraft; *US* Blue Ribbon.

OSTRICH

The ostentatious plumes of the world's largest extant bird were once of huge commercial importance to the millinery trade. Fashions change and the decorative use of ostrich (and other plumage) in hats and garments is minimal by comparison with former times. For years, ostriches have been farmed in their native Southern Africa: still for their feathers, but now more importantly for their protein rich, low cholesterol meat. There are even ostriches now being farmed commercially in Oxfordshire!

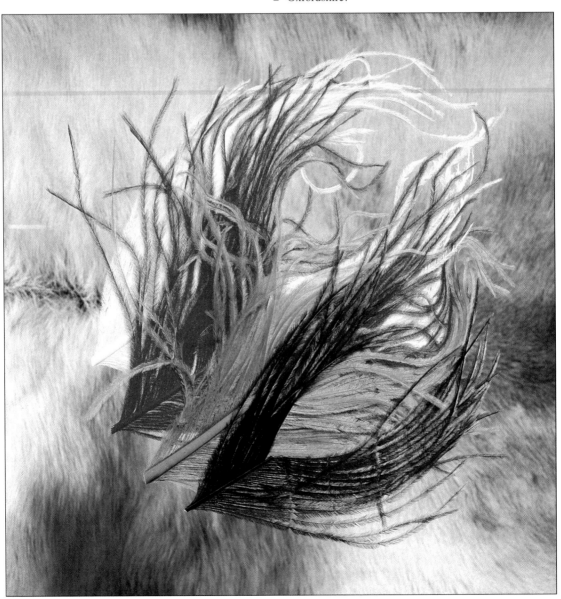

Ostrich plumes: a useful material for ribs, wings, bodies and many other applications.

Pheasant feathers: (from left) Argus, Reeves, Ring-neck (x2), Golden (x2).

Ostrich herl is a traditional material for 'butts' and 'joints' in salmon flies and is used for tails, bodies and thoraces in some trout flies. The white plumes dye readily. Also available as 'micro herl', used for tiny nymphs and emergers. Mike Tucker of Custom Aquatics markets a range of custom dyed 'Liqui Scud-Herl' in the following colours: sand, silver grey, big horn orange, early spring, miracle mile, olive grey, green river special and rust. Generally widely available in many colours.

AUS Alpine; *UK* Sportfish, Saville, Niche, Walker, Slater, Lathkill, Rooksbury, McHardy, Norris, Watercraft; *US* Hook & Hackle, MM, E.A.T., Cabela, Gorilla, Hunter, Marriott; *INT* Orvis. For Liqui-scud Ostrich Herl: *US* Custom Aquatics.

OWL

Barn and Tawny
The small mottled brown hackles on the upper edge of the tawny's wing was used in some old North Country patterns, The blue fur from the base plumage was used for dubbing, and the larger wing feathers for winging large moths or night flies.
Primary and secondary wing feathers from the barn owl provided wings for large night flies.
US Fly & Field

PARTRIDGE

Brown
AUS Alpine; *US* Fly & Field.

Cinnamon
US E.A.T.

Chukar

The soft hackles from this bird are often substituted in the United States for the French Partridge used in Britain. An Eurasian breed introduced into Nevada in 1935 it is now present in a fair range of the western and northern states of the US.

US E.A.T. (Standard, Blond and Barbary), Blue Ribbon, Marriott.

French (Red-legged)
The French partridge's principal offering to the flytyer is its distinctive body plumage. These wedge-shaped feathers are pale grey at the base, with bands of cream and black and a cinnamon/chestnut tip. They are used principally for mayfly patterns, both as fan wings and as wound hackles (eg. Straddlebug and other Irish mayflies). The chestnut tails of French partridge are also useful for winging sedge patterns. Sold as whole skins; packs of tail feathers and small packs of selected hackles.

AUS Alpine; *JAP* Sawada; *UK* Sportfish, Saville, Niche, Walker, Slater, Rooksbury, McHardy, Watercraft.

Grey
The grey partridge is sometimes called the English or Hungarian partridge. Partridges have declined in Britain: adversely affected by changes in agricultural practice. The speckled brown back and speckled grey breast feathers are used in many traditional patterns (Orange Partridge, Yellow Partridge, March Brown, mayflies, etc.). The barred and blotched and cinnamon quills from wings and tails are traditionally used for various sedge wings. The grey breast feathers dyed in yellow and olive shades are favoured in many mayfly and damsel nymph patterns. The small downy feathers make fabulous beards and sides on Sculpin-type lures. Sold as whole skin, paired wings, matched wing quills, tail feathers and

packs of grey breast or brown back hackles.

AUS Alpine; *GER* Brinkhoff; *JAP* Sawada; *UK* Sportfish, Saville, Sparton, Niche, Walker, Slater, Lathkill, Rooksbury, McHardy, Watercraft; *US* Kaufmann, Hunter, Fly & Field.

Hungarian
US E.A.T., Cabela, Blue Ribbon, Marriott, MM; *NL* Kelson; *INT* Orvis.

Japanese
JAP Sawada

PARROT (see Macaw)

PEACOCK

Widely used in flytying, peacock plumage is magnificently endowed with iridescent blues and greens. The eyed tail feathers provide the famous herl, used for the wound bodies of many patterns (Black & Peacock Spider, Royal Wulff, Coachman, etc.). The stripped herls from the eye provide the 'quills', used in many famous patterns (Orange quill, Beacon Beige, etc.). From the base of the bird's tail are the brilliant iridescent 'sword' feathers, used for the wings of the Alexandra and as a wound herl in the Green Insect grayling pattern. The peacock's speckled wing quills are similar to those of the American turkey and are useful for salmon fly wings and Muddler Minnows. The electric blue neck hackles are used for the Goat's Toe seatrout fly and for throat hackles on other seatrout, steelhead and salmon flies. Available as single eyed tail feathers, strung herl, paired swords and wing quills. The blue neck plumage is usually sold in small packets.

Widely available from fly tying retailers.

AUS Alpine; *GER* Brinkhoff; *JAP* Sawada *UK* Sportfish, Saville, Sparton, Niche, Walker, Slater, Lathkill, Rooksbury, McHardy, Norris, Watercraft *US* E.A.T., Kaufmann, Cabela, Hunter; *INT* Orvis

---

PEAHEN

Often overlooked by the tyer in favour of the Peacock, the soft, ruddy feather of the wing is good for close-winged flies (eg. Welshman's Button, stoneflies). Soft feather from back also used for winging. Herl is naturally greenish or black and dun.

US Slater.

PELICAN

Primary wing quills are a perfect substitute for condor. Wing coverts are light grey with a distinct silver sheen. The lesser wing coverts are small narrow feathers not unlike the anhinea (dark silver colour, when tied Matuka-style make perfect sandeel imitation).

NL Kelson.

PHEASANT

Argus
The wing quills and tail feathers from this magnificent bird have been incorporated into many of the modern fully dressed salmon flies (eg. several of the 'art' salmon flies created by the Japanese tyer, Ken Sawada). The secondary feathers are amazingly long in fibre and feature the most magnificent eyes, or 'moons' that look as if they have been painted on artificially. Rare and very expensive. Normally sold as 4" sections of quill.

JAP Sawada; *US* E.A.T.

Blue-eared
Widely used as a heron feather substitute for spey flies.

US E.A.T., Hunter, Marriott, Blue Ribbon.

Copper
Saddle feathers are copper coloured with white edges

NL Kelson; *US* E.A.T.

Elliot's
A kaleidoscope of colours are contained in the plumage of this bird

NL Kelson

Golden
The various plumages from the oriental golden pheasant undoubtedly feature more frequently in salmon fly tying than those of any other bird. As well as the famous neck (tippet) and crest (topping) feathers, golden pheasant provide many other useful feathers, some of which can be used as substitutes for rarer plumages. These magnificent birds have been domesticated and are eaten in the far east. There are feral populations in Britain. The plumage is thus plentiful and relatively cheap.

The red and the yellow body feathers are used in prawn and shrimp patterns (eg. General Practitioner), while the red spear feathers from the base of the tail are used as 'feelers' on prawn imitations. The tail is marked with irregular dark brown barring over a tan background and again is found in the dressings of many mixed wing Atlantic salmon flies. It is frequently specified as a substitute for Florican bustard. Full skins (less tail and head) are available cheaply. Crests and tippets are so frequently used that there is little sense in buying other than the complete head/neck.

Generally widely available.

AUS Alpine; *JAP* Sawada; *UK* Sportfish, Saville, Niche, Sparton, Walker, Slater, Lathkill, Rooksbury, McHardy, Watercraft; *US* Dan Bailey, E.A.T., Kaufmann, Cabela, Gorilla, Hunter, Fly & Field, Marriott, MM, Hook & Hackle; *INT* Orvis.

Impeyan Monal
Black plumage with a blue metallic sheen
NL Kelson; *US* E.A.T.

Grey peacock

Body feathers are metallic-eyed, dark grey with white flanks. Various sizes, including thumb-size for cheeks. Tail feathers and covert feathers have two eyes. Not cheap.

US E.A.T.

Hardwick

Breast and body feathers range from black with a light centre to cinnamon.

NL Kelson.

Lady Amherst

The Amherst pheasant has similar fly tying uses to the golden pheasant. The tippet feathers are similar, but more rounded and are snow white, tipped iridescent black (used in such salmon patterns as Evening Star, Colonel's Lady and Pas River). They can be usefully dyed such colours as fluorescent green and fluorescent yellow. The Amherst's crest has blood red lustrous feathers, but there are far fewer of them than the 'toppings' found on a golden pheasant's crest. The striking tail feathers are very long: white with broad bars and irregular finer stripes of iridescent greenish black. The very long fibre length at the base of the tail can be employed in very large sizes of full dress salmon flies (eg. Childers, Champion and several Canadian patterns). The tail fibres are also used for the tails of some mayfly patterns. The bright orange spears from the base of the tail are used as feelers and legs of prawn and shrimp patterns. Sold as complete skins, single tails (natural and dyed), complete crest/tippet collars and in small packs of selected tippets.

AUS Alpine, *US* Dan Bailey, E.A.T., Kaufmann, Hunter, Fly & Field, Marriott, Blue Ribbon, MM; *UK* Sportfish, Saville, Niche, Walker, Lathkill, Rooksbury, McHardy.

Manchurian

Body feathers are light grey, brown and black. Being very soft they are well suited for smaller Spey patterns.

NL Kelson

Melanistic

US Fly & Field

Metallic

JAP Sawada

Peacock

Brown and buff speckled feathers with a small peacock eye at the tip. Feathers are used as cheeks or whole feather wings.

JAP Sawada; *NL* Kelson; *US* Marriott.

Red

AUS Alpine; *US* Montana Master.

Red Temminks

The most common of the five species of Tragopan. Red with pale blue/grey spots on the neck, back and body feathers. Used for cheeks, wings red collars and throats.

US E.A.T.

Red Tragopan

Back and body feathers are naturally red with white and light blue spots, as called for on some salmon patterns. Can also be used on streamers, or as nymph legs and tails.

US E.A.T.

Reeves

The hen bird has the colouring of Ruffled Grouse with finer barrings and larger than grouse.

AUS Alpine; *NL* Kelson; *UK* Saville; *US* E.A.T.; Marriott.

Ring-necked

The most common of the pheasants and easily obtained. The ring neck pheasant is arguably the most useful single bird to the fly dresser: just about every feather on the bird can be used. The small church window feathers on the back are used as wings in many patterns (Houston Gem), while the coppery black tipped neck feathers are used to imitate the Bracken Clock and Cockchafer beetles. The small white feathers from the neck ring itself can be dyed to produce substitutes for such rarities as toucan and Indian crow. The green rump feathers are used (in three pairs) for the Mrs Simpson Lure, from New Zealand. The tail feathers provide tails for mayflies; legs for craneflies and the herl for probably the most famous nymph pattern of all. And that is just the cock bird!

The hen ring neck pheasant is hardly less useful, with beautifully marbled plumage in shades of brown, mottled over pale buffs and tans and almost olive khakis. The hen pheasant's tails furnish the wing for the famous Invicta, while the wing quills are used in a number of caddis patterns.

Sadly, relatively few of the plumages from either cock or hen pheasants are sold commercially. It is a great pity that whole, cured skins of both sexes are not more widely available. The great usefulness of the ring neck pheasant in fly tying is further extended by the common occurence of melanistic, light phase and albino variations from the normal coloration.

Sold as cock and hen tails (natural and dyed) and as matched hen wings and quills. Infrequently as whole skins.

AUS Alpine; *GER* Brinkhoff; *UK* Sportfish, Saville.Niche, Walker, Slater, Lathkill, Rooksbury, McHardy, Norris, Watercraft; *US* Dan Bailey, E.A.T., Kaufmann, Cabela, Gorilla, Hunter, Blue Ribbon, Marriott, Hook & Hackle, MM; *INT* Orvis

Satyr Tragopan

Small feathers of rich red brown and at the tip a small grey eye with a black circle. The medium sized feathers are used for Matuka style wings or as the underwing in salmon patterns.

NL Kelson; *US* E.A.T.

Lemon Wood Duck sides (left), Barred Wood Duck (centre below), Teal (right)

Shepsters
US Fly & Field

Silver
The white, black barred body feathers of the silver pheasant are used for the sides and cheeks of a few trout and salmon patterns and notably in some famous N. American streamer patterns, such as the Grey Ghost. The tail of the bird is also sometimes used for similar applications to common ring neck pheasant tail.

AUS Alpine; *JAP* Sawada; *UK* Saville, Slater; *US* E.A.T., Marriott, MM; *NL* Kelson.

Yellow Golden
Selectively bred to have a washed-out, bleached look. Dominant colours are: white, light brown, bright yellow. Yellow hackles make a good toucan substitute.

US E.A.T.

PLOVER, GOLDEN

Neck, breast, back and shoulder provide beautiful hackles - either dyed or natural. They make good legs. The broad fibres from the quills were used by Halford in his Goose Dun. Fibres from the broad breast feathers can be wound to make good bodies

JAP Sawada; *UK* Lathkill, Saville, Walker, Rooksbury, McHardy, Watercraft; *US* Fly & Field

---

PRAIRIE CHICKEN

A grouse-like bird (tan, brown and black) with elongated neck feathers

US E.A.T.

PUKEKO

Normally now available as a substitute as a dyed blue-black feather to replace the original breast and flank used for night fishing patterns.

AUS Alpine

QUAIL

Various species are available to the tyer (eg. California, Coturnix, Gambel's, Scaled), of which Mearns (also known as Harlequin or Montezuma) is one of the most underrated birds in flytying. The heavily mottled feathers have a wide range of sizes, which are ideal for soft hackle flies, underwings and legs for nymphs. The female birds range in colour from tan to dark brown and the males from brown to dark dun with spotted black and white

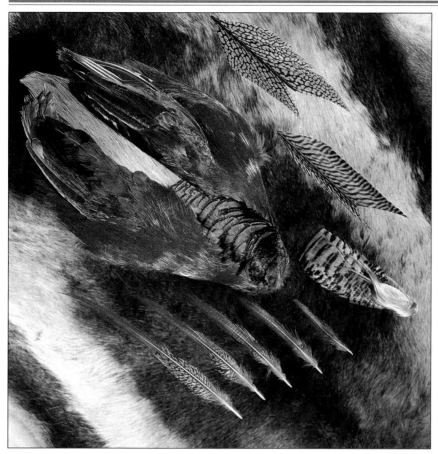

LEFT: The Golden Pheasant has long been a favourite of the flytyer providing a range of vivid colours and textures. Whole skin (top left), two tail sections (top right), head and neck topping and crest (right), red tail spears (bottom).

BELOW: Ordinary white wing quills can vary considerably in strength, length, and suitability for taking dyes: goose (left), swan (middle), duck (right)

feathers (similar to guinea fowl). It can also be used as a jungle cock substitute.

NL Kelson; *UK* Angling Pursuits; *US* Blue Ribbon Flies, E.A.T., Marriott, Montana Master.

RHEA

A small South American Ostrich, with feathers similar to Ostrich plumes but very much smaller. The fibres are dense and of even length, making them useful for nymphs.

US E.A.T., Marriott.

ROSELLA

Both Beautiful and Penant types have attractive feathers - purple/blue, purple, orange/yellow, brownish/red and green, black with yellow edges etc. Good substitutes for Toucan or as cheeks on salmon flies.

JAP Sawada; *NL* Kelson.

SCHLAPPEN

Webby feathers, from between the saddle and tail feathers of fowl, giving 6 to 8" of solid web, and used for steelhead, salmon and saltwater patterns, and for palmering.

AUS Alpine; *UK* Lathkill, Slater, Angling Pursuits; *US* Dan Bailey, Kaufmann, E.A.T., Cabela, Hunter, Marriott, MM; *INT* Orvis

SNIPE

The common snipe is used for in several English North

Country patterns, such as Snipe and Purple (rump hackle), Blue Dun (wing quills) etc. The small dark grey spoon shaped coverts from near the 'elbow' and the rump feathers are the most useful. If unobtainable the same feathers from the golden plover can be used as a substitute (starling at a pinch). Sold usually as paired wings.

JAP Sawada; *UK* Sportfish, Saville, Niche, Walker, Slater, Lathkill, Rooksbury, McHardy, Norris, Watercraft; *US* E.A.T., Fly & Field, Blue Ribbon, Marriott

SPEY HACKLE

see Heron (page 16) and Blue-eared Pheasant (page 20).

UK Lathkill, Angling Pursuits, Slater; *US* Kaufmann, Cabela, Hunter, Marriott, Hook & Hackle, MM; *GER* Brinkhoff.

STARLING

The common starling provides a number of useful feathers. The wing quills are commonly specified for the wings of traditional dry flies and many wet patterns (eg Olive Dun, Black Gnat). Starling is also used as a substitute for plumage that is now protected (eg, for hen blackbird in Greenwell's Glory and for Dotterel).

The glossy tan tipped body plumage is a splendid hackle for spider type wet flies (Stewart's Black Spider) and has been used as a jungle cock substitute. Starling is readily obtainable as the bird is regarded as a serious pest in some parts of the world. Sold as whole skin, paired wings, wing quills and small packs of body hackles.

JAP Sawada; *UK* Sportfish, Saville, Sparton, Niche, Walker, Slater, Lathkill, Rooksbury, McHardy, Norris, Watercraft; *US* Blue Ribbon Flies, Marriott, MM.

SUPER SOFT WEB HACKLE

Offered as an improved hackle suitable for a wide variety of streamer, steelhead, trout and bass patterns. The short, webby hackle feathers are lightly impregnated with CDC oil after dyeing, rendering them shiny, soft and supple. Sold in packets of approximately 20 hackles and are available in: Black, White, Olive, Mallard Grey, Bright Yellow, Purple, Red, Bright Blue, Hot Pink and Hot Orange.

US Montana Master.

SWAN

Wing quills and shoulders come in a variety of dyed colours, eg. white, black, red, orange, teal blue, olive, brown, claret.

NL Kelson; *UK* Saville, Slater.

SWIFT

The secondaries are used for winging. A shabby black

colour, the primaries are too short in fibre for any flies but the smallest. The dark brownish black hackles from the back and under the wing have some uses.

UK McHardy, Watercraft; *US* Blue Ribbon.

TEAL (Green-winged Teal, N. America)

The very distinctively marked flank feathers from the teal (black bars on a white background) are used extensively for the wings of traditional wet fly patterns for trout and seatrout (eg. Peter Ross, Teal Blue & Silver), but are also used for the sides of many classic salmon flies and even as a hackle on one or two (Ackroyd).

Teal breast feathers are used most commonly for fanwing mayfly patterns (Grizzle King) and the wings of salmon flies (eg. Black Doctor, Blue Charm, Green Highlander, Jock-Scott). The grey wing quills can be used in the same way as mallard primary and secondary feathers. The black barred white flank feathers of widgeon are very similar and the two are interchangeable, to all intents and purposes.

AUS Alpine; *JAP* Sawada; *US* Dan Bailey, E.A.T., Kaufmann, Cabela, Hunter, Marriott; *UK* Sportfish, Saville, Sparton, Niche, Walker, Slater, Lathkill, Rooksbury, McHardy, Norris, Watercraft

TOUCAN

The various toucans come from the rain forests of South and Central America and are now protected. The yellow breast and deep red rump feathers were widely incorporated in Victorian salmon flies, mostly for body veilings, but also as throats and tails on some dressings. The genuine feathers are unobtainable by any legal or morally justifiable means. A number of substitutes have been tried, with varying success. For the yellow plumage, the small rounded feathers from the very top of a golden pheasant crest and Amherst pheasant neck feathers have been tried. Hareline Dubbin offer a dyed substitute. The deep red rump feathers can be substituted with golden pheasant rump.

GER Brinkhoff; *JAP* Sawada; *NL* Kelson *UK* Sportfish, Saville, Sparton, Niche, Slater, Lathkill, McHardy, Watercraft; *US* Hunter, MM.

TURKEY

The native American wild turkey and its domesticated descendants - both bronze and white - have proved a rich source of feathers for flytying. The large quill feathers from tail and wings occur in a range of mottled and barred effects in a variety of shades, from pale buff tans to rich chocolate brown. Turkey feathers are also available in a wide range of dyed colours. The large size of turkey feathers permits the tying of large traditional salmon patterns. The speckled feather known as 'oak turkey' is the correct wing material for the famous original Muddler Minnow, while the range of turkey coloration lends itself to sedge wings, stonefly and other nymphal wing cases, grass hoppers, etc. Turkey can provide a pretty good substitute for speckled bustard and, of course, the much used substitute for marabou stork. Spirit River, Umpqua, Benecchi, House of Harrop offer a vast range of turkey products, including Ozark original speckled turkey quills, Ozark mottled turkey quills, mottled turkey flats, white turkey, genuine oak turkey quills, biots and stripped quills. Much turkey material is now available CDC impregnated.

UK Sportfish, Saville, Niche, Slater, Lathkill, Rooksbury, McHardy, Norris, Watercraft; *AUS* Alpine; *JAP* Sawada; *US* E.A.T., Kaufmann, Cabela, Hunter, Marriott, MM, Blue Ribbon.

Oak/Mottled Turkey

UK Saville, Sparton, Walker, Slater, Rooksbury; *AUS* Alpine; *US* E.A.T., River Edge, MM, Cabela, Hunter, Blue Ribbon, Marriott; *INT* Orvis.

Biots

Longer than Goose biots and make good segmented bodies.

US Kaufmann, Cabela, Hunter, Blue Ribbon, Marriott

Flats

For tying wings on thorax-style flies.

US Kaufmann, Cabela, Hunter, Marriott, Whitetail, Hook & Hackle, MM. Some are CDC impregnated, as with House of Harrop products.

WEAVER BIRD

With its numerous small orange/red and deep black feathers it makes one of the very best Indian Crow substitutes. Being small they are only suitable for veilings and tails.

NL Kelson.

WHITE PEACOCK

It has pure white eye feathers, with off-white, creamy herls and soft marabou-like body feathers. The neck hackles are 2" long and extremely soft.

US E.A.T; *NL* Kelson.

WIDGEON

The white, black barred flank plumage is very similar to that found on the teal, but is even more vividly marked. The feathers are used in the same way for the wings and sides of Atlantic salmon and seatrout flies, such as Peter Ross and Teal Blue & Silver. Widgeon is markedly less prone to splitting than similar plumages from other ducks, making it ideal for beginners or those who have difficulty with teal wings. The neck feathers are used for salmon fly hackles. Sold as flank, and wing quills.

American Widgeon varies from deep reddish brown with black barring to a rosy tan with fainter bars. It is not the same as European Widgeon as called for in some salmon flies. European Widgeon is much closer to the flank feathers of the Northern Pintail in America.

JAP Sawada; *US* E.A.T.; *UK* Slater, Lathkill, McHardy, Watercraft.

WOODCOCK

The wing quills of this elusive woodland game bird are of principal interest to the flytyer, used for winging the woodcock 'series' of flies (eg. Woodcock & Yellow, Woodcock & Mixed). The bird's entire plumage is characterized by a distinctive orange caramel marbled appearance. The body hackles are used in some wet spider patterns. Sold as paired wings and small packs of plumage.

AUS Alpine; *JAP* Sawada; *UK* Sportfish, Saville, Sparton, Niche, Walker, Slater, Lathkill, Rooksbury, McHardy, Watercraft; *US* E.A.T., Fly & Field.

WYANDOTTE HEN

Feathers are white and light brown, and the wings quills white with a black edge (which dye well). Other wing quills are light brown with a black list.

NL Kelson.

Hairs & Furs

(other than deer hair)

AMERICAN OPOSSUM

White with black tips (see Opossum)

US E.A.T.

AFRICAN GOAT / ANGORA GOAT

Guard hairs 5-6" (125-152mm) long and thus ideal for winging the largest tube flies and saltwater patterns. The fur is shinier, smoother in texture, and more mobile than bucktail, and can be a substituted for polar bear. The under-fur is extremely soft and can be substituted for seal's fur, offering similar translucency whilst slightly softer, in nymphs, steelhead, seatrout and salmon flies.

The under-fur dubbing is marketed by Orvis as 'Angora Goat Dubbing' (see Dubbings section). African Goat is usually sold on small patches of hide, sometimes under the name 'Angora Goat'

US Hunter, Cabela, Kaufmann, Marriott; *INT* Orvis.

BADGER

Badgers are now protected in the UK and not available from flytying retailers. The fur can still be obtained (if you are lucky) from jumble and garage sales. The hair from old shaving brushes is invariably too worn to be of any use, but road kills are another possibility. The N. American badger is a different species, though the fur has similarities.

The cream/tan under-fur can be used for dubbing, but it is the guard hairs 1-2 inches in length- that are of principal interest to the fly tyer. Cream in colour with a black and white barring at the tip and very finely tapered, they are used for hair wing salmon and seatrout flies. The hair tends to compress and reduce in size when wet, so a larger than normal bunch of hair may be used to good effect. Badger dyes well, emphasizing the natural barring. Grey

squirrel is the usual substitute.

AUS Alpine; *JAP* Sawada; *US* Hunter, Gorilla, Kaufmann, Marriott, E.A.T.

BASSARISK (see Monga Ringtail)

BEAR

Black

Guard hairs are about 3" long with a 'crinkled' base grading to a fine, straight, glossy tip. The hair is very flexible and 'mobile' and good for hair-wing salmon tube flies and streamers. The dense dark grey to black under-fur dubs well. Accepted substitutes for black bear are fitch tail or buck tail. Black bear is usually sold as small patches of tanned hide.

AUS Alpine; *JAP* Sawada; *NL* Kelson *UK* Saville, Niche, Slater, Sparton, Rooksbury; *US* Hunter, E.A.T., Hook & Hackle.

Black Bear Masks

These are not cheap and come in two sizes: very large and medium.

US E.A.T.

Brown/Grizzly

Fur colour varies widely from pale cafe-au-lait to dark chocolate, with guard hairs up to 3-4" in length, similar in texture to black bear with a crinkly base grading to a straight fine tip. A very mobile fur used for salmon, steelhead and streamer patterns. The soft under-fur makes useful dubbing.

UK Saville ('Ginger'), Watercraft; *US* E.A.T.

Polar

A creamy white hair - up to 5" in length - renowned for

LEFT Turkey feathers: (from top) Ozark speckled, Barred wing quill, Oak, Peacock, White-tipped.

translucency and brilliant lustre. It is used in salmon, steelhead, saltwater and streamer patterns. Generally protected,supplies are extremely limited and costly. As a result, several natural and synthetic substitutes have appeared. A limited amount of the real fur is sometimes available.

JAP Sawada; *NL* Kelson; *UK* Saville, Slater, Rooksbury; *US* Cabela.

BEAVER

A very fine fur, full of natural water-repelling oils and thus ideal for the smallest of dry flies. It dyes well and is available on its own or blended with other fibres. The under-fur is light to dark dun grey and is frequently blended with muskrat for such patterns as the Adams and Blue Dun. As it is glossy it is often mixed with Muskrat to make spinning easier.

AUS Alpine; *JAP* Sawada; *UK* Saville, Slater, Watercraft, Angling Pursuits; *US* Hunter, Cabela, Blue Ribbon, Gorilla, Kaufmann, Marriott, E.A.T.

BOAR, CHINESE

Fine very robust hairs (bristles) make good tails, feelers and legs,especially for shrimp and prawn patterns. The natural colour ranges from off white to black. In light shades it dyes well. Also used as ribbing and body material for dry flies. Available in packs of mixed colours, or individually: golden stone, white, black, cream, brown and grey.

NL Kelson; *US* AA, Marriott, E.A.T.

BOBCAT

Very soft fur suitable for leech patterns, or as an alternative to rabbit.

US E.A.T.

BUCKTAIL

Usually comes from the male N. American white-tail deer. This long hair is stiffer and thicker than goat, but some fly-dressers prefer it for large tube flies and saltwater patterns, particularly for use in fast water currents. The natural colours are light brown and white, the latter allowing strong bright dyed colours.

Bucktail is simple to dye, but the high natural fat content requires degreasing prior to dyeing. Bucktails are available in a wide range of colours, with those sourced in N. America generally being of a higher quality than those offered for sale in Europe.

JAP Sawada; *GER* Brinkhoff; *NL* Kelson; *UK* Saville, Niche, Slater, Lathkill, Sparton, Sportfish, Watercraft, Rooksbury, Norris, McHardy, Walker; *US* Hunter, Cabela, Gorilla, Bailey, Kaufmann, Marriott, E.A.T.; *INT* Orvis

BUFFALO

The real thing from Bison down on the range. Has the appearance of a combination of sheep and bear. Not as straight and coarse as bucktail, the shorter hairs are fine and soft. Natural colours are from medium brown to almost black. Approx. 2-6" in length. Used for winging large salmon, steelhead and streamer patterns, buffalo has a very dense under-fur that can be used for dubbing bodies on large flies. Substitutes: black bear and bucktail. Also available as 2" squares of hide (short dark brown hair). Used for dubbing mixes, or spikey nymph dressings.

US E.A.T., Marriott

CALF

Body Hair

Much straighter than calf tail, but has the same natural colours. It is used frequently for the wings and tails of hair wing dry flies, but is generally too short to be of use in larger streamer patterns. Normally sold as small patches of tanned hide.

AUS Alpine; *JAP* Sawada; *NL* Kelson; *UK* Slater, Watercraft, Rooksbury, McHardy; *US* Cabela, AA, Gorilla, Bailey, Kaufmann, Marriott, E.A.T.; *INT* Orvis.

Tail (Kip)

Calf tails produce a fine hair of variable length: shorter at the root of the tail and longer towards the tip. Natural colours are white, brown and black. It is a solid, relatively incompressible hair, that usually has some degree of crinkliness and curl. Shorter, fine calf tails are used for winging dry flies, while extra large tails can be used for very large streamers and specialised patterns, such as the Collie Dog (for salmon).

Calf can be used as a substitute for bucktail in smaller streamer and salmon flies. A range of dyed colours is usually available. Some tails can have very crinkly hair, so careful selection may be important. Calf tail is often called Kip tail in N. America. Widely available.

AUS Alpine; *JAP* Sawada; *GER* Brinkhoff; *NL* Kelson; *UK* Saville, Lathkill, Sparton, Watercraft, Rooksbury, Norris, McHardy, Walker; *US* Hunter, Cabela, AA, Gorilla, Bailey, Kaufmann, Marriott, E.A.T.; *INT* Orvis.

CAMEL

Fine, soft and short fibred, this hair is used for dubbing dry flies, having a similar floatability to rabbit but absorbing floatant well. It has a nice rough-hewn 'buginess' for nymphs as well. The Wapsi Fly Company first introduced this to flytyers commercially.

GER Brinkhoff; *UK* Watercraft; *US* Marriott.

CHINCHILLA

Once prized for fur coats, these South American rodents are now more popular as pets. They have a truly gorgeous thick pelt that protects them from the cold in their native Andes. The soft grey mottled fur can be substituted as dubbing where rabbit or hare are usually specified, or where a pale grey colour is required. Sold as small pieces of hide.

US Marriott, E.A.T.

COYOTE

North American wild dog which gets its name from an ancient Aztec word. Coyote fur is often obtainable from road kills in N. America, but is virtually unknown in the UK as a flytying material. The guard hair of the coyote varies in colour from a rusty red to a brown/black, with creamy white bars and a dark base. The hair is used in much the same way as grey squirrel and makes an excellent hair wing material for various streamer patterns. Sold as small patches of tanned hide.

AUS Alpine; *NL* Kelson; *US* Marriott, E.A.T.

COYPU (see Nutria)

CROSSCUT RABBIT

Similar to a Zonker strip, but differing in that the strip is cut across the hide. When wrapped around the hook shank, like a hackle, the pile of the fur lies naturally backwards along the hook shank - in effect a fur hackle. This is a useful material for hackling large nymphs (eg. Dragonflies) and streamers (Bunnies, Leeches, etc.). Sold in packs of pre-cut strips, in a range of colours.

AUS Alpine; *GER* Brinkhoff; *US* Hunter, Cabela, Kaufmann, Marriott; *INT* Orvis.

DONKEY

African

Extremely soft 4" to 5" hair which can be used in leech patterns instead of marabou, and is more durable.

Spanish

A white and brownish grey hair about 4" long.

NL Kelson

ERMINE

The stoat in its winter colours. The hair is white at the bottom of the tail and then turns to black at the tip.

AUS Alpine; *UK* Watercraft, Slater.

FISHER

A large N. American marten with black/brown stiff shiny hair and light underfur.

US E.A.T., Marriott.

FITCH

A collective fur trade name given to various members of the ferret family. Tail hair is used in the wings of some salmon fly patterns and the under-fur, creamy yellow to grey in colour, is considered good for both wet and dry fly dressings.

JAP Sawada; *UK* Watercraft; *US* Hunter, Marriott, E.A.T.

FOX

Arctic

Highly mobile and extremely soft white fur which takes dyes well. Used for hairwings and streamers, and as breathers on nymph and emerger patterns. Stronger than Marabou, with a pulsating action.

UK Saville, Niche, Slater, Lathkill, Sportfish, Anglian, Watercraft, Rooksbury; *US* Hunter, Fly & Field, E.A.T.

Red

Also occurs in melanistic (silver) and cross phases as well as red. The fox provides a fine under-fur in a range of natural shades. Fly tyers now make much use of fox guard hairs, and the tails are excellent for hair wing salmon and streamer flies.

AUS Alpine; *JAP* Sawada; *GER* Brinkhoff; *SWE* Berqvist; *NOR* Bergqvist; *UK* Slater, Lathkill, Watercraft, Angling Pursuits; *US* Hunter, Kaufmann, Marriott, E.A.T. *INT* Orvis.

Grey

Guard hairs, are black, white and black-tipped, and are used in the wings of the Rat series of flies - rusty, silver and black. Generally more expensive than red fox.

AUS Alpine; *JAP* Sawada; *UK* Slater, Lathkill, Angling Pursuits; *US* Hunter, Kaufmann, Marriott, E.A.T.

Silver

NL Kelson; *US* Hunter, Marriott, E.A.T.

GOAT

A fine mobile hair up to 4 inches long that is used in various hair-winged salmon and streamer flies. It has a good underwater action and is a good hair to learn to tie hair-winged flies with as it does not flare and is easy to control. Available in a range of dyed colours.

GER Brinkhoff; *NL* Kelson; *UK* Saville, Niche, Slater, Lathkill, Sportfish, Watercraft, Rooksbury, Norris, McHardy, Walker; *US* Hunter, Kaufmann, E.A.T.

Snow goat

A 6" long white hair with light buff tinge that can be used as a substitute for polar bear.

NL Kelson.

GROUNDHOG (see Woodchuck, page 36)

HARE

The hair of the European brown Hare's ear, or mask, is specified in many patterns. The mask and ears range in colour from pale tan, through ruddy brown to almost jet black. The texture and length ranges from fine under-fur to almost bristle-like long guard hairs. The ears are covered with a very close, fine hair with almost no under-fur. A mixture of the fur from the ears and the mask gives the true dubbing for the Gold Ribbed Hare's Ear and March Brown.

Hare and leveret (young hare) body fur is also extremely useful for dubbing, providing beautiful creamy under-fur and long guard hairs. While the European hare provides the authentic material for many traditional British patterns, many other rabbits and hares furnish useful dubbing and should not be ignored. No flytyer should be without at least two hare's masks on his tying bench to ensure a good range of colours. Widely available and sold as whole masks with ears, or as paired ears (both natural and dyed colours) and as tanned skins. Hare is also sold as pre-plucked dubbing (natural, dyed and/or blended with other fibres).

AUS Alpine; *GER* Brinkhoff; *JAP* Sawada; *NL* Kelson; *UK* Saville, Niche, Slater, Lathkill, Sparton, Sportfish, Watercraft, Rooksbury, Norris, McHardy, Walker; *US* Hunter, Cabela, AA, Fly & Field, Gorilla, Bailey, Kaufmann, Marriott, E.A.T.; *INT* Orvis.

A range of furs: (clockwise from top left) Racoon, Lynx, Badger, American opossum, Skunk, Woodchuck and Coyote (centre),

Tails: (from left to right) Mink, Grey Fax, Bassarisk and Opossum

Snowshoe Hare

Sometimes incorrectly referred to as 'snowshoe rabbit', the coarse fur from the hind feet of this N. American hare bears some resemblance to seal's fur in texture and has a similar translucence. The material has been popularized in the US with a pattern called 'The Usual Pattern' and is now used by Orvis for their CDC Rabbit's Foot Emergers. Snowshoe hare foot is an excellent dry fly dubbing, floating higher and longer than most other materials. Sold as single feet. In Scandinavia, Arctic hare foot is a reasonable substitute.

US Marriott; *INT* Orvis.

HORSE HAIR

In the times of Walton and Cotton, horse tail hairs were used for fly lines, leaders and tippets. The hair from a stallion's tail is surprisingly strong and our angling fore-bears could land quite large trout on a single strand!

As a flytying material, horse hair is used for winding bodies, giving translucent and segmented effects (e.g. Bucknall's Footballer midge pupa). The natural colour of horse hair ranges from cream, to brown and almost jet black, and it can be dyed.

JAP Sawada; *UK* Saville, Niche, Slater, Watercraft,

McHardy *US* E.A.T.

JAVELINA (see Peccary, page 33)

KANGAROO

The fine rust or grey bottom fur is useful for nymphs and hopper bodies.

UK Watercraft; *US* E.A.T.

KIP TAIL (see Calf Tail, page 28)

KIWI RABBIT STRIPS

These are 1/2" wide strips used in saltwater, sculpin, and bass patterns. Colours: natural brown, olive, yellow, black, white, natural grizzly.

LLAMA

Grey kinky wool-like fur used as a woolhead material and for Spuddlers.

US Marriott, E.A.T.

LYNX

The body fur from this wild cat is soft and fine. It makes marvellous dubbing for nymphs. Not unlike hare's mask, but with more mobility, this is an uncommon material but it is available.

US EAT

MARMOT (see Woodchuck, page 36)

MARTEN

A shiny dubbing in black or brown which is especially good for nymphs.

UK Saville, Slater; *US* Marriott, E.A.T.

MINK

The N. American mink became the staple of the luxury fur trade, being widely farmed for its fur in N. America and Europe. Farm escapees have resulted in mink becoming widely established ferally, outside their natural range, and a pest. The natural colour is a glossy brown (northern forms are darker) with a white patch under the chin. The fur is characterized by the thick rich underfur and the lustrous longer guard hairs.

Farmed strains have produced a range of colours: white, blue greys, browns and black. The underfur is water repellant and is useful for dry flies. With the attendant guard hairs, it makes a thick spiky dubbing. Thin strips, cut with the grain of the pelt (like Zonker strips) are the crucial component of the Minkie lure and, it is said, a salmon egg hook dubbed heavily with mink makes the best imitation of a trout pellet! The guard hairs are glossy and it is advisable to use some securing cement or varnish on the the thread on the hook to prevent hair loss.

AUS Alpine; *JAP* Sawada; *NL* Kelson; *UK* Saville, Slater, Watercraft, Rooksbury; *US* Hunter, Marriott, E.A.T.

MOHAIR

Mostly available in the form of coarse and fuzzy yarn from knitting suppliers it can be used for extra hairy nymph dubbing. It can also be obtained in coils of untwisted long fibres and, in this form, has many applications for wings, tails and dubbed bodies of salmon and streamer patterns. Top quality mohair has a wonderful lustre and can be dyed easily to brilliant, rich colours. Chopped mohair (of good quality) is an effective substitute for seal's fur.

UK Saville, Niche, Slater; *US* Hunter, Marriott, E.A.T.

MOLE

The smoky blue/grey fur is very short and even in length and has the appearance and feel of thick piled silk velvet.

The structure of the individual fibres prevents the animal's fur becoming fouled by mud during its habitual burrowings.

Mole fur is regarded by many as the finest dubbing for small dry fly patterns and the natural colour is ideal for blue dun and iron blue dun imitations. Mole is relatively easy to dub. The fur is best removed from the skin with a sharp craft knife blade, rather than scissors, as this obtains a longer fibre length.

Usually sold in its natural colour as whole, or as cured or tanned skins, it is sometimes overdyed in colours such as olive, chestnut, black and claret. Very occasionally, one can find paler colours dyed over pre-bleached mole skins: pale olive, orange, golden olive and amber shades.

AUS Alpine; *JAP* Sawada; *NL* Kelson; *UK* Saville, Niche, Slater, Lathkill, Sparton, Sportfish, Watercraft, Rooksbury, Norris, McHardy, Walker; *US* Fly & Field, Marriott, E.A.T.

MONGA RINGTAIL (Bassarisk or Ringcat)

These naturally black and white banded tails are extremely useful for small to medium hair wing salmon and seatrout patterns. It is also used for lower wing layers on bucktail flies. Dyed in a variety of popular colours, it makes a good substitute for plain dyed squirrel, which is more expensive since it requires pre-bleaching in order to remove the barring from the individual fibres to achieve a plain colour. The white hairs sometimes have dark tips and these will still show up after dyeing. The texture is not dissimilar to grey squirrel, but silkier and straighter. Sold as whole tails, or pieces of mixed colours.

UK Saville, Slater, Watercraft, McHardy; *US* Hunter, Marriott, E.A.T.

MONGOOSE

Has guard hairs banded in colours ranging from cream to black. Very fine tapered, almost like bristle. Excellent for hair wing caddis and useful for smaller Atlantic salmon and streamer patterns. Normally sold as small packs of pre-sorted selected guard hairs.

NL Kelson; *US* Marriott, E.A.T.

MONKEY

Usually a barred ginger/black fine hair which is good for nymph tails or smaller hair wings. Silver monkey fur was recommended by Kingsmill Moore for the body of his Grey Ghost Bumble.

UK Saville, Slater (Silver).

MUSKRAT

The natural belly underfur is very soft and the colour, of this member of the rodent subfamily, that includes voles and lemmings, is a rich blue dun making excellent dubbing. Some colours are cream or dark brown and are good for dry fly tails. The fur is highly water-resistant.

AUS Alpine; *JAP* Sawada; *NL* Kelson; *UK* Saville, Niche, Slater, Lathkill, Watercraft, Rooksbury, McHardy; *US* Hunter, Cabela, Gorilla, Hook & Hackle, Kaufmann, Marriott, E.A.T.; *INT* Orvis

NUTRIA (Coypu)

'Nutria' is the fur trade name for the fur of the coypu, a large South American water rodent, which has become popular as a dubbing material in recent years. The soft mid-brown underfur is relatively easy to dub and is sold as small pieces of tanned hide.

AUS Alpine; *NL* Kelson; *UK* Slater; *US* Marriott, E.A.T.;

OPOSSUM

The American opossum which has a pale cream translucent fur is rarely sold in the flytying trade. It is the Australian opossum that is offered with its much greater range of colourings - grey, cream, reddish brown and tan. Soft and easy to spin the fur makes excellent nymph and dry fly dubbing. When dyed, it also blends nicely to give a good gradation of colour.

AUS Alpine; *JAP* Sawada; *NL* Kelson; *UK* Slater, Watercraft, McHardy, Angling Pursuits; *US* Cabela, Kaufmann, Marriott, E.A.T.

OTTER

A thick dense fur from winter skins which is brown with guard hairs. Used in flies such as the Trueblood Otter and Matt's Fur Nymphs.

JAP Sawada; *US* Kaufmann, Marriott, E.A.T.

PECCARY (Javelina)

This wild pig is the only one native to the south-western USA and Mexico. The bristly fibres are 1-4" (25mm-102mm) long and banded black and white with a black tip. Fairly stiff, yet flexible, it and frequently used for the antennae of shrimp and stonefly patterns. The bristles can be softened by soaking in warm water for a few minutes. They can then be wound onto a hook shank to make effective segmented, tapering bodies for various imitative patterns. Sold as small pieces of hide.

AUS Alpine; *UK* Lathkill; *US* Hunter, Marriott, E.A.T.

PIG BRISTLES

Stiff bristles used for prawn and shrimp fly tails and whiskers, available in red and orange.

UK McHardy.

PORCUPINE

An option when bristly fibres are wanted for quill bodies. Tough and resilient.

JAP Sawada; *US* Marriott.

RABBIT

Like its cousin the hare, the rabbit's fur is used extensively as a dubbing material, both in the natural form and dyed. The fur dubs and 'bonds' easily, making it easy to blend with other, less malleable materials, including synthetics. Hareline Dubbin offers it in an astounding 32 colours.

Rabbit guard hairs can also be used for mobile hair wings and tails in such patterns as damsel fly nymphs. Poul Jorgensen employs the fur with the guard hairs intact for his Fur Caddis Pupa. Rabbit skins also provide Zonker strips when cut lengthways from the hide and Cross-cut strips when cut across the hide. Rabbits hind feet supplied by Marriott, E.A.T. and Hunter.
Rabbit is widely available.

AUS Alpine; *NL* Kelson; *UK* Saville, Niche, Slater, Lathkill, Sparton, Sportfish, Watercraft, McHardy, Walker; *US* Hunter, Blue Ribbon, Fly & Field, Gorilla, Bailey, Marriott, E.A.T.

RACOON

The N. American racoon has very fine medium brown underfur that can be used for dubbing neat compact bodies. The guard hairs can also be used for winging streamer patterns but, like badger, the hair seems to 'reduce' in volume when wet.

AUS Alpine; *JAP* Sawada; *UK* Watercraft; *US* Marriott, E.A.T.

SEAL

The classic British dubbing fur for many patterns. As stocks of quality fur have diminished many man-made substitutes have been offered in the market place. The coarse, shimmering fibres from the Atlantic Seal is the one favoured by tyers, although the Pacific Seal has a soft and velvet-like underfur. Good seal fur is still obtainable, but inspection of a sample is advisable before bulk purchase. When well dubbed it has a unique translucency that the traditionalist tyer still loves.

AUS Alpine; *UK* Saville, Niche, Slater, Lathkill, Sparton, Sportfish, Watercraft, Rooksbury, Norris, McHardy.

SHEEP

Wool

From the fleece (as opposed to spun knitting yarn), it can be used for the heads of sculpins and muddlers, where the buoyancy of spun deer hair is undesirable and the fly

Hare Masks: (from left) dyed olive, natural, golden

is required to achieve depth quickly. Fleece also has a lively mobile action underwater and is considerably more durable than marabou.

A versatile material that can be spun onto a hook shank in a similar way to deer hair and trimmed to shape to make realistic minnow bodies. It takes colour well from waterproof marker pens. Sold in single colours: Brown, Dark Brown, Silver (minnow), Olive, Dark Olive, Orange, Purple, Red, Rust, Yellow, Black, White, Blue, Pink, Chartreuse and Tan.

AUS Alpine; *UK* Watercraft; *US* Hunter, Cabela, Bailey, Marriott.

Icelandic

Looking almost synthetic in appearance and texture, this hair has remarkable natural length, 6-9" (152-226mm), making it applicable for tube, streamer and all but the very largest saltwater patterns. Normally supplied in natural, bright white, it dyes well. Usually sold as patches of tanned hide.

NL Kelson; *UK* Saville, Watercraft; *US* Hunter, E.A.T.

Tiewell Mara Wool

A very fine, clean and soft-tanned wool whose fibres are translucent and 3" long without wrinkling. Makes for easier tying of sculpins, and saltwater streamers with large heads. It can be spun like deer hair and clipped to shape. Colours: white, black, grey, chartreuse, fl. green, pale blue, hot pink, red, olive, purple, white/black tips, grey/black tips.

AUS Alpine; *US* Marriott, Montana Master.

Dall Sheep

A mountain sheep found in Alaska, British Columbia and the Rockies. It has very dense white hair (similar in tex-

ture to caribou). Usually just under 1" long, sometimes a little longer, it is soft and spins well. Best for small spun dry fly bodies. Not easily obtainable. A phone call to Chris Helm at Whitetail might give you a lead.

SKUNK

The tail is of primary interest to the tier. The long black fibres are glossy, while the white portions have an almost translucent sparkle. A magnificent hair for large salmon flies and streamers. Skunk is not readily obtainable in the UK - or even the US - not least because of the strong stomach required to collect a roadkill and its lingering after-effects at home! Probably most appropriate for bachelor tyers.

AUS Alpine; *JAP* Sawada; *UK* Saville, Watercraft; *US* Marriott, E.A.T.

SQUIRREL

The tails of these ground and tree-dwelling rodents are probably the most important hair for winging hair wing salmon, seatrout and streamer flies. The longest fibres come from the top third of the tail. Squirrel tails may be pre-bleached to remove the natural banding to obtain plain dyed colours, but this can make the hair brittle and tends to result in hairs being shed from the tail.

There are 267 squirrel species around the world and all could probably be used for flytying! The most commonly used species are the grey squirrel, pine squirrel, red squirrel, and the fox squirrel. While squirrel tails are renowned for hair wings, the body furs of various squirrels make outstanding dubbings. Pine and grey squirrels have beautiful salt and pepper grizzling and can be dyed and blended to further extend their usefulness.

AUS Alpine; *JAP* Sawada; *NL* Kelson; *UK* Saville, Niche, Slater, Lathkill, Sparton, Sportfish, Watercraft, Rooksbury, Norris, McHardy, Walker
US Hunter, Cabela, Blue Ribbon, Kaufmann, Marriott, E.A.T.; *INT* Orvis.

STOAT

Stoat tails are becoming scarcer and hard to obtain. Specified in comparatively few patterns, notably the popular hair wing salmon flies of the Stoat's Tail family (Silver Stoat, Thunder Stoat, etc). Most flytyers will substitute black dyed squirrel tail, which has the advantage of allowing larger sizes to be tied. Fitch, Weasel and Mink have also been tried. When available, sold as single tails.

NL Kelson; *UK* Niche, Saville, Slater, Lathkill, Sparton, Watercraft, Norris, Walker; *US* E.A.T.

TANUKI TAIL

Japanese Raccoon. A brown and ginger hair, useful for streamers. The underfur makes excellent dubbings.
US E.A.T.

TUSCANA LAMB

A bright, white extra fine hair which is virtually a natural polypropylene imitation! Can be used for dubbing and coloured with Pantone pens, or dyed.
US E.A.T.

WALLABY

The fur is bushier and longer than that of the kangaroo. Works well on Bass flies and has a leech-like look when wet.
AUS Alpine, *US* EAT

WEASEL

The tails are about 6" (150mm) long with a very rich mid-brown hair. Slightly longer than stoat and more expensive.
AUS Alpine; *UK* Watercraft.

WOLVERINE

Large voracious mustelid (family includes badgers,

A range of dyed fox hair patches, from Mustad.

martens, weasels, etc.) of the N. American and European Arctic. The hair is not quite as long as bear, but is fine, soft and dark whilst nevertheless being almost translucent. The guard hair is excellent for hair wing and streamer flies. The underfur also makes a fine dubbing. Sold as patches of hide.

US E.A.T.

WOODCHUCK (Ground Hog / Marmot)

One of the most versatile hairs available to the tyer, 4 - 5 cms long. Unlike deer hair, it is not hollow but floats very well. Guard hairs make good caddis wings (eg. the Chuck Caddis) and can also be used for upwing mayflies. With its very mobile and lively action underwater it can be used as wing material substitute in the Llama series of flies (often underrated fish catchers).

Underfur can be clipped and blended for dubbing that can be used in place of hare's ear, giving a nice scruffy nymph effect. Guard hair natural colour is barred black, tan and black brown, with white tips. Usually sold as small patches of tanned hide.

AUS Alpine; *US* Hunter, Cabela, Kaufmann, Marriott, E.A.T.

ZONKER STRIPS

Thin strips cut from soft-tanned rabbit skins, in the longitudinal direction of the hide. Used in the Zonker series of flies and tied in at the rear of the hook shank and at the head, somewhat similar to 'Matuka' style tying.

Zonker lures need specially prepared flexible rabbit strips, so check the hardness of these products before buying for this particular purpose. The tying principle can also be used for various bait fish or leech imitations. Orvis has tested several width's of this material and believes its own 1/8" (4mm) wide Zonker strips are the best compromise for tying flies in sizes 2-12.

Cross-cut Rabbit Strips are superficially similar to Zonker strips, but are cut across the skin, being designed to be wound onto the hook as a hair hackle.

Orvis sells Zonker strips in packs of five linear feet of strip, individually up to 12" long and available in 15 colours.

AUS Alpine; *GER* Brinkhoff; *JAP* Sawada; *NL* Kelson; *UK* Saville, Niche, Slater, Sparton, Sportfish, Watercraft, Rooksbury, Norris, McHardy; *US* Hunter, Cabela, Gorilla, Kaufmann, Marriott.

YAK

Used for streamer, steelhead and salmon fly wings, including tubes and Collie Dog patterns, and also for elver patterns as it can be ten inches in length, usually not less than six. Naturally brown, it is often dyed black, but also available in blue, yellow, orange, red.

UK Saville, Watercraft.

Deer Hair

THE PROPERTIES of deer hair, and its abundant availability, have made it an integral part of the North American flytying scene. In Britain, after the introduction of the muddler head from across the Atlantic, tyers knew that deer hair was good but were very inexperienced in its use. Moreover it was felt that deer hair was a variable, sometimes unreliable material that did not always achieve the required tasks.

The 1990s have seen all this change for the better, due largely to two Americans - Steve Kennerk of Rocky Mountain Dubbing Co. in Wyoming, and Christopher Helm from Toledo, Ohio, who now runs Whitetail Fly Tieing Supplies. Firstly, Steve introduced quality hair into the UK market, and then Chris made several visits to the UK and Europe. Through his demonstrations, seminars and articles a whole new understanding was opened up for British tyers.

Good deer hair is now available from most flyshops, but that bearing the Whitetail or Rocky Mountain label is to be commended. Steve Kennerk and British photographer Terry Griffiths produced in 1994 a four-page leaflet entitled *A Hair's Difference - the ultimate guide to tying with hair* which is a very helpful introduction to the selection of the right type of hair for the job in hand.

Chris Helm's seminar notes entitled 'Tips for Selecting Deer Hair' are also an invaluable aid, and contain maps showing the range of mule deer subspecies, ranges of whitetail deer subspecies, and a numbered diagram of the skin of a Northern Woodland whitetail deer indicating the types of hair available and their primary applications.

Another source of premium deer hair is Jeff Mack's Longhorn Flies and Supplies.

The term 'deer hair' loosely describes hair from seventeen subspecies of whitetail deer, eight subspecies of mule deer, elk, antelope, caribou and moose. The quality and characteristics of any of these animals' hair will vary depending on age, sex, diet, and heridtary influence. If that were not enough of a headache to sort out, climate, where it lived, and how long ago it was killed will provide further important variables.

The two species of deer most commonly processed for the flytying industry are Northern Woodland whitetail and Rocky Mountain mule deer. Other hairs that are commonly in use are those of the Texas whitetail and the West Coast Columbian whitetail. 'Coastal' deer hair is today a general term referring to hair from the western coast of the US. Rocky Mountain Dubbing markets coastal hair from early season male deer (short, straight, and with uniform tips and barring) which stacks well. Other coastal 'substitutes' which are used include Texas whitetail, Virginia whitetail, Florida whitetail and early season Northern Woodland whitetail.

Deer hair is often described as 'hollow', and many types are. However, this is not hollow like a drinking straw but, rather, each hair is filled with a multitude of tiny cellular air pockets like a honeycomb. Hair textures fall into three categories:

Fine: Not noted for flaring, but ideal for down-wing flies and tails.

Medium: Flares to around 45°; excellent for Caddis and Comparadun.

Bucktails: (from left) dyed yellow, natural, dyed orange.

Coarse: Flares up to 90° and is used for clipped-body flies, Muddlers and Bass flies.

Deer hair comes dyed in many colours. It is generally sold as small patches of tanned hide. The principal hairs available, their properties and applications are listed in this section.

ANTELOPE

A very thick, hollow-bodied, coarse hair, with a varying length of 1"-2.5". The natural colour of the hair is a grey base shading to a brownish tan at the tips. It has a reputation for being rather brittle, but Rocky Mountain Dubbing uses a special tanning and dyeing process aimed at elimination of the brittleness problem. An excellent spinning hair, but not recommended for stacking. Highly buoyant.

BASS HAIR

Bleached and dyed cow elk and the most durable hair for all spun and clipped deer hair body patterns. The special dyeing process produces sharp and vivid colours.
Colours: green, olive, orange, purple, red, yellow, black, bleached, blue, pale yellow, chartreuse.

BUCKTAIL (see also page 28)

On the white side of the tail, the upper 70% of the hair towards the tip of the tail is best suited to streamers, as this hair will not flair to any extent. The hair nearest the rump becomes coarser and will flare with moderate thread pressure. On the dark side, the hair is finer with many having a black tip while the remainder is dark brown. The brown hair was once used in dry flies for tails and wings (eg. original Wulff patterns), but now fine body hair is used for wings, and moose hair for tails.

CALF BODY (see entry on page 28)

CALF TAIL (see entry on page 28)

CARIBOU

A light grey deer hair (snow white on the belly) that is spongy, and packs well. Caribou is excellent for smaller flies requiring a spun deer hair body (eg. G&H Sedge, Irresistible). This short, soft hair is too fine and delicate for flies much larger than about size 10.

CHAMOIS

The familiar 'shammy leather' used for cleaning cars and windows is also used in such patterns as the Chamois Leech. Specially developed by Rocky Mountain Dubbing

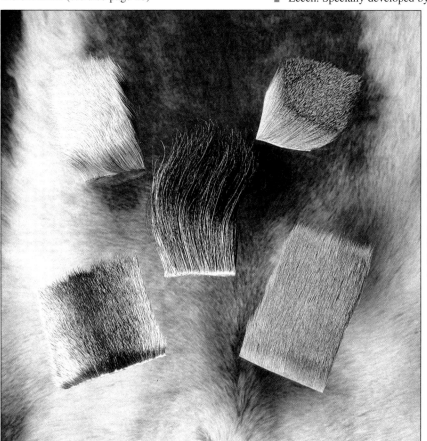

Deer hair has so many uses for the flytyer and the properties of the hair will vary according to whether the animal has been culled in winter or summer, its age, sex, diet, and so on. Clockwise from top left: Reindeer, Roe Deer (winter), Roe Deer (summer), Moose hock, Moose mane (centre).

to minimize drying and stiffening after being fished. Sold in packaged tanned pieces of approximately 12" square. Colours: brown, grey, olive, purple, red, rust, yellow, black, cream, white chartreuse, tan and claret.

COASTAL DEER HAIR

Used for Comparaduns (wings and tails). Medium texture with a length between .25" and 1" with well-defined barred tips. The hair carries no micro growth so stacking is easy and, with its small diameter, flies of sizes 18-20 can be tied. The medium texture makes it usable for small clipped bodies but, being a little heavier than Texas whitetail, it is not suitable for spinning.

DEER MASK

This is the entire face area of various species of deer (most commonly white-tailed deer) including the ears. Essential for tying deer hair winged dry flies in small sizes (eg. Sparkle Dun, Comparadun, various caddis patterns). As with hare's mask, deer's mask provides a wide range of natural colours, from speckled brown, to light dun, to cream. Deer mask furnishes the right textures and lengths of hair for flies from size 8 down to the tiniest. This is a 'must' for the caddis specialist, but seems to be available from relatively few retailers. English Angling Trappings is one.

ELK

Wapiti are known as 'elk' in North America. The deer that Europeans call elk, are known as 'moose' in North America. However, elk hair provides the broadest range of hairs to meet nearly every tying situation. Elk is sold in various categories:

Bull Elk: Medium textured with long pale golden tips making good wing material.

Cow Elk: Coarse textured with steeply tapering tips. Excellent spinning properties

Elk Hock: From the upper leg of cow or bull elk. Stiff hair used for caddisflies in sizes 14-16 and for dry flies. Depending on thread pressure it will flare to 45°. A very short hair at $^1/4$" to $^5/16$" in length, the natural colour ranges from tan to dark brown.

Elk Mane: From the neck of cow or bull elk at a length of 3" to 6" coloured medium to light brown. It is very fine and does not flare but is good for tails, especially divided ones.

Yearling Elk: A one-year-old immature hair from $^3/4$"-$1^1/2$" long. Coloured naturally soft grey to tan it has a uniform thickness to the tip allowing very small Comparaduns to be tied down to size 22. The hair compresses and conforms to thread pressure very close to the tip and it does not roll. Yearling Elk is also used for spun hair bodies on dry flies and for muddler heads. It is about half the diameter of Cow Elk. Humpies and

Goofus Bugs are tied with this hair.

IMPALA

Very fine short hair suited to tails on dry flies for size 16 and smaller.

MOOSE

This huge deer is known as 'elk' in Europe. The dark brown to jet black body hair is very coarse and between 2" and 5" in length. It is extremely buoyant and is used for the tails and wings of dry flies, eg. the Wulff series. Moose mane is a salt and pepper mix of black, brown and grey hairs. As much as 6" long, moose mane has long been used for winding 'quill' bodies. For this purpose, an individual hair is first flattened between finger nail and thumb.

MOOSE BODY HAIR

Very stiff and not suitable for spinning, but very buoyant. Excellent for dry fly tails and nymph feelers. Ranges from very short to long.

MOOSE MANE

Very long, 3-8" and not suitable for spinning. Good for creating two-tone bodies on dry flies. This is done by taking a white hair and a black hair, soaking them in water for half an hour, tying the tips in and wrapping both hairs together, creating a neat segmented body. The body should be given a coating of varnish after it dries. Mosquito bodies can be made by the same process, and the hair is also useful for long tails.

MULE DEER

Excellent spinning hair, but a little shorter than whitetail. Light grey to off-white in colour, it dyes well.

NORTHERN WHITETAIL

Excellent hair for spinning and used for a wide range of patterns that incorporate spun and clipped deer hair, such as Muddlers, Dahlberg Divers, Bass Bugs, Buck Bugs, etc. Light grey stem with black barring at the cream tip.

REINDEER

A very fine, soft and compressible hair with a slight crinkle. It is finer and softer than Caribou, and highly regarded as a spinning hair. Its fragility does not lend itself for the folded body on a Humpy.

ROE DEER

The winter hair of the European roe deer is highly buoyant and excellent for spinning and stacking for wings. The summer coat is equally good for winging tiny Comparaduns and Micro caddis. Pelts range in colour from very light red/brown of the summer coat to the thick grey/brown of the winter coat. The pure white rump of the winter roe will provide the tyer with about 20 square inches of excellent hair for dying.

SITKA WHITETAIL

Similar to Northern Whitetail but with more distinctive markings. Good for Muddlers, Hoppers, Caddis and Hairbugs.

TEXAS WHITETAIL

Comes from a sub-tropical climate so the hair is very fine. Up to 2" long. Good for tails and downwings (eg. Caddis). The hair is hollow only in the lower third and is strongly variegated.

WESTERN BLACK-TAILED MULE DEER

A good hair for deer hair winged patterns in small and medium sizes. The hair is 3-5cm long and relatively fine. Natural colours: pale brown and tan shades. Some 'Coastal' deer often has a very fine soft under-fur. Tyers can leave this 'underfluff' as it gives the hair wing extra support and helps soften the hard line of the guard hairs. Sold as small patches of hide - natural and bleached.

AUS Alpine; *GER* Brinkhoff; *JAP* Sawada; *NOR* Rakkelhanen; *SWE* Bergquist; *UK* Lathkill, Anglian, McHardy, Sportfish, Niche; *US* Whitetail, Longhorn, Marriott, Kaufmann, Bailey, Gorilla, Blue Ribbon, E.A.T, Hunter, Cabela; *INT* Orvis

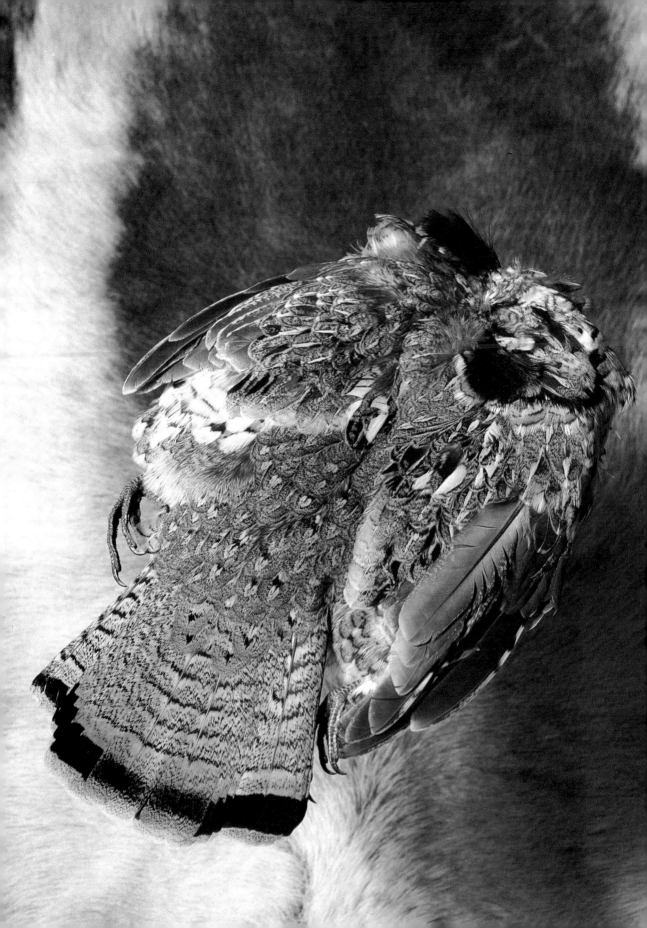

Hackles

Hackle feathers traditionally arouse the greatest passion amongst tyers. Cock hackles of particularly good or rare colour and those with sufficiently short barb length to enable small dry flies to be tied have always been prized. Thirty years ago it was a common complaint that good dry fly capes were scarce - to the extent that many of the 'traditional' natural colours were virtually unobtainable. Dyeing and other methods such as blending two hackles were used to replicate difficult to obtain hackles specified in old patterns.

Things have improved dramatically in recent years due to the efforts of specialist breeders and modern techniques of fowl husbandry. Many traditional colours have re-appeared in qualities that far exceed anything that was obtainable in the past. These developments come at a price however and the tyer will have to pay for top flight cock neck or some saddle from the best known American 'genetic' hackle farms - particularly if bought outside the US.

HACKLE USE

The differences between cock and hen hackles

Cock hackles are longer and more pointed than those from the hen birds which are shorter and more rounded. The 'barbs' of good cock hackles are 'sharp' stiff and glassy in appearance whereas the fibres of hen hackles are softer 'webbier' and have a duller more opaque appearance.

Cock hackles are used for the wound hackles on dry flies where a stiff ruff of hackle fibres assists flotation. They are also used for palmering on bodies for the same purpose. Hen hackles are used mostly for wet flies where the soft absorbent fibres allow the fly to penetrate the water surface easily. The soft hen hackles move more flowingly under water. These are general distinctions and there is nothing hard and fast here as cock hackles are frequently used in wet flies and hen hackles may be incorporated in dry flies.

Undoubtedly it is dry fly quality cock capes that flytyers get excited about. Hen hackles have many important applications in fly dressing but they are far easier to come by in acceptable qualities. For this reason what follows is principally concerned with cock hackles.

CHOOSING COCK CAPES

When choosing any cape particularly one with a hefty price tag it is well worth selecting very carefully. Capes come from individual birds each with distinctive characteristics. One cannot expect the sort of uniformity one would find in bags of sugar from a supermarket. For some tyers mail order purchases may be the only realistic option.

If at all possible, however, it is a far better proposition to visit a specialist retailer with a really good stock through which to rummage. Do not simply take the first off the rack but look through the whole pile and pick the best of the bunch. Most high quality hackle capes are sold in 'Zip-loc' plastic bags and one can only really gauge a cape's quality by taking it out of its packet and examining it - preferably in natural light. Only by close visual and tactile examination can one fully appreciate the qualities in a hackle cape. Indeed this is true of all natural fly dressing materials.

An appreciation of quality hackle comes with

LEFT: Grouse and partridge feathers feature prominently as hackles in many fly dressings of old. This wonderfully varied skin is of the Ruffed Grouse.

practice of viewing and handling many kinds and grades of hackle cape over time. Some of the most important points to look for are:

Colour

Usually the first consideration. The best capes have even and uniform colour that conforms to one of the accepted colour designations referred to later. It is worth remembering however that where a cape lacks uniformity of colour or is of 'nondescript' colour it might be of excellent quality in all other respects. Such capes can often be had at bargain prices: either for use as they are (the trout invariably seem not to mind) or for dyeing to more useful shades.

Condition

The healthiest and strongest birds produce the best conditioned feathers. Dr Tom Whiting owner of Hoffman Hackle has said that when choosing birds for breeding he considers not only colour and quality but also the character of the birds. No matter how good a colour a bird may appear to have a poor spirited bird will not get a good deal in the pecking order thus its health and condition - and therefore feather quality - are unlikely to be of the best. Such a bird rarely produces a top quality cape or makes a worthwhile contribution to the bloodline.

The overt appearance of a cape is often a good first indicator of general condition if not ultimately of quality. Birds in good health and condition seem to 'glow' and the individual feathers are clean and springy. Poor condition often manifests itself as a tatty pecked appearance with thin spots possibly indicating poor diet infestation or disease.

Feather Count

It is clearly desirable for a cape to have as many feathers of useful sizes as possible. Some indication of feather density can be gained just by feeling between finger and thumb the thickness (depth) of a cape where the thin end (the head) starts to widen into the neck proper. Bending the cape at this point will cause the feathers to stand proud from the skin and separate from one another. By doing this individual hackles can be examined and some assessment of the numbers and size distribution can be made.

The 'best' quality necks (supposedly) have high numbers of hackles with barbs short enough to tie the tiniest dry flies. These capes command the highest prices and cater largely to the American market where some tyers consider a size 16 gross! If one's tying is normally on a more 'macroscopic' scale it is clearly a pointless waste of money buying capes featuring lots of size 24-28 hackles. Indeed if one's tying mainly involves sizes 12-16 then a 'lower' grade neck -or even a saddle- will not only be cheaper it may actually also have better hackles for one's needs.

Useable Hackle Length

Look closely at the characteristics of individual hackle feathers. The best cock hackles furnish the highest barb density along the shaft (stem) and which provide the longest portion of 'useable hackle'. This part of the feather also known as the 'sweet spot' is where ideally the hackle barbs are of uniform length. The stem along the sweet spot should also be fairly thin and flexible to allow easy winding onto the hook. Stems that are so thin as to be fragile and those that are so thick that they are inflexible and bulky when tied in are both undesirable. Hackle stems that are brittle - possibly through age or poor dying technique- are almost useless.

The best hackles have long sweet spots and a high barb density along the shaft, allowing more hackle to be wound on to the hook. The longest sweet spots of all are to be found on some of the super grades of saddle hackle. These are so long that several densely hackled dry flies can be tied from a single feather.

Grading of Hackles

Genetic Capes are generally sold in Three Grades (1, 2 and 3) with Number 1 being the best and the most expensive.

CLASSIFICATION OF HACKLE COLOURS

Different methods of classification of hackle colours have been employed from time to time. Frank Elder discusses this aspect in *The Book of the Hackle*. The system dividing colours into the three categories of Single Colours, Bi-Colours and Duns has been widely used. It was originated by C.F.Walker in *Fly Tying as an Art*. There is no perfect system whatever methodology is used as there are two different aspects involved - colour and marking. The variants are enormous as indicated by the fact that Jacqueline Wakeford's *Flytying Tools and Materials* includes photographs of 44 different hackle colourings. Elder's division into five categories (Single Colours, Bi-Colours Barred Duns and Off-Colours) seems as helpful as any for use here to illustrate some examples of capes currently offered.

SINGLE COLOURS

White

Pure white capes are quite rare: most tending to be creamy or having splashes of other colours. While pure white hackles have limited direct applications in fly tying they are much sought after as a base on which to dye other colours.

Cream

Ranges from off-white to dark cream. More easily obtained than white cream hackles can also be over dyed with other colours.

Ginger

From dark cream to pale red.

Light Ginger
The glowing colour of cinnamon and honey which Metz describe as 'the colour of golden wheat at harvest time'. Sometimes splashed with a hint of yellow.

Red
From pale red to dark red this group are sometimes described as 'brown'.

Red Game
Colours range from a rusty red/brown to that of dried blood. Red game (and the black centre listed varieties that come from it) is a staple colour of fly dressing and used in countless patterns.

Black
Jet Black by definition but Jet black in a natural (undyed) cape is a rarity. Natural blacks are more commonly very dark reddish brown or have a dark grey 'bleached charcoal' appearance. The undersides of natural black hackles are invariably disappointingly pale. Dense jet black can really only be attained by dyeing.

BI-COLOURS

Badger.
Black list (centre) with outer being white or cream with the barb tips sometimes black.

Yellow Badger.
Black list with outer from cream to pale or medium ginger with the barb tips sometimes black.

Furnace
Black list with outer from ginger to dark red with the tips of barbs sometimes black -very often seen as red hackles with a black centre. It extends in range from Greenwell's (pale ginger) to Coch-y-bonddu. Furnace hackles have many uses in fly dressing but are particularly for good for patterns imitating adult caddis flies.

Coch-y-bonddu
A very dark furnace. Coch-y-Bonddu is the Welsh name for a red and black beetle that hatches prolifically in mid-summer (literally: black with a red base). The name describes also the artificial fly that imitates the insect and the appropriate hackle colour as well.

BARRED

Cuckoo
Black and white bars. Also called 'Grizzly', 'Irish Grey', 'Monkey' and 'Grey Hen'

Cree
Like Cuckoo but ginger or red instead of the black. Crossing Rhode Island Red with Plymouth Rock will produce this effect. Darker Cree hackles can be used to create an 'instant Adams' since only one feather is needed instead of the usual grizzle and red game wound

together in the conventional way.

Barred Ginger: A creamy ginger accented with bars of light brown.

Grizzle
Not really a colour reference but a description of the barred markings. Using this principle a Cree could be regarded as Ginger Grizzle.

Grizzle hackles are silver or cream/white marked with alternating chevrons of black. These impressive hackles from the fowl breed known as Plymouth Rock are used in many fly patterns. Perhaps the most famous are the Hoffman Super Grizzle saddles. These extraordinary feathers are intensely marked and incredibly long. Selective breeding has produced birds that grow saddle hackles several inches long yet with barbs short enough to tie small dry flies.

Barred Cream: A very pale yellow/cream hackle barred with sandy dun

Barred Sandy Dun: A cream to pale dun background barred with sandy dun.

Rusty Dun: Dun to Blue Dun hackles with edges (barb tips) shading to honey or red.

DUNS

Dun
Pale dun colour all over

Sandy Dun: A Metz special breeding giving a pale sandy tan shade sometimes with hints of cream in mid-rib and tips. Some capes of this designation are almost a khaki giving the faintest impression of having an olive cast. The nearest british equivalent is an Andalusian.

Chocolate Dun: A Metz bred colour that is dark brown blue dun rather than dark grey blue dun which.has the appearance of a medium to dark brown but lacking the warm mahogany redness found in Red Game shades.

Blue Dun
From pale grey to near black with a brownish overtone to a greater or lesser amount.

Iron Blue Dun: Hackles range from almost a natural black to pale khaki and sandy shades. Iron Blue Dun is at the dark end of the dun spectrum: a very dark slaty blue grey

Rusty Dun
Blue Dun spangled with rust colour. If pale medium or dark is used in the description this should refer to the shade of the blue dun.

Honey Dun
A blue dun list with the outer normally honey colour but it can be from cream to near red. If pale medium or dark is used in the description this should refer to the shade of the blue list. A cape that is now difficult to get in good quality but Paul Filippone of Donegal Inc. in Roscoe New York is always worth contacting about these

A collection of rooster neck capes, from Hoffman

OFF-COLOURS

All other hackles which cannot conveniently be placed in the previous four categories.

White Splashed

Essentially a white cape 'marred' by having some of its hackles wholly or partially coloured black and/or dark dun.

Variant

This broad categorization refers to any cape with a variation in its hackles or consists of a combination of rare or unusual colours or markings.

NOTE: Caution should be exercised when comparing names of natural capes from the US with British classifications as different names may be used. For example Light Ginger (US) is Dark Honey (UK), Sandy Brown (US) is Light Red Brown (UK), and Dun (US) is generally a Dark Blue Dun (UK).

INDIAN AND CHINESE CAPES

A great many capes offered for sale are of Chinese or Indian origin. They dye very well but are not as stiff as genetic hackle having the feel sometimes of stiffish hen. That said some excellent 'finds' are possible for the diligent sifter of these capes in stores. For many tyers they may well meet all their needs particularly for stillwater trout angling and they do not hurt the pocket in

the way genetic capes do. Chinese capes are much larger than Indian.

SOURCES OF GENETIC HACKLE

CHANTICLEER

This company is no longer in business but its products are still sometimes available. Not quite as long as Hoffman hackles but extremely good value. Cock Necks are graded 1, 2, 3 and Cock Saddles 1 and 2. A Cock Unit (ie.neck and saddle) at Grade 4 is available as are Hen Sets and Whole Hen Skins at Grade 1.

Colours: grizzly, light ginger, light dun, cream, silver badger, brown, splash dun, dark dun, black variant, dark ginger, medium dun, sandy dun, white, gold badger, barred dun. Also offered in: white, dark blue, red game, honey dun.

UK Rooksbury McHardy.

COLLINS

Produces feathers with short stiff barbs and the minimum of web. Cock capes come in Grades 1, 2 and 3 and Commercial and Hen and Spade hackles are also available. **Colours**: Duns (all shades), grizzly, brown, black, cream, 'One of a kind', barred creams, barred duns, barred ginger, variants, cree, white, splash, badger, ginger, barred, white.

US Collins.

DJ HACKLE

Martin Fitzgerald runs the DJ Hackle Farm in England producing a limited colour range of rooster necks which are excellent value for money.

Available in: grizzle, pure white (perfect for dyeing), dyed black, genetic silver and golden badger.

UK Saville, Niche, DJ Hackle.

EWING

From one of the smaller breeders based in Iowa, the saddles offer excellent value for money in:

Natural: grizzly, natural white.
White dyed: red, yellow, orange, blue, green, coachman brown, olive, claret, ginger, black.
Grizzled dyed: olive.

UK Rooksbury Lathkill Sportfish

HEBERT

Three grades of neck are available from Ted Hebert:
1 Classic
2 Standard
3 Pro Grade
Colours: *natural*: pale watery dun, cream, brown, medium and dark dun, ginger, badger, cree, chinchilla.
Cold dyed: chocolate dun, light dun, medium dun, dark dun, black.
Saddle patches: In same colours and same three grades as the necks they tie mostly in sizes 10 and 12.

AUS Alpine; *US* Hunter AA.

A range of natural hen capes from Hoffman (top two rows) and Metz (bottom row)

HOFFMAN

In the mid-1960s Henry Hoffman started breeding fowl to produce grizzle hackles. At the time he was a passionately keen flyfisherman and also tying flies commercially.

He was fortunate to start his activities with exceptionally good initial stock -birds already possessed of good (for the time) saddles providing 'dry fly quality' hackles of good useable length. Having been raised on a poultry breeding farm he quickly realized the flytying potential of these unique barred Rock Plymouth bantams. By his own assessment Hoffman reckons that the quality of his initial stock probably saved him ten years of development time.

For about ten years he concentrated solely on grizzly before introducing white and ginger to his gene pool. By the 1970s the Hoffman Grizzly hackle was becoming recognized as the best available and by the 1980s Hoffman's saddles had become almost legendary and amazed anyone who saw them for the first time. The stock of white birds progressed rapidly providing excellent hackle for dying and further establishing the Hoffman name.

It was basically a family operation only producing around 2,200 roosters a year and concentrating on quality rather than quantity.

In 1989 Dr Thomas Whiting struck a deal with Henry Hoffman to acquire the Hoffman stock and name to further develop and expand the already unique gene pool. A life-long poultry and game bird enthusiast, Whiting brought industrial breeding and production experience to the Hoffman hackle endeavour not to mention his three university degrees which include a PhD in poultry management and genetics.

To ensure continuity Henry Hoffman agreed to act as a consultant for five years. Additional stocks where acquired in order to develop dun and other colours as well as natural blacks. The enterprise has also expanded into 'exotic' plumages aimed at the classic salmon fly market. Whiting farms with 100,000 roosters in summer 1996 plans to continue expanding to meet the ever-growing demand for 'the world's finest hackle'. Their newest venture, American Hackle, promises to be a most versatile feather for the tyer.

The full Hoffman range (until 1997) should include the following but it would always be wise to check availability of particular colours:-

Necks

These are widely considered to be the finest rooster necks available. Grade 1 necks should contain 300 or more perfect hackles in the sizes listed.
Grade 1 Neck: suitable for flies from size 10 down to 26.
Grade 2 Neck: suitable for flies from size 10 down to 24.
Grade 3 Neck: suitable for flies from size 10 down to 20.

Saddle

A Hoffman saddle hackle averages between 8" to 10" in length and can tie some five or six flies per hackle in sizes mostly 12-14 with some suitable for sizes 10 and 16.

Soft Hackle Matuka Patches

Used for Crowley Lake matuka patterns, as the wide feather gives a good perch profile, and the downy feathers make pulsating collars. Also used for steelhead flies.

Natural: grizzly, white, brown, barred medium ginger, light ginger, golden badger, variant, honey dun, grizzly/variant, barred ginger, medium ginger, silver badger, furnace.

Dyed: black, coachman brown, light dun, medium dun, dark dun, orange, red, pink, purple, yellow, chartreuse

Grizzly dyed: Grizzly/olive, grizzly/brown, grizzly/ orange, grizzly/red, grizzly/pink, grizzly/ purple, grizzly/yellow, grizzly/chartreuse, grizzly/ dun.

US Marriott.

Hen Sets

These sets include both the neck and saddle from the hen bird and represent very good value. Hoffman hen hackles are as outstanding as the company's cock hackles. They have good length and nice round tips and are particularly suited to 'soft hackle' and 'burnt wing' applications.
Colours: *Natural*: grizzly, white/cream, barred ginger, brown/furnace, light ginger, golden badger, variant.
Dyed: light dun, medium dun, dark dun, black, bleached white.
Grizzle dyed: olive brown, dun, coachman brown.
The above colours are all available as cock neck capes and saddles, hen sets (neck plus saddle) and 'Chickabou'.

Chickabou (*see* Feathers section) is similar to turkey marabou substitute (but smaller and finer) and is available dyed over plain white or grizzle in colours: orange, red, pink, purple, yellow, chartreuse.

AUS Alpine; *GER* Brinkhoff; *UK.* Niche, Slater, Watercraft, Rooksbury, Lathkill, Anglian, Saville, Sportfish, McHardy, Angling Pursuits; *US* Cabela, Hunter, AA, Gorilla, Bailey, Kaufmann, Marriott.

HOWARD'S HACKLE

This Canadian company currently specialises in grizzly necks (grades 1, 2 and 3) and grizzly saddles (grades 1 & 2), and natural blacks and are looking to develop their breeding stock further. They also provide Coq de Leon feathers.
CAN Howard.

KEOUGH

Both cock capes and saddles come in three grades (1, 2, 3). The hackles are very thin in profile and long stemmed. The colours which are all true natural duns are:

brown, cream, ginger, black, light dun, medium dun, dark dun, variant, ginger, cree, honey dun, grizzly furnace, dun, grizzly.

Hen Necks

Ultra Grade 1. Colours: black, cream, grizzle, red game, ginger, blue dun.

UK Slater, Rooksbury; *AUS* Alpine; *US* Hunter; *INT* Orvis.

LONGHORN NECKS & SADDLES

Good for patterns requiring long and consistent webby feathers, such as streamers. The saddles contain many long feathers. All the colours are dyed over grizzly and are used in Wooly Buggers, and as legs for Bass Poppers and Tarpon Streamers. Colours: natural, orange, chartreuse, yellow, green, purple, olive, red.

US Marriott

METZ

Metz is probably the best known name in high quality hackle from birds bred specifically for fly tying and is now run as a division of Umpqua Feather Merchants.

NECKS

Metz rooster necks are available in three grades:
*Grade 1 necks have a full range of hackles from size 8 through to 24 (and often as small as 28).
*Grade 2 necks are almost identical in feather quality but have marginally fewer feathers in the smallest sizes and may display slightly more web or some other minor imperfection. Metz grading standards are so stringent that none of these flaws would be significant and Grade 2 necks are priced at a very worthwhile discount to the Grade 1 capes.
*Grade 3 necks may have a little more web, broken tips or pin feathers than Grade 2 but still have plenty of top quality dry fly hackles. This grade will have fewer hackles in the very smallest sizes but may nevertheless have an impressive count of high quality feathers suitable for sizes larger than 16 and cost about half the price of the Grade 1 necks.

SADDLE PATCH
*Grade 1
Feathers suitable for dry flies of size 14 and larger as well as outstanding long hackles for streamer and saltwater patterns and dry fly tails.
*Grade 2
Slightly shorter feathers with few suitable for smaller dry flies. This grade nevertheless provides many hackles suitable for salmon dry flies; palmered woolly buggers; saltwater streamer and bass patterns.

Metz also offers 'Micro Barbed Saddles' suitable for smaller dry flies than catered for by the normal Grade 1 saddle.

Metz cock necks and saddles are available in colours:

black, grizzly, variant, brown, barred ginger, light ginger, barred cream, cream, white splashed, cree, barred sandy dun, chocolate dun, light blue dun, dun, medium dun.
The cock capes and saddles are also available in dyed colours.

HEN CAPES

Soft webby feathers for wet fly and soft hackle applications as well as for spinner wings (unadulterated) and for cutting or burning to other wing shapes. Metz natural hen capes and saddles are available separately or in sets in colours: black, grizzly, brown, light ginger, cream, white splashed, chocolate dun, dun, medium dun.

AUS Alpine; *GER* Brinkhoff; *US* Cabela, E.A.T., AA, Bailey, Kaufmann, Marriott, Hook & Hackle; *UK* Niche, Slater, Watercraft, Rooksbury, Sparton, Lathkill, Anglian, Saville, Sportfish, Norris, Walker, McHardy.

SHANNON'S FANCY HACKLE

Shannon Owen started collecting dry fly quality birds of various colours in 1972 since which time he has been heavily involved in a breeding programme. Until recently he sold materials in only limited quantities but now plans to expand. High quality dry fly hackles strictly graded and quality controlled in natural colours: grizzly brown, coachman brown, barred brown, cree, ginger barred ginger, light dun, medium dun, barred dun, badger furnace, white, cream.

US Cabela

SPENCER'S HACKLES

A large range of high quality hackle in natural and dyed colours with the top grade necks having notably thin and flexible hackle stems. The slightly different grading nomenclature in the following descending order of quality is:

Supreme
Extra Select
Select
Choice

Available in the following colours: *Natural*: cream (neck & saddle), white (neck), barred ginger (neck), brown (saddle), ginger (neck), coachman brown (neck), brown (neck), grizzly (neck, saddle, bleached, hen neck, hen saddle).

Dyed: (all available on white or grizzly) blue dun, purple, blue, fl. pink, claret, red, orange, black, fl. yellow, fl. chartreuse, pale morning dun, yellow, olive, light olive, dark olive, brown.

US Spencer.

Dubbings

MANY OF THE HAIRS and furs previously listed are commonly used as dubbing material. The marabou fluff of feathers is also used for dubbing such things as collars. However, with the reduced availability of some natural materials, recent years have seen an explosion of ready-packeted dubbing materials. Some of these are natural materials, others man-made, and yet others a blend of the two. Some dubbings now come ready-dubbed on a central core material, looking not unlike pipe cleaners.

Many tyers have become used to blending their own particular shades and style of dubbing at home. Commercially available dubbings come in an enormous range of colours and reflective properties, and are often then mixed and refined to the tyer's own personal formula. Colour systems and charts are available to aid the tyer, but one person's perception of a precise shade is not necessarily that of others.

Each year seems to produce even more products, some of which are available labelled by their originating source and others by the retailer. Thus, the tyer entering a store with a large range of dubbings can be somewhat overwhelmed and puzzled by what confronts them. Furthermore, many stores put together their own blends of dubbing as well - such as the beautifully translucent (when wet) Scud Dubbing created by guide Mac Fogelsong at Montana Troutfitters Shop which comes as orange grey or olive.

We have attempted to weave a way through the contemporary maze of the world of dubbings. The journey is by its very nature representative of what is out in the market place, rather than a comprehensive and complete catalogue, and space dictates that some selectivity has been exercised both as to products and colour listings. By way of signposts we have referred to some brand names most likely to be encountered, which may well be the wholesaling source, but we have also indicated suppliers who carry the material for purchase by the public. Because of the variety of differing local conditions encountered by anglers, a supplier may not necessarily carry in current stock the whole range of colours available: however, if they are already working with the manufacturer of the product, they should be able to order your required colours.

DUBBING IN PACKETS

ANGORA GOAT

A perfect substitute for seal with its distinctive spike, sparkle and translucency, much liked by nymph, salmon and steelhead tyers who insist on natural materials. When mixed with fox, rabbit or Spectrablend, the effect is softer and more subtle. Available in the following colours: fiery brown, mahogany, brown, dark brown, black, light dun, medium dun, dark dun, light olive, medium olive, dark olive, brown olive, orange, burnt orange, red, yellow, amber, salmon, cream, ginger, claret, green highlander, insect green, blue, purple, white, light yellow, hot orange, green, natural.

US Marriott, Cabela, Hunter, Kaufmann; *GER* Brinkhoff; *INT* Orvis.

Left: The soft under-feathers of Hoffman Chickabou 'capes', some natural, some dyed.

ANTRON DUBBING
Antron was popularized by Gary LaFontaine in his book *Caddisflies* in which he showed the use of the shine of this tri-lobal material to represent the pupal cases of emerging caddis pupae. Colours: clear, cream, ginger, gray, caddis green, light olive, olive gray, dark olive, yellow, golden stone, light brown, brown, dark brown, black, gray brown, amber.

US Marriott, Cabela, Kaufmann; *GER* Brinkhoff; *INT* Orvis.

ANTRON/HARE BLEND
75% rabbit and 25% Antron, the rabbit provides the qualities of natural fur, while the Antron adds the bright sparkle: cream, buff fox, tan, dark brown, rust, yellow, caddie green, gray, blue dun, amber, light olive, dark olive, black, golden stone, light hare's ear, dark hare's ear.

INT Orvis.

ANTRON SPARKLE DUBBING
Extremely soft but with lots of sparkle. Colours: white/clear, light yellow, light grey, light olive, Cahill cream, black gnat, golden tan, chocolate, march brown, golden stone, hexagenia, rust, medium olive, light olive dun, golden olive, olive damsel, fox squirrel belly, hare's ear, dark olive, crawdad orange, bright yellow, claret, green highlander, chinese red, shrimp pink, fl. yellow, fl. orange, fl. fire orange, fl. chartreuse, fl. pink.

UK Lathkill.

AUSTRALIAN POSSUM DUBBING
An extremely versatile fur, blended with a little Antron, available in 14 colours: brown, natural, march brown, natural gray, dark dun, olive, light olive, sulphur orange, rust spinner, sulphur yellow, black, cream, caddis green, tan.

US Marriott, Cabela.

AUSTRALIAN OPOSSUM
Extremely fine dry fly dubbing, from the natural fur of the Australian Opossum. Colours: light natural, dark natural, dyed black, dyed olive, dyed dark olive, dyed rusty brown, dyed dark brown, dyed dark gray.

US Marriott.

AWESOME POSSUM
Blended guard hair and the soft underfur from Wapsi.

US Marriott.

BEAVER BLEND PLUS
Beaver belly fur with the addition of tri-lobal nylon for added sparkle. Available in the same colours as 100 Per Cent Beaver (see page 57).

US Marriott

BEAVER DUBBING
Beaver fur is used in many standard and new nymph patterns. Rocky Mountain Dubbing has a special technique of bleaching the underfur and dyeing it to the 'true' colours needed for the most popular fly patterns.

Available in 16 colours: natural, brown, blue dun, pale morning dun, adams gray, light olive, olive, dark olive, olive brown, stone fly rust, sulphur yellow, black, cream, Hendrickson pink, chartreuse, tan.

US Marriott, Cabela, Hunter; *INT* Orvis.

BLENDED MUSKRAT DUBBING
Extra fine Muskrat, with guard hairs removed, excellent for small dry fly bodies. Available in nine colours: natural, brown, light gray, pale morning dun, olive, light olive, black, cream, pale yellow.

US Bailey.

BLENDED RABBIT DUBBING
Rabbit fur is one of the most popular natural dubbing materials. With its long fibres it is easy to dub and useable from the tiniest dries to giant dragonfly and stonefly nymphs. Available in 25 colours: red, blue, purple, yellow, pale yellow, green, dark green, gold, orange, olive, pale olive, dark olive, golden olive, rust, brown, dark brown, tan, pink, chartreuse, gray, dark gray, black, natural white, hare's ear, cream.

UK Sportfish.

CADDIS EMERGER DUBBING
Simulates highly translucent aquatic insects and the dubbing traps air bubbles to convey an appearance much like gas emission. Colours: black, yellow, white, march brown, green, tan, Hendrickson pink, gray, brown, olive, peacock, muskrat, rust, cream, gray olive, rust olive, amber, olive brown, olive yellow, pheasant tail.

US Cabela, Blue Ribbon.

CAMEL DUBBING
Real camel underfur, with fine, long, staple fibre allowing very tight spinning onto the thread for the thin bodies of small dry flies: black, natural tan, Cahill cream, dark brown, rusty brown, olive, dark olive, dirty yellow, light yellow, gray, light orange, brown, mahogany brown, squirrel belly, Hendrickson pin, golden stone, Cahill cream, camel.

US Marriott, Kaufmann; *GER* Brinkhoff; *INT* Orvis.

CHARLES JARDINE SIGNATURE SERIES
A range of blends from Upstream Innovations of Oregon and marketed through Gordon Griffiths in the UK.
Stillwater/Emerger: light olive caddis, dark olive, early black, orange, claret, ginger midge, Blagdon green, red, blae and black, orange silver, yellow, cream, ginger sedge, sea green, amber, medium olive.
Hoppers: hopper claret, hopper light olive, hopper red, hopper dark olive, hopper orange, hopper fiery brown.
Rivers Dry Fly: BWO, sunset, apricot, light baetis, dark baetis, march brown, mayfly-danica, terrestrial brown, terrestrial black, BWO spinner, general ephemeroptera, pale watery cream.

UK Anglian, Rooksbury.

CRYSTAL SEAL

A sparkly and somewhat crinkly/coarse synthetic, not unlike Angora goat, but with greater reflective properties. Used especially for mini leeches and shrimp (scud) patterns. Colours: light olive, olive, light gray, tan, black, fl. orange, red, burgundy, cream.

US Kaufmann

DAVE'S BUG DUB

A Davy Wotton product that is 100% hare's fur. It is a mixture of soft underfur and spikey guard hairs. Produces good bodies and, if used with a dubbing twirler or loosely dubbed onto the thread, makes realistic looking legs. Colours: light olive, green olive, dark olive, brown olive, golden olive, orange, red, claret, black, grey medium brown, natural.

UK Wotton; *US* Fly&Field.

DAZL-TRON

A synthetic dubbing blend with highlights of pearlescent fibres adding a life-like gleam. Slightly finer than most Antron dubbings, it can be used for both wet and dry flies. Available in 12 colours: black, medium brown, rust brown, tan, cream, medium olive, blue wing olive, callibaetis, pale morning dun, Adams gray, golden stone, sulphur yellow.

US Kaufmann.

DAZL HARE'S EAR

A super 'buggy' blend being mainly shaved hare's ear with some dyed rabbit. Dazl-Tron is added as a binder to make dubbing easier and to provide subtle colour highlights. Extremely easy to use, it is excellent for nymphs, wet flies and emergers. Colours: black, rust brown, natural hare's ear, cream dark olive, golden olive, blue wing olive, dark dun, light dun, sulphur yellow, burnt orange, light shrimp pink.

US Kaufmann, Marriott.

EVER-FLOAT

A Hobbs product that comes in waterproofed, hank form. It is said to dub as well as the old Spectrum.

US Blue Ribbon, MM.

FAUX SEAL

A synthetic seal's fur substitute in bright colours: crimson red, scarlet red, green, purple, fiery brown, black, yellow, orange, pink, blue.

US Marriott

FINE AND DRY

Very fine polypropylene, with a fibre gauge of approx. 1.2 denier, and which can be used for the tiniest dry fly flies. Permanently water-proofed and incorporating a small amount of Antron to give colour highlights and a little sparkle. Colours: black, rust brown, march brown, hare's ear, light tan, light Cahill, creamy white, medium olive, light olive, blue wing olive, hexagenia, pale evening dun, blue dun, pale morning dun, Adams grey, golden stone, sulphur yellow, creamy yellow, amber, Hendrickson pink.

US AA, *INT* Orvis.

FLASHABOU DUBBING

Described as 'a multi-purpose synthetic dubbing', this is made from Flashabou shredded into short lengths. Flashabou is a metallic or pearlescent synthetic material of the Mylar type. It is, perhaps, most suited to saltwater patterns and caddis case imitations. Colours: silver; gold, pearl, copper, red, green, dark blue, electric blue, orange, purple, lime green, chartreuse, gun metal gray, black, rainbow, fuchsia, olive black, yellow, magenta, ice blue, pink, sand, medium brown, dark bronze.

US Marriott.

FLY-RITE CLARET POLYPROPYLENE DUBBING

Produced especially for the UK market to fill a gap in the colour scheme.

UK Niche.

FLY-RITE EXTRA FINE POLY DUBBING

Extra fine polypropylene dubbing material developed in the US. The colours are based on the Borger Colour System which was developed after 20 years of research into insect colouration by the well known American flyfisher, Gary Borger. The manufacturer prides itself on the accuracy and consistency of its colours. Sold singly or in a portfolio of 44 colours:1 white (BCS 107), 2 black (BCS 118), 3 dark olive (BCS30), 4 bright yellow (BCS 45), 5 rust (BCS 76/77), 6 chocolate brown (BCS 87/98), 7 dark grey (BCS 114), 8 golden olive (BCS37), 9 golden yellow (BCS 47), 10 blue wing olive (BCS 40/43), 11 orange (BCS 73/77), 12 cream (BCS 36), 13 grannom green (BCS 18/19), 14 golden amber (BCS 38), 15 light olive (BCS 40), 16 chartreuse (BCS 21), 17 golden brown (BCS 60/62), 18 rusty orange (BCS 77), 19 light tan (BCS 91/95), 20 dark tan (BCS 99), 21 light grey (BCS 110), 22 Cahill tan (BCS 58), 23 olive sulphur (BCS 44), 24 tiny blue wing olive (BCS 24), 25 cream variant (BCS 39), 26 Adams grey (BCS 110/114), 27 speckled dun/light Hendrickson (BCS 95), 28 dark reddish brown (BCS 65/66), 29 western olive (BCS 37/32), 30 march brown (BCS 68), 31 pale morning dun (BCS 55), 32 rusty olive BCS 59), 33 orange sulphur (BCS 53), 34 Quill Gordon/brown drake yellow (BCS 32/40), 35 inchworm green (BCS 24/21), 36 ginger cream (BCS 54), 37 grey drake/grey fox (BCS 92/95), 38 pale watery yellow (BCS 49), 39 medium brown/dun variant (BCS 99), 40 caddis pupa green (BCS 20), 41 pale olive (BCS 27), 42 dark olive (BCS 34), 43 camel (BCS 58/61), 44 ecru (BCS 104)

US Marriott, Kaufmann, Bailey, Fly-Rite, Hook & Hackle; *UK* Niche, Saville, Rooksbury; *JAP* Sawada.

FLY-RITE NATURAL DUBBING

A natural floating dubbing made up of 100% natural

wool fibres unblended. Colours: white, golden olive, amber, primrose, rust, tan, pale morning dun, olive speck, pale olive, caddis tan, caddis green, dark brown, chartreuse, dark gray, march brown, olive, black, gold, kelly green, pale gray, pink, yellow, gray, golden brown, hot orange, golden yellow, reddish brown, orange burgundy, red quill.

US Marriott, Fly-Rite.

FOX FUR DUBBING

This almost cashmere-textured dubbing is produced from humanely farmed Norwegian fox. Popularised and promoted by Torill Kolbu, it can be used for all sizes of fly bodies, from the smallest midge to the largest salmon fly, and dubs easily onto any type of tying thread, including monofilament. This product is also sold in a longer hair form as Fox Hair which enables a wider range of uses. Available in 24 colours: bright green, red, claret, magenta, orange, bright yellow, purple, dark blue, blue, lilac, aquamarine, green highlander, light brown, medium olive, light olive, pink, golden yellow, white, blue dun, black, grey, light blue, brown and dark brown. Sold individually, or in 12 colour dubbing dispenser boxes.

GER Brinkhoff; *NOR* Bergqvist; *SWE* Bergqvist.

FROG'S HAIR DUBBIN'

Made from 100% natural fibres and ties well down to size 26. Colours: black, white, golden yellow, golden brown, amber, tan, pink, yellow, primrose, pmd, green,

olive, olive speck, caddis green, caddis tan, rust, red brown, burgundy, salmon, sulphur, red quill, insect, brown drake, pale grey, pale olive, dark brown, orange, hot orange, dark gray, Adams gray, chartreuse, march brown, gold, golden olive.

US Bailey.

HARELINE DUBBIN

Natural dubbing consisting mainly of rabbit fur, a fur which has relatively few guard hairs making for neat and easy dubbing, even in the smallest sizes. Colours: light Cahill, march brown, Adams gray, hare's ear, dark hare's ear, dark dun, black, pale yellow, yellow, bright yellow, olive, light olive, insect green, caddis green, orange, hot orange, rusty orange, brown, green damsel, red, light gray, stonefly, rust, chocolate brown, cinnamon caddis, dark olive, amber, antique gold, olive dun, olive brown, purple, olive tan, seal brown, olive hare's ear, peacock, white, cream, golden brown, dark olive brown, creamy olive, sand, tan & yellow, ginger, creamy gray, dirty yellow, Hendrickson pink, fl. orange, fl. coral, fl. yellow, fl. pink, fl. lime green, fl. coachman red.

US Marriott, Cabela, Hunter, Kaufmann, Whitetail; *UK* Lathkill; *AUS* Alpine.

HARELINE SHEARED DUBBING

Muskrat Belly, Muskrat & Antron, Beaver, Beaver & Antron. Natural fur sheared from the pelt and blended.

US Marriott.

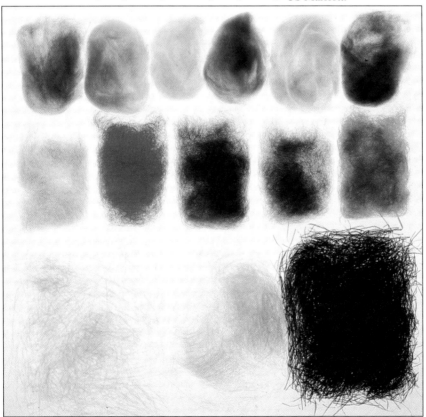

Dubbing materials are now available in an extraordinary variety of colours, textures, degrees of coarseness and softness. Pictured left are: Umpqua's Super Fine (top row), Partridge's SLF (middle row), Spirit River's Lite Brite and Magnum Lite Brite (bottom row)

HARE-TRON DUBBIN

A rabbit and Antron blend in colours: light Cahill, march brown, gray, golden brown, light olive brown, dark dun, black, pale yellow, yellow, golden stone, olive, creamy olive, olive dun, caddis green, pale olive, dark brown, burnt orange, ginger, dark olive, seal brown, light gray, cinnamon caddis, olive tan, olive brown, pink shrimp.

AUS Alpine; *US* Marriott, Kaufmann, Whitetail; *UK* Lathkill.

HARE'S EAR PLUS DUBBIN

Antron added to the Hare's Ear makes this good for nymphs, with the buggy guard hairs spiking out. Colours: natural hare's ear, natural dark hare's ear, insect green, black, reddish brown, olive, tan, chocolate brown, gold, olive brown.

UK Lathkill; *AUS* Alpine; *US* Marriott, Hunter, Kaufmann, AA, Whitetail.

HARETRON DUBBING

With the extra 'g' at the end, this is the Lureflash rabbit and Antron blend in: white, pink, lime, orange, red, cream, olive, light brown, black, brown, yellow, magenta.

UK Rooksbury, Watercraft.

HARROP DUBBING

Very fine natural dubbing conditioned with CDC oil for waterproofing. Colours: pale morning dun, light Cahill, blue wing olive, light olive, mahogany, callibaetis, trico, rusty spinner, olive, muskrat gray, black, Hendrickson, brown, gray olive, sulphur orange, tannish yellow, dark tan, pale olive, yellow, caddis green, brown olive, Colorado green drake, light grey, dark honey, pink Albert, ephrum white, pale yellow.

US Marriott.

IDAHO SEAL DUBBING

A blend of natural furs seeking to simulate seal's translucency and shimmer. Colours: cream, olive, burgundy, dun, purple, yellow, light olive, fiery brown, black, tan, hot orange, red, brown, green, brown olive.

US Marriott

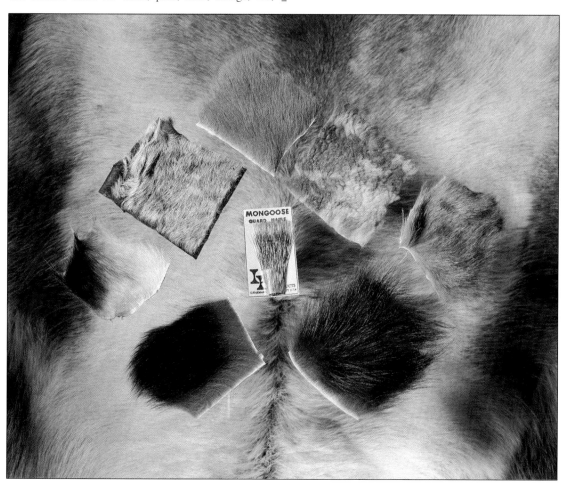

Various natural furs useful for dubbing and winging: (clockwise from top) Kangaroo, Llama, Bobcat, Fisher, Wallaby, Fitch, Chinchilla, Mongoose guard hair (centre).

INTER-TAC DUBBING

Long rabbit hair dubbing from Phil Camera's company: effective for both dry flies and nymphs. Colours: white, amber, yellow, ginger, red, olive, tan, brown, gray, blue dun, black.

US Gorilla.

IRISE DUB

A blend of several dubbing fibres along with a special Mother of Pearl filament from Lureflash in the following colours: black, white, brown, olive, lime, red, claret, green, grey, orange.

UK Rooksbury, Watercraft.

KAUFMANN NYMPH BLENDS

Dubbings designed especially for Randall Kaufmann's famous stone fly nymphs and shrimp (scud) patterns. Colours: black stone, golden stone, brown stone, olive scud, tan scud.

US Marriott.

KAUFMANN'S RABBIT DUBBING

All the natural colours have the guard hairs left in. Colours: *Natural*: light Cahill, march brown, gray, hare's ear. *Dyed*: black, olive, insect green, caddis green, orange, hot orange, rusty orange, light gray, rust, chocolate brown, cinnamon caddis, dark olive, amber, antique gold, olive dun, olive brown, seal brown, olive hare's ear, peacock, white, golden brown, dark olive brown, creamy olive, sand, dirty yellow. *Fluorescent*: orange, coral, yellow, pink, lime green, royal red.

US Kaufmann.

K-DUB (Kapok)

Kapok is a natural vegetable fibre obtained from the seed pod of the Kapok tree. Because of its floating qualities, it is used as a filling for life jackets. Kapok compresses extremely well, which allows the flytyer to dress very fine compact bodies on small dry flies.

   The natural colour is a creamy off-white, but it is readily dyed. Colours: female Hendrickson pink, dark olive, yellowish grey, medium grey with a bluish tint, cream yellow with an orange tinge, chocolate brown, pale yellow cream, caddis green, cream, black, light red brown, yellow orange, creamish olive yellow, tan, white, slate grey, male Hendrickson tan pink, olive brown, dark red brown, isonychia maroon brown, yellow brown with orange tint.

US Marriott.

KRYSTAL DUB

Extremely fine soft dubbing easy to use and with a noticeable sparkle. Useful for nymphs and emergers. Colours: hare's ear, dark hare's ear, gray, black, olive, tan, caddis green, rust, cinnamon caddis, medium brown, olive brown, peacock green.

US Marriott, Cabela; *UK* Lathkill; *GER* Brinkhoff.

LAZER LIGHT

Although used as a wing material it can also be spun, wrapped or dubbed. A synthetic hair with heathering (blended colours). Available in: black, hot green, minnow blue, peacock, chartreuse, hot orange, minnow green, purple haze, glacier white, hot pink, minnow grey, rainbow.

AUS Alpine, *US* Marriott, AA.

LIGAS ULTRA TRANSLUCENT DUBBING

An earlier 'model' of Scintilla, which may still be found.

US Hook & Hackle, E.A.T.

LITE BRITE

A striking dubbing that consists entirely of fine strands of metallic or pearlescent, Mylar-type material. Lite Brite has been most enthusiastically received in the US and is now gaining popularity elsewhere. It can be used on its own, or mixed with other dubbing materials. It is perfect for streamer patterns such as the Clouser Minnow, and a few strands added to the marabou on Woolly Bugger and Leech patterns make them really come alive. Lite Brite can be dubbed straight onto pre-waxed thread to create cased caddis bodies, which are especially effective when used with a gold head bead. It also represents a major development for the bodies of salmon and steelhead patterns as, dubbed and teased out with Velcro, the material spikes out like seals' fur, but with ten times the sparkle!

Colours: black, bronze/brown, river green, dark olive, gold, yellow, copper, purple haze, silver, ruby red, ocean blue, burgundy, salmon pink, minnow blue, pearl/blue flash, pearl/green flash, fire fox peacock, polar pearl, rainbow, hot yellow, copper/pearl.

UK Lathkill, Anglian; *US* Marriott, Kaufmann, Whitetail; *INT* Orvis.

LOON DUBBING

Three new lines of dubbing which have recently come into the marketplace: 1. Llam-a-Rama (furry); 2. Pyle-on Nylon (iridescent and shiny); 3. Knottin' Cotton (dry). Available in: light grey, dark grey, black, red-red, gold, rusty orange, natural, tan, rusty brown, mahogany, dark chocolate, light olive, avocado, forest green, pale yellow, bright yellow.

US Loon (contact for local suppliers)

LUREFLASH LIFELIKE DUBBING (LLD)

A ready-mixed blend of trilobal, translucent and other circular fibres in: red, insect green, light brown, yellow, green highlander, white, black, grey dun, dark brown, olive, orange, claret.

UK Anglian, Watercraft.

LUREFLASH SELFBLEND DUBBING (LSD)

The three elements of the completed LLD colours in one pack for blending together at home for desired shade. It is claimed that over 10,000 colours and blend mixtures can be obtained from this system.

UK Anglian, Watercraft.

MAD RIVER BEAVER DUBBING

Capable of being dubbed down to size 28, with some excellent dry fly colours, this beaver dubbing can be purchased in singly or in a 24 compartment set. Colours: 1 ephron white, 2 sulphur yellow, 3 natural dun, 4 rust, 5 rusty spinner, 6 red, 7 cream, 8 rusty orange, 9 black, 10 light claret, 11 olive brown, 12 tan, 13 olive, 14 pale evening dun, 15 isonychia, 16 dark Hendrickson, 17 blue dun grey, 18 dark olive, 19 light olive, 20 Adams grey, 21 pink fox, 22 medium brown variant, 24 march brown, 25 sulphur orange.

US Hunter.

MAGNUM LITE BRITE

A coarser fibred version of Lite Brite for larger saltwater and bass patterns. Colours: dark olive green, gold, purple, silver, ruby red, ocean blue, salmon pink, minnow blue, polar pearl, pearl blue, pearl green, hot yellow.

US Contact Spirit River for local supplier of this larger version.

MIX AND MATCH (see Star Fire, page 60)

MUSKRAT DUBBING

Colours: natural gray, brown, pale yellow, cream, olive, black, pale morning dun, light shaded natural, light olive.

US Marriott, Hunter; *UK* Lathkill.

100 PER CENT BEAVER

Sheared beaver belly fur that has some of the guard hairs left in. Versatile and easy to use, it is well worth the consideration of any tyer who has a strong preference for natural dubbing materials. Colours: black, rust brown, natural brown/grey, olive (damsel), golden stone, ginger.

US Contact Spirit River for local suppliers.

NATURE'S SPIRIT DUBBING

Made from finely carded wool treated with CDC preen oil for floatation. Dyed to exact shades that match the natural well, this is regarded as a quality product. Colours: pale morning dun, infrequens, blue wing olive, olive, light olive, pale olive, gray olive, brown olive, deep olive, rusty spinner, light Cahill, yellow, pale yellow, tan yellow, sulphur orange, muskrat gray, light gray, dark honey, light honey, caddis green, green drake, dark tan, brown, trico, pink Cahill, callibaetis, Hendickson, mahogany, ephron white, slate, red, orange, black.

US Hunter.

PAXTON'S BUGGY NYMPH

A medium-coarse woolly dubbing for hairy 'buggy' patterns, and large nymphs and streamers. Colours: rust, dark brown, tan damsel, pale olive, lava brown, gray, blue olive, caddis, sage green, tan, black, cinnamon, dark brown, light brown, light hare's ear, golden stone, dark

hare's ear, olive, light olive, brownish olive.

US Contact Umpqua for local suppliers.

PERMATRON DUBBING

(see entry for Permatron, page 82)

US Marriott.

PETER MASTER'S DUB

Professional flytyer Peter Masters' own brand of Antron dubbings which blended to imitate natural insect colours. There are 39 shades ranging from Green Highlander to Light Orange, and some interesting mixtures such as parrot mixed olive, rainbow black and bloodworm red.

UK Masters.

POLAR BEAR DUBBING

Colours: red, purple, yellow, claret, black, hot pink, olive, brown, hot orange, chartreuse, green highlander, silver doctor blue.

US Marriott.

POLY II

A fine, medium-length fibred polypropylene felted into sheet form, from which dubbing can be teased as required. The sheets can be stored extremely compactly and obviate the mess frequently associated with loose dubbings. While rather less convenient than loose fibred dubbing for actual tying, it is ideal for the travelling flytyer's kit. Each 4" x 5" sheet contains a deceptively large amount of material - sufficient, it is claimed, for 250 size 16 fly bodies. Poly II can also be cut to shape and used for wings. Colours: western olive, Cahill cream, black, chocolate brown, medium golden olive, medium grey, white, creamy pink, mahogany brown, pale yellow, rust, dark cream, pale watery olive, nymph, creamy orange, tan, dark olive green, dark grey, pale grey dun, pale rose dun.

Also in fluorescent colours: fl. yellow, fl. green, fl. red, fl. orange.

UK Niche, Rooksbury; *US* Fly-Rite.

POLY-SEAL SPARKLE FIBRE

A coarse sparkle dubbing with fibre length of approx. 2", intended for use as a seal's fur substitute. Colours: pink fluorescent (BCS79), red fluorescent (BCS84\85), orange fluorescent (BCS73), chartreuse fluorescent (BCS24), yellow fluorescent (BCS73\77), blue fluorescent (BCS133), green fluorescent (BCS19), purple fluorescent (BCS79\80), white sparkle (BCS 107), black sparkle (BCS118), medium grey (BCS105), tan (BCS58\61), rust brown (BCS63\73), chocolate brown (BCS98), western olive (BCS43\40), dark olive green (BCS 11\14)

US Marriott, *UK* Niche.

POLY-WIGGLE

Sparkly long-fibred (6") polypropylene, slightly coarser than Poly II. Ideal for streamers and nymphs and available in a range of bright colours suited to salmon, seatrout, steelhead and saltwater patterns. Available in 17 colours: white (BCS 107), black (BCS 118), blue (BCS 140), yellow (BCS 47), orange (BCS 73\77), red (BCS 89), pink (BCS 79), chartreuse (BCS 16\17), chocolate brown (BCS 98), rust brown (BCS 63\73), tan (BCS 58\61), dark olive green (BCS 11\14), western olive (BCS 43\40), pale watery olive (BCS 13\16), pale yellow (BCS 49), medium grey (BCS 105), purple (BCS 126\127).

UK Niche; *US* Fly-Rite.

PSEUDO SEAL
Synthetic seal's fur substitute from Spirit River with the same lustrous sheen and look as the natural, but not quite so stiff and easier to dub. It can be used wherever seal is traditionally specified. Colours: black, polar white, olive, green, golden yellow, burnt orange, purple, red, fluorescent fire orange, fl. chartreuse, fl. shrimp pink, fl. orange.

US Marriott.

RABBIT HARETRON
A rabbit and Antron blend highly recommended in Randall Kaufmann's *Fly Tyers Nymph Manual*. Colours: light Cahill, march brown, gray, golden brown, light olive brown, dark dun, black, pale yellow, yellow, golden stone, olive, creamy gray, olive dun, caddis green, pale olive, dark brown, burnt orange, ginger, dark olive, seal brown, light gray, cinnamon caddis, olive tan, olive brown.

US Kaufmann.

RAINY'S SPARKLE DUB
A blend of a spectrum of sparkling colours, perfect for matching the hatch. Single line dubbing for small flies is recommended, but a dubbing loop brings out a nice 'buggy' effect on larger nymphs. Colours: white, mother of pearl, light Cahill, tan, pale yellow, creamy yellow, sunshine yellow, shrimp pink, chartreuse, golden olive, olive, olive brown, peacock, plush peacock, honey amber, amber, pale sulfur orange, sulfur orange, smokey orange, flaming orange, light cinammon, medium cinnamon, dark cinnamon, rust, golden stone, golden brown, brown, light hare's ear, dark hare's ear, misty grey, Adam's grey, iron grey, black, black/aqua splash, black/blue splash, black/xmas splash, black/emerald splash, black/orange splash, black/purple splash, black/red splash, black/fuchsia splash.

US Marriott, Rainy.

SALMON AND STEELHEAD DUBBING
A dynamic combination of rabbit and Lite Brite. Both the rabbit guard hairs and spiky Lite Brite create a translucent, highly reflective, shaggy dubbing that is perfect for streamer style and saltwater patterns. Colours: black, purple, red, yellow, fl. chartreuse, fl. shrimp, fl. hot pink, fl. cerise, claret, kingfisher, orange, hot orange.

US Kaufmann.

SALMO-WEB DUBBING
Bright and sparkling for shaggy bodies on nymphs and streamers, and blends well with other materials. Colours: bright seal, lemon yellow, fl. yellow, yellow, pink, orange, hot orange, fl. red, medium red, dark red, purple, light claret, medium claret, tan, fiery brown, brown, dark brown, light blue, medium blue, super crystal, light olive, green highlander, fl. green, bright green, golden olive, blue dun, black, medium olive, dark olive.

US Marriott; *JAP* Sawada.

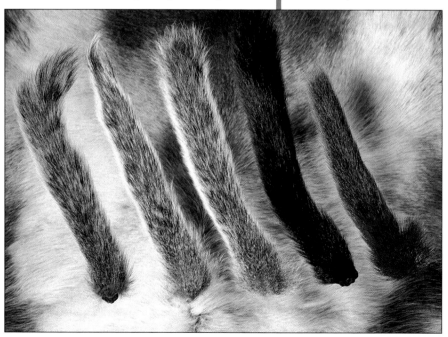

Grey Squirrel tails: the natural (centre) and four dyed colours.

SCINTILLA DUBBING

Kenn Ligas' Scintilla is a synthetic dubbing material available in a wide range of single and blended colours designed to match various natural insects. Along with a colour description, each shade is cross-referenced to the Borger Colour System Available in 85 colours: 1 gingery black (BCS9), 2 coal black (BCS118), 3 pale olive green (BCS1), 4 pale bluish grey (BCS105), 5 smoky pink (BCS 79), 6 pale creamy shrimp (BCS72), 7 smoky grey (BCS110), 8 pale rusty brown (BCS 125), 9 rusty dun (BCS121), 10 transparent grey (BCS106), 11 fiery rust (BCS76), 12 honey cream (BCS48), 13 fiery claret (BCS90), 14 dark chocolate (BCS64), 15 pale yellowy olive (BCS 38), 16 rich olive (BCS43), 17 sooty olive (BCS 33), 18 smoky olive (BCS25), 19 pale cinnamon (BCS74), 20 chroma green (BCS18), 21 creamy pinkish grey (BCS122), 22 pale primrose grey (BCS46), 23 very pale yellow (BCS42), 24 orangish black (N\A), 25 orangish sepia (BCS63), 26 honey amber (BCS51), 27 smoky dun (BCS 108), 28 light hare's mask (BCS95), 29 dark hare's mask (BCS65), 30 pale olive brown (BCS32), 31 golden brown (BCS67), 32 vivid red (BCS85), 33 hot orange (BCS77), 34 fiery amber (BCS50), 35 transparent pearl (BCS93), 36 sooty pale yellow (BCS17), 37 pale brownish grey (BCS61), 38 transparent pink (BCS69), 39 smoky beige (BCS 95), 40 transparent white (BCS107), 41 purplish brown (BCS117), 42 purplish olive (BCS35), 43 dark rusty brown (BCS86), 44 blood and brown (N\A), 45 blood and black (N\A), 46 peacock (N\A), 47 iridescent indigo (BCS144), 48 emerald and black (BCS146), 49 rich magenta (BCS127), 50 juicy chartreuse (BCS21), 51 salmonella (N\A), 52 neon pink (BCS80), 53 crawdaddy (BCS73), 54 ultra violet (BCS130), 55 teal green (BCS147), 56 royal blue (BCS140), 57 bright lime (BCS19), 58 garden hackle (N\A), 59 smoky orange (BCS71), 60 hot fuchsia (BCS126), 61 siphlonurus gray (BCS109), 62 pale amber (BCS46), 63 medium amber (BCS 47), 64 dark amber (BCS53), 65 medium olive brown (BCS29), 66 dark olive brown (BCS34), 67 medium cinnamon (BCS74), 68 dark cinnamon (BCS86), 69 light chocolate (BCS58), 70 medium chocolate (BCS61), 71 primrose (BCS 42), 72 pale beige (BCS91), 73 medium rusty brown (BCS66), 74 pale olive (BCS27), 75 medium olive (BCS37), 76 grandis green (BCS 28), 77 pale ginger (BCS51), 78 ginger (BCS 62), 79 dark ginger (BCS59), 80 medium hare's mask (BCS99), 81 golden olive (BCS44), 82 dark golden olive (BSC41), 83 ripe olive (BCS23), 84 rhyacophila green (BCS4), 85 damsel blue (BCS 136).

also available is:

Scintilla Caliente Scintilla Dubbing that is blended with long thin and supple strands of synthetic flash material. Available in dispenser packs or individual packets. Colours: cherry bomb red, intense tangerine, ardent orange, black & blue, sunburst yellow, copper & black, jazz bo blue, snazzy salmon, spiced cherise, highlighted

ABOVE: deer masks are useful for coarse dubbings and certain caddis and muddler patterns.

lime, juicier chartreuse, walnut & copper, speckled shrimp pink, awesome olive, jewelled ebony, hot flash fuchsia, ultra violet & ruby, diamonds & white, scuzzy leech brown, black & ruby, electrified garden hackle, hyped hare's mask, golden olive glitter, prettier peacock.

US Marriott, Cabela, AA, Hunter, Bailey; *INT* Orvis.

SCOTIA COMPLETE TARTAN DUBBING

Magnus Angus, its creator, describes it as 'a beaut buggy, leggy dubbing which makes a great thorax on nymph patterns'. Colours: black, iron grey, claret, fiery brown, natural, blood, pink purple, orange, blue, warm olive, insect green, olive, cinnamon, ginger, aphid green, amber.

UK Scotia.

SEAL-EX

A seal's fur substitute developed by Poul Jorgensen (and now in the Rocky Mountain Dubbing stable). It is slightly coarse and full-bodied for nymphs, salmon and steelhead flies, and available in 27 colours: isonychia, brownish black, light golden brown, pale amber, pale olive gray, medium olive, dark olive, pale olive, olive brown, dark brown, medium brown, grass green, pale green, golden amber, creamish white, buff, yellowish cream, black, yellow, hot orange, light orange, red, fiery brown, green highlander, silver doctor blue, claret, gray.

US Marriott.

SEAL'S FUR (natural)

The classic British dubbing material. See entry in Hairs & Furs.

SEALTRON DUBBING

A mix of seal's fur and Antron from Lureflash in: black, grey, olive, green, blue, claret, red, yellow, orange, brown, light brown, cream.

UK Watercraft.

SHEARED BEAVER

Natural beaver fur sheared from the hide. A super-fine dubbing that goes on the thread easily. It incorporates a small proportion of guard hairs and exhibits good floating qualities for dry flies: 60 coffin fly cream, 61 sulphur yellow, 62 quill gordon, 63 rust, 64 rusty spinner, 68 trico black, 70 baetis olive, 71 tan 72 blue wing olive, 73 pale morning dun, 75 Adams gray, 77 light olive, 78 medium olive, 80 Hendrickson pink, 81 brown, 83 march brown, 84 light orange, 85 pale yellow.

INT Orvis.

SILK DUBBING

This 100% silk dubbing is very fine and long fibred, naturally water resistant and has a real translucency. It will tie the smallest of dry flies and holds its colour well. Colours: black, white, cinnamon brown, pale yellow, dark hare's ear, light Cahill, march brown, Adam's grey, olive hare's ear, olive brown, dark dun, light gray.

US Hunter.

SPECTRABLEND

For the flytyer who prefers natural materials but can do without the bother, mess and inconsistency of mixing his own, Spectrablend has 26 pre-blended colours for nymphs, dries and wets: black hare's ear, royal coachman red, green damsel, Hendrickson pink, Hendrickson nymph, white, cream, light Cahill, march brown, gray, hare's ear, dark hare's ear, olive hare's ear, dark dun, black, pale yellow, yellow, light olive, caddis green, sulphur orange, burnt orange, light gray, rust, chocolate brown, cinnamon caddis, dark olive, amber, olive, seal brown, peacock, olive dun, olive tan, claret.

INT Orvis

SQUIRREL BLENDS

Dyed squirrel hair blended with highly refractive Antron. The material dubs easily gives a spiky and natural look to nymphs. Colours: black, dark hare's ear, medium hare's ear, tan, dark olive, medium olive, dark dun, natural gray, antique gold, sulphur,
rust, burnt orange.

US Kaufmann.

SQUIRREL BRITE

Blended Squirrel Blend and Lite Brite. Tyers in the US had been shredding Lite Brite and mixing it with their dubbing for some time and Spirit River was asked to produce a pre-blended mix. A relatively coarse dubbing with super sparkle that lends itself to nymphs and many other sub surface flies. Available in 12 colours: black, dark hare's ear, medium hare's ear, tan, dark olive, medium olive, dark grey, natural gray, antique gold, sulphur, rust, burnt orange.

US Kaufmann.

SQUIRREL DUBBING

Grey natural, fox natural, bleached ginger, olive, golden olive, dark olive, brown, rusty, dark brown, black, green, orange.

US Marriott, Kaufmann; *UK* Lathkill; *GER* Brinkhoff.

STAR FIRE

A British synthetic blend dubbing from John Hunt that comes in three preparations under the name 'Mix and Match': **Nymph, Fire hair, Fire fur.**
Colours include: red, natural, hot orange, claret, brown, fl. orange, fl. red, green brown, dark green, amber, ginger, bright green. Also blends for midge pupa, sedge pupa, damsel nymph, shrimp and corixa.

UK Lathkill.

STEELHEAD/SALMON DUBBING

A seal's fur substitute, easily applied allowing spiky and buggy bodies, especially when using a dubbing loop. Colours: black, purple, red, yellow, chartreuse, fl. shrimp, fl. hot pink, fl. cerise, hot orange, claret, kingfisher blue, orange.

US Marriott.

SUPER FINE DUBBING / SUPER FINE DRY FLY DUBBING

Very fine denier (1.2) with a smooth texture and treated with a permanent DuPont waterproofing, for tying the smallest dry flies. Colours: Adams gray, amber, black, blue dun, brown, brown olive, dark tan, golden olive, gray olive, Hendrickson pink, light Cahill, mahogany brown, olive, pale
evening dun, pale morning dun, sulphur orange, tan, caddis green, callibaetis, cinnamon caddis, pale yellow, rusty brown, fl. chartreuse.

US Marriott, Cabela, Hunter, Kaufmann; *UK* Lathkill; *GER* Brinkhoff.

SUPER-POSSUM

A blend of Australian opossum and Antron, with minimal guard hair content, it can be dubbed to make very smooth neatly tapered dry fly bodies, or picked out for 'buggy' nymphs. Australian opossum is one of the finest dubbing furs available and the Antron adds a touch of sparkle to the base colour: brown, black, white, sulphur yellow, sulphur orange, orange, pale morning dun, march brown, tan, rust, rusty spinner, Hendrickson pink, caddis green, olive, dark olive, cream, dark dun.

INT Orvis.

SYNTHETIC LIVING FIBRE (SLF)

Developed by Davy Wotton and marketed by the well known English hookmakers Partridge, SLF rapidly developed a world-wide following among tyers as a seal's fur substitute, greatly helped by Davy's personal appearances at shows and flytying days at which he demonstrated many innovative ways of applying the material. It is now available in many forms:

SLF Standard
Available in 48 colours, some of which are blends: 1 bright green, 2 green highlander, 3 insect green, 4 dark green, 5 medium olive, 6 dark olive, 7 green olive, 8 light olive, 9 olive dun, 10 golden olive, 11 brown olive, 12 dark claret, 13 fiery claret, 14 light claret, 15 hot orange, 16 fiery orange, 17 crimson, 18 fiery red, 19 fiery yellow, 20 yellow, 21 light blue, 22 kingfisher blue, 23 dark blue, 24 teal blue, 25 magenta, 26 purple, 27 violet 28 grey, 29 iron blue, 30 blue dun, 31 dark grey dun, 32 summer duck, 33 gold, 34 brassy gold, 35 fiery brown, 36 dark brown, 37 rust brown, 38 cinnamon, 39 beige, 40 ginger, 41 black, 42 white, 43 fluorescent yellow, 44 fl. red, 45 fl. orange, 46 fl. lime green, 47 fl. pink, 48 natural seal.

SLF Finesse
A finer textured version suited to smaller nymph and dry fly patterns: 3 insect green, 4 dark green, 5 medium olive, 7 green olive, 8 light olive, 9 olive dun, 10 golden olive, 11 brown olive, 12 dark claret, 15 hot orange, 17 crimson, 20 yellow, 24 teal blue, 28 grey, 29 iron blue, 30 blue dun, 34 brassy gold, 36 dark brown, 38 cinnamon, 39 beige, 40 ginger, 41 black, 42 white, 48 natural seal.

SLF Master Class
Blends of several different SLF Finesse colours for imitation of specific natural insect colours, in two series:

Oliver Edwards series
River & Stream MC1 Baetis/Brown Olive, MC2 Baetis/Green Olive, MC3 Baetis/Yellow Olive, MC4 Baetis/Dark Iron Blue, MC5 Baetis/Pale Watery, MC6 Heptagenid/sulphurea nymph (yellow may), MC7 Heptagenid/sulphurea dun and emerger (yellow may), MC8 Ephemerella/Blue- Winged Olive, MC9 Ephemera danica (mayfly), MC10 Rhyacophila/sand fly pupa, MC11 Limnephilis lunatus (cinnamon sedge), MC12 Isoperla (yellow sally), MC13 Perla (large stoneflies), MC14 Gammarus pulex (shrimp /watery olive), MC15 Gammarus pulex (shrimp breeding orange).

Davy Wotton series
Stillwater MC16 black (midge pupa), MC17 green (midge pupa), MC18 claret (midge pupa), MC19 golden dun (midge pupa), MC20 red (midge pupa), MC21 olive (midge pupa), MC22 orange silver (midge pupa), MC23 green (caddis), MC24 amber (caddis), MC25 yellow (caddis), MC26 orange (caddis), MC27 brown (caddis), MC28 dark (damsel nymph), MC29 light (damsel nymph), MC30 mayfly nymph.

SLF Hanks
SLF is also available in hanks, for use in 'hair' wings, tails, etc. Colours: 4 dark green, 5 medium olive, 15 hot orange, 17 crimson, 20 yellow, 22 kingfisher blue, 26 purple, 28 grey, 29 iron blue, 41 black, 42 white, 43 fl. yellow, 44 fl. red, 45 fl. orange, 46 fl. lime green.

SLF Midge
The finest form of the dubbing for the smallest of flies, available in 15 shades: 3 insect green 5 medium olive 7 green olive 8 light olive 11 brown olive 15 hot orange 20 yellow 28 grey 30 blue dun 36 dark brown 38 cinnamon 39 beige 41 black 42 white 48.

SLF Supreme
Available in 15 colours, these are some of the standard dubbings combined with 'flash' attractor materials: SU2 green highlander plus SU4 dark green SU13 fiery claret SU16 fiery orange plus SU18 fiery red plus SU20 yellow plus SU22 kingfisher blue SU23 dark blue SU25 magenta SU28 grey SU33 gold SU35 fiery brown SU36 dark brown SU41A black SU41B rainbow black.

SLF Poul Jorgensen signature series
A series of 24 high visibility dubbings for the salmon and steelhead flytyer: 1 peacock 2 magenta flame 3 purple haze 4 electric blue 5 fiery blood red 6 claret black 7 highlander 8 copper king 9 fall green olive 10 golden 11 sunset orange 12 blue horizon 13 lemon silver 14 fall brown 15 fiery red brown 16 silver salmon pink 17 silver purple 18 silver grey 19 purple fiery claret 20 fire orange 21 red fiery claret 22 fiery golden yellow 23 fluorescent fire orange 24 jaffa orange.

UK Saville, Lathkill, Sportfish, Anglian, Rooksbury, *US* Marriott, Fly & Field, Hunter, Kaufmann, Whitetail, *GER* Brinkhoff; *JAP* Sawada.

TOUCH DUBBING
Used by Gary LaFontaine for his sparkle dun pupa bodies, and for other patterns. Colours: olive, cream, yellow, light grey, dark green, medium green, white, burnt orange, brown, pink, medium grey, gold russet.

US Marriott

ULTRA DEER HAIR DUBBING
A Rocky Mountain Dubbing product Incorporating a special blend of deer hair with other fibres that has proved especially useful for chironomid and caddis emerger patterns, allowing the fly to float in rather than on the surface film. Originally designed specifically for cased caddis imitations as the chopped up deer hair makes very buggy, twig-like flies. Available in six colours: natural, caddis brown, caddis olive, flame emerger, hot spot black, cream.

US Marriott, *UK* Sportfish.

ULTRA-DUB
A very simple and versatile Acrylic dubbing that can be applied to most threads without pre-waxing and with which it is relatively easy to maintain a neat compact body.

Colours: yellow brown with orange tint, cream yellow with orange tint, tan, cream with a touch of pink, creamish olive yellow, dark olive, caddis green, slate grey, female Hendrickson pink, pale yellow cream, black, light red brown, chocolate brown, dark brown, yellow orange/sulphur yellowish grey, white, male Hendrickson tan pink, isonychia maroon brown, olive brown, dark red brown.

US L&L Products (contact for local suppliers)

UMPQUA SPARKLE BLENDS DUBBING
Very sparkly and translucent synthetic dubbing lending itself to a wide range of applications from small dries to salmon and steelhead flies.

Colours: Cahill cream, chestnut, chocolate, ginger variant, dark stone, golden olive, mint, frosty olive, march brown, hexagenia, light olive dun, callibaetis, blue grass, golden stone, medium olive, hare's ear, black gnat, vanilla, charcoal gray, light olive, olive damsel, light gray, sand, golden tan, dark olive brown, green, squirrel belly, fluorescent chartreuse, fl. fire orange, chinese red, deep purple, crawdad orange, fl. pink, fl. orange, bright yellow, shrimp pink.

US Marriott

UPSTREAM DUBBINGS
Oregon Upstream Innovations have a series of five dubbings:

Dry Fly
Very fine synthetic dubbing. Colours: black, white, light grey, medium grey, dark grey, red, dark brown, light brown, dirty orange, peach, cream, creamy tan, golden brown, light tan, dark tan, blue wing olive, blue grey, red grey, pale green, olive tan, golden tan, light olive, olive grey, rust, yellow, amber, rusty brown, sulphur dun, pale morning dun, rusty tan, dark olive, chartreuse.

Caddis
Designed to match the colours and translucency of caddisflies. Colours: yellow, tan, cream, amber, brown, rusty olive, grey olive, grey, olive, green, rust, black, muskrat, pheasant tail, olive yellow, peacock,

LEFT A super grizzle saddle cape, showing the exceptionally long hackle length which enables the tyer to use each feather for several flies.

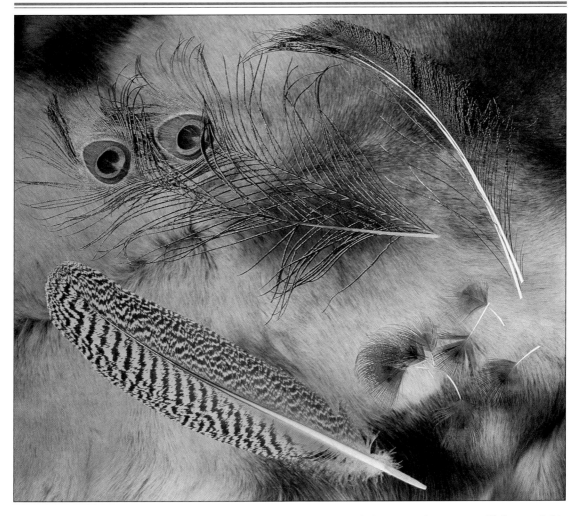

ABOVE peacock feathers: eyes (top left), sword (top right), blue neck (bottom right), wing quill (bottom left)

clear/white, hendrickson pink, march brown, olive brown, super hare's ear, mosquito larvae, light olive, blood midge.

Antron Fibre

Colours: white, black, grey, cream, orange, tan, brown, rust, dark olive, light olive, amber, yellow.

Nymph

Blended synthetic and natural fur for shaggy bodies. Colours: rust, olive brown, brown, light olive, light tan, rust hare's ear, dark tan, cream, black, grey hare's ear, light hare's ear, dark hare's ear, dark olive, olive yellow, golden brown, muskrat grey, light grey, dark grey, sand, dark rust, creamy grey, olive hare's ear, brown stonefly, black stonefly, golden stonefly, cream caddis, aqua caddis, light scud, medium scud, dark scud.

Big Bug

Various materials combined for bigger flies such as baitfish and leeches. Colours: sculpin belly, olive sculpin belly, sculpin head, grey shad, olive shad, brown trout, brook trout, rainbow trout, baby bass, salmon smolt, gill red, rusty crawfish, cinnamon woolly bugger, brown woolly bugger, black woolly bugger, brown leech, black leech, olive grey leech, western cranefly, blue damsel/dragon, golden stonefly, brown stonefly, black stonefly, October caddis, white minnow belly.

US Marriott, Blue Ribbon, Montana Master.

DUBBING BRUSHES AND THREADS

ANTRON DUBBING BRUSH

Antron put into a dubbing loop created with two strands of soft copper wire. Colours: cream, golden yellow, crawdad orange, light grey, red, brown olive, black gnat, march brown, rust, medium olive, chartreuse.

US Marriott.

DREW'S DUBBING BRUSH

Made of peacock herl and thread. Gives a stronger peacock herl body.

US Marriott.

EASY-DUBBING

Ready to tie pre-dubbed thread that comes ready to wind as a fly body. The thread is 'flocked' with dubbing by a process that applies the optimum amount of material. A body wound with this material produces a beautifully buggy look that is a cross between hare's ear and pheasant tail in appearance. Sold in single colour packs, containing 1.5m of the material and as 'fine' and 'extra fine' Colours: black, dark dun, medium dun, chocolate brown, medium brown, light brown, sand, olive brown, medium olive, rust, mahogany, orange, pale morning dun, chartreuse.

NOR Bergqvist; *INT* Orvis

EZ - BODY DUBBING

Another ready-to-tie pre-dubbed thread on a thin copper wire that comes in a variety of colours. Has a fuzzy, furry appearance with a strong sheen.

US Anglers Choice

LUREFLASH

Dubbing Bristles

Available in: fl. white, fl. orange, light brown, grey, claret, green highlander, fl. lime, fl. lime, dark green, fl. red, medium olive, black.

Hare & Flash Dubbing Brushes

Mother of pearl filaments added to the natural fur

Cul de Canard Dubbing Brushes

A mixed colour pack

Soft Dubbing Brushes

Soft-cored with no weight

Marabou Dubbing Brushes

Marabou on a soft copper wire

Shimmer Bristles

Metallic tinsel on a wire core, in both long and short fibre

Mosaic Bristles

Many tyers lamented the loss by fire of the factory that made the extraordinary Mosaic winging fibres. Now the deadly colours are reproduced as a body material.

Natural Fibre Dubbing Brushes

Available in: white, black, charcoal, dark olive, light olive, damsel, damsel green, light hare's ear, dark hare's ear, light tups, dark tups, claret, yellow, brown, dark brown.

UK Saville, Watercraft

MAGIC DUB

Consists of dubbing material spun between two strands of soft copper wire. As well as giving the finished fly some extra weight, the copper core glints attractively through the dubbing with almost a self-ribbing effect. Easy to wind and the soft copper wire is surprisingly easy to cut if taken well into the gape of normal fly dressing scissors. Comes in the following varieties:

Squirrel: natural gray, black, dark brown, brown, rusty brown, dark olive, golden olive, old ginger, natural fox.

Hare's Ear Plus: natural, dark natural, black, chocolate, red brown, olive brown, olive, tan, insect green

Antron: brown, dark reddish brown, green olive, olive, golden olive, golden amber, golden yellow, tan, gray, orange

Marabou: black, brown, olive, yellow, tan, green, gray, red, white, chartreuse

US Marriott; *INT* Orvis.

NEW DUB

Dubbing on a string from Benecchi. Fine dubbing attached to a strong thread. Colours: black, brown, cream, dark grey, dark olive, green, light olive, orange, red, yellow.

UK Sportfish.

RAINY'S NO DUB

Fuzzy thread comprising two twisted strands, which can be separated for tying patterns smaller than size 16. Sold on the card in colours: white, Cahill, tan, chocolate brown, cinnamon, rust, avocado, olive, insect green, chartreuse, pale yellow, bright yellow, golden stone, carrot orange, red, misty grey, dove grey, Adams grey, iron grey, black.

US Marriott, Cabela, Rainy.

SIMAN PRODUCTS

Jan Siman and his family produce a large range of the original dubbing brushes (copper cored) and soft-dubs (thin thread cored).

JS Dubbing

A special blend of hare, rabbit, fur and antron in: white, black, reddish brown, brown, tan, light grey, red, orange, yellow, light yellow, olive, dark olive, grey, yellowish grey, dark brown

JS Dubbing & Deer

Blended hare, rabbit fur, antron and winter deer hair. The colour range is the same as JS Dubbing

Crystal Antron

Synthetic material of triangular cross-sectioned fibres with high refractive index of light in: White, lemon, gold, gold olive, beige olive, dark olive, olive, light olive, grey olive, chartreuse, insect green, green highlander, tan, light brown, brown, cinnamon, dark red brown, light orange, medium orange, dark orange, raspberry, hot red, red, light scarlet, scarlet, blue dun, iron blue, black.

Marabou

A blend of cut marabou feathers on the brush or dub in: white, black, brown, olive, tan, red, yellow, purple, chartreuse, hot orange, hot pink, pink, grey, golden olive, fl. orange, fl. cerise, fl. white, fl. yellow, fl. red, wine, green, fl. blue, lime green.

Crystal Antron and Marabou

Triangular cross sectioned fibres and marabou feathers combined in the same 23 colours as for Marabou

Squirrel Plus

A blend of 50% squirrel and 50% hare's ear in 15 colours: cream, natural, dark natural, dark grey, black, reddish brown, chocolate, dark brown, dark olive, olive, golden olive, light olive, insect green, yellow, orange.

Mohair
Pure mohair dubbing in 13 colours: white, lemon, golden olive, insect green, grass green, dark green, orange, red, chartreuse, light blue, blue dun, brown, dark brown.

Mohair & reflex
A blend of mohair dubbing and sparkling synthetic fibres in the same colours as Mohair.

CDC Plus
Fine cut CDC feather fibres blended with squirrel hair or antron fibres in 12 colours: white, natural grey, mallard grey, slate grey, black, cinnamon, olive, yellow, woodcock gold, salmon pink, fl. orange, fl. chartreuse.

Fine mylar
The same principle with metallics in 29 colours: gold, blue, grey, yellow, turquoise, orange, dark blue, copper, dark brown, light brown, brown, dark orange, dark red, dark green, chartreuse, bright blue, red, lime, green, purple, bronze, silver, fuchsia, black, pink, burgundy, pearl/blue, pearl/purple, pearl/green, pearl/gold.

CZ Siman

SLF TWISTS
Dubbing twists or brushes have become popular since their introduction by Jan Siman from the Czech Republic. They consist of short, chenille-like lengths of dubbing twisted between two strands of thin wire. These are tied in with the tying thread and wound to form a body in the same way that chenille is used. Colours: 5 medium olive, 6 dark olive, 10 golden olive, 11 brown olive, 15 hot orange, 20 yellow, 28 grey, 36 dark brown, 39 beige, 41 black, 42 white, 44 fluorescent red, 46 fluorescent lime green

UK Saville; *GER* Brinkhoff.

UNI-YARN MOHAIR
Very buggy looking Mohair wool trapped between two twisted threads. Good for larger nymphs and streamers. Colours: black, brown, charcoal, cream, fuchsia, grey, light grey, olive, red, white, wine.

US Marriott.

UNI-YARN
Spooled body material to produce a dubbed effect without dubbing. Colours: black, burnt orange, brown, bronze, cream, golden brown, gold, green olive, grey, insect green, khaki, dark brown, dark grey, light, yellow, magenta, olive, orange, purple, pale yellow, red, sun yellow, white, wine, fl. green highlander, fl. orange, fl. chartreuse, fl. chinese red.

US Marriott.

VENIARD DUBBING BRUSHES
Hare's Ear Blend: natural, natural black, black, chocolate, golden, insect green, olive, olive brown, red brown, tan.

Crystal Seal: black, black/gold, blue dun, gold, hot

orange, insect green, olive, red, red brown, yellow.

UK Saville, Sportfish, Anglian, Rooksbury, Norris.

WRAP-A-DUB
Comes on a bobbin spool as a dubbing flecked thread in: creamy gray, cream, tan, chocolate brown, yellow olive, dark olive, slate, red brown, caddis green, olive brown, greyish tan, medium gray.

US Marriott; *UK* Lathkill.

NOTE ON COLOUR SYSTEMS

The blending of different coloured dubbings to produce a particular desired effect has long been practised by flytyers. The shades needed have sometimes been referenced to particular colour systems and charts. Kingsmill Moore, for instance, in his *A Man May Fish* referenced the colours for his flies in the Kingsmill Series and Bumble Series to the Colour Charts of the Royal Horticultural Society. These were, for some time, hard to come by, but they have now been republished by the Society in one volume (unfortunately at a price of £100). The Society can be contacted at 80 Vincent Square, London SW1P 2PE (Tel. 0171-834-4333).

Al Caucci and Bob Nastasi published their *Fly-Tyer's Colour Guide* in 1978, which was advertised as 'the first colour standard for the fly-tyer'. In 1986, Gary Borger copyrighted his Borger Colour System (BCS) and this is featured in his book *Designing Trout Flies* (1991). Kenn Ligas used the BCS for referencing Scintilla Dubbing to the fly patterns in *The Fly-Fisher's Manual* (1992)

Borger Colour System (BCS)
After 20 years of research, Gary Borger, the well-known American flytying writer, developed a system for describing 147 colours used in imitative fly dressing. The Borger system seems to eliminate interpretive error (one man's buff is another man's tan, etc.) since colours can be matched accurately against the BCS standard. The heart of the system is a convenient little booklet, in which the entire BCS colour range is printed on waterproof paper. The 4"x 6" booklet can be carried by anglers while out fishing. Instead of having to collect natural specimens, which have a tendency to fade anyway, the angler needs only to compare an insect against the BCS and note the colour match. Millimetre, inch and hook scales are also included, so that the size of natural food organisms can be recorded conveniently.

UK Niche; *US* Cabela

Manmade materials

I T SEEMS THAT hardly a day goes by without a new manmade product being brought to the market place. The explosion of these materials over the last twenty years or so has been quite remarkable. This has arisen partly due to the reducing availability of more traditional materials, and partly through the advance of science. Tyers have reacted in various ways to the new arrivals, with older ones like Darrel Martin stating 'I am ambivalent about synthetics. I gently resent them and yet I admire what they do'. He has also drawn attention to the the three main approaches that tyers can take to synthetics:

Minimalist:
Incorporating a sparse amount to help produce an effect found in nature.

Utilitarian:
Recognizing that natural and synthetic fibres have differing attributes, and opting for the manmade because it provides the better properties for the particular fly being tied.

Synthetics only:
Moving over completely to tie flies with no natural materials in them.

Whichever way the tyer goes, manmade materials are here to stay. Many have become indelibly associated with the name of their supplier or distributor (eg. Hedron, Lureflash, Moser, Oregon Upstream, Partridge, Spirit River, Umpqua, Wapsi, Wotton), and new faces constantly appear to challenge the conventional European and American sources, such as companies like the Australian Tiewell.

In general, synthetics scatter and shatter light better than natural materials, thereby giving more reflection, translucence or iridescence. The twisting or crinkling of fibres gives angled surfaces for reflection, and iridescence (the prismatic quality caused by differential refraction) can be purpose built into manmade materials. Some thoughts to bear in mind when selecting manmade materials are:

Water absorption
Natural fibres contain water at 10% or more and some wools, for example, can absorb up to 30% or more of their own weight. Synthetic fibres have little if any such absorptive properties.

For example, at 95% humidity, Nylon has a 6.5% moisture content, Acrylics 2.5%, and Polyesters 2%. Fibres that have low absorptive products usually have static cling. Additionally, some manmade materials have been waterproofed to reduce absorption even more.

Specific gravity
The specific gravity of manmade materials is an important consideration when considering floating or sinking flies. With the specific gravity of water taken at 1, Polypropylene is lighter at 0.91/0.92, Polyesters are heavier at 1.32/1.38, as are Acrylics at 1.7 and Nylons at 1.14.

Denier
The description of a Denier refers to the fineness of

LEFT Manmade materials for the flytyer: (clockwise from top left) Crystal Hair, Mobile, Krystal Flash, Spandex, Holographic Fibre, Floss Flex, Flashabou Accent (centre).

a fibre. Technically it is the weight in grammes per 9,000 metres of yarn. The lower the denier, the finer the material. Thus ultra-fine fibres may have a denier around 1.2 while Polypropylene is between 2.8 or 3.

Glow materials

Those with inbuilt glow properties should be used sparingly. Casting an ultra-violet light in a darkened room over flies created with fluorescent materials will show the likely picture to be produced under water, always bearing in mind the filtering out of the effect on colours at different depths.

Foam

This material has become very popular. Thought needs to be given to the properties of the type of foam to be used. Open Cell Foam contains open pockets and absorbs water. Closed Cell Foam has airtight pockets making it watertight and buoyant.

Sometimes foams are categorised as hard or soft/flexible. Soft foams come in three types - Polyurethane, Vinyl, Polyethylene. Polyurethane foams tend to break down under ultra-violet light - as Skip Morris puts it 'they rot in the sunshine'.

Vinyl foams will react with some solvents, as anyone knows who has the bright idea of coating a suspender ball in varnish! They melt when they come into contact with glues and cements.

Polyethylene foam, such as EVA (Ethyl Vinyl Acetate), does not react to solvents and stands up well to sunshine. Some EVA's can be rigid unless a plasticiser is added during their making. The size of the bubbles in a particular foam is another variable.

Beads

The trend for using small glass beads in flies is growing - even for whole body sections. Thought should be given to the style of bead best-suited for the purpose required. Beads come in many forms:

Iris - iridescent, rainbow effect.
Lined - translucent, clear or coloured, with a lined centre of a different colour.
Lustre - rich, shiny finish on opaque and translucent beads.
Matte - frosted effect.
Opaque - solid, flat colour.
Pearl/Ceylon - solid colour with shiny finish.
Rainbow - iridescent effect of matte.
Silver-lined - translucent, clear or coloured, with a lined centre of a different colour.
Translucent - see-through, rather like stained-glass.

BACKS

BODY STRETCH

Similar to Scud-Back but with stronger colours and more suitable for shrimp backs. Highly stretchable material which is good for nymph bodies as well.
Colours: black, clear, brown, olive, pink, cinnamon, yellow orange, fl. yellow.
UK Lathkill, Sportfish.

BUG BACK

Patterned sheet that can be coloured with a pen. Two sheets per pack.
UK Sportfish.

FLASHBACK

Another form of flexible prismatic film for backs.
US River Edge

FLEXIBODY

Originated by Hans de Groot, sold by the single sheet and popularised by Oliver Edwards in his *Flytyers Masterclass* book. Colours: dark olive, medium olive, light olive, black, red, grey, yellow, clear, orange, brown, shrimp, fl. yellow, fl. orange, fl. green.
UK Lathkill, Sportfish; *US* Fly & Field.

PEARL SHELL-BACK

The Lureflash equivalent to Spectra-Flash.
UK Rooksbury, Saville, Sparton, McHardy, Watercraft.

PEARLESCENT SHEET

Pre-cut sheet for Flashback nymphs.
UK Lathkill; *US* Marriott, MM.

PRISMATIC FILM BACK

A flexible plastic prismatic film for shrimp backs that will pick up the colour of the material it is placed over.
US Fly & Field.

RAFFIA

The real thing in buff, brown, yellow, light green, orange.
UK Sparton, McHardy.

RAFFENE / ARTIFICIAL RAFFIA / SWISS STRAW / RAYON STRAW

Comes in red, white, orange, black, green, ruby, olive, golden olive, brown.
AUS Alpine; *GER* Brinkhoff; *UK* Sparton, Rooksbury, Niche, Saville, Lathkill, Slater, Walker, Norris, McHardy,

Watercraft; *US* Marriott, Hunter, Cabela, Kaufmann, BR, Montana Master.

SCUD BACK

A transparent elastic textured strip that is extremely flexible and versatile. It is particularly useful for shrimp 'shell backs' and for thorax covers, wing cases, etc. Can be used to imitate trailing shucks or wound to form life-like bodies on midge pupae imitations. Available in $1/8$" and $1/4$" widths. Colours: red, tan, light olive, dark olive, orange, pink, grey and clear.

AUS Alpine; *GER* Brinkhoff; *UK* Lathkill; *US* Marriott, Cabela, AA, Bailey, Whitetail, Blue Ribbon, Montana Master; *INT* Orvis

SPECTRA-FLASH

Ultrafine pearlescent fabric in sheet form with a sparkling translucency. Use rough side up. Pearlescent Colours: grey, olive, light brown, dark brown, pink, yellow, mother of pearl.

UK Niche; *US* Fly-Rite.

BEADS, BUBBLES AND BULLETS

BEAD HEADS (Gold Head Beads)

Bead Head flies are now popular the world over. Drilled, metal beads are sold in at least four sizes (2mm, 3mm, 4mm, 5.5mm) coloured gold, silver or copper. The best quality beads have a non-tarnish finish and are countersunk on one side, to help threading the bead onto a hook (which is also helped by selecting shallow barbed and round bended hooks). Instant Gold Heads can be made by threading a bead onto the leader before knotting the fly (NB. ensure the countersunk side faces the knot and the hook eye). Usually sold in packs of 10 or 15, and widely available.

AUS Alpine; *GER* Brinkhoff; *UK* Sparton, Lathkill, Rooksbury, Niche, Saville, Sportfish, Anglian, Sparton, Walker, McHardy, Watercraft; *US* Marriott, Hunter, Cabela, AA, Bailey, Gorilla, Kaufmann, Montana Master; *INT* Orvis.

BRITE BEADS

From Spirit River, these have a small hole, with one end smaller to prevent the bead slipping over the eye, while the other is enlarged to allow it to slip over the barb. Weighting material can also be inserted in the larger end. Can also be used on the water as an instant bead head on any pattern by letting the bead run freely on the leader. Colours: gold, copper, nickel.

US Marriott, Blue Ribbon.

BT's PINCH EZY BEADS

Pinch-on brass beads that give the 'bead-look' with less weight. Pliers are used to pinch them on. Useful when getting a bead over a barb is a problem.

US BT, Marriott

CONE HEADS

Another name for Bullet Heads (see Bead Heads)

CYCLOPS EYES

For Bead Head nymphs and Wooly Buggers. Available in brass, nickle, copper or black in sizes: small $3/32$", medium $1/8$", extra large $3/16$". Sold in packets of 25.

AUS Alpine; *US* Marriott, Hunter.

GLASS BEADS

Many iridescent colours in many sizes are available from craft shops, including those which have their holes off-centred giving interesting refracted light effects. Useful for heads or whole bodies.

UK Beadworks, Hobby Horse, Anglian, Watercraft; *US* Beadworks, Marriott, Hunter, Cabela, Kaufmann, MM.

GOLD HEADS (see Bead Heads)

GOLDEN BULLETS

Gold plated, bullet-shaped brass beads are a development from Gold head beads, and dramatically change the appearance and action of any streamer pattern tied with them. Ideal for large streamers for pike, saltwater, etc. Available in large and small sizes, for hook sizes 8 to 2/0.

GER Brinkhoff; *US* Marriott, Hunter.

KILLER CADDIS GLASS BEADS

A series of eighteen colours in three sizes. Heavier than plastic equivalents, but no larger in size. Uniform size and shape is guaranteed.

US Temple Fork.

SCINTILLATOR BUBBLES

Translucent iridescent bubbles giving the illusion of trapped air on caddis, midge and mayfly patterns. Use the oval beads over a dubbed body for caddis emergers and the round beads for the head of midge and mayfly imitations. They help emergers float in the surface film and come in four sizes: 3x6mm oval for size 14-18 flies, 3mm round for size 16-24 flies, 4mm round for size 16-24 flies, and 5mm round for size 16-24 flies. Oval bubbles are sold in packs of 36, round beads 40. Supplied with full tying instructions from Kenn Ligas for The Original Scintillator .

ABOVE Winging materials: Poly II Wings, Shimazaki Air Thru Wing, Wyngs, Organza wing material, Fantastic Wing, Microweb Wing, Scintilla wing film, Lace Wing, Fake Wing, Zing, Wasp Wing.

US Blue Ribbon Flies, Marriott, Hunter, AA, Bailey, Gorilla, MM, BR.

TIN HEADS (see Bead Heads)

TUNGSTEN BEADS

Twice as heavy as comparable brass beads and heavier than lead so the nymph really gets down quickly. Available in brass, nickel, copper and black at sizes $3/32$", $1/8$", $5/32$", $3/16$" with 25 in each pack.

US Marriott, MM, Kaufmann; *INT* Orvis.

BODIES

CADDIS CASES

These represent the larval caddis case. Made from nylon blended with polyester and Chinese boar bristle strands. Extremely easy to use: insert the hook through the material and tie in at the head. Additional security can be achieved with a drop of cyanoacrylate glue, and trim to shape with scissors. The colour of fly is determined by the colour of underbody. Sold in packs of six strands (enough, it is claimed, for 50 flies), with tying instructions.

US Marriott.

CORK BODIES

Cork cylinders for bodies to aid buoyancy. For larger trout and bass popper patterns.

UK Saville, Anglian, Watercraft; *US* Hunter, Cabela; *INT* Orvis.

DETACHED BODIES

Ready-made extended body sections that simply require attachment. Removes the need to built the body up during the tying process.

Mayfly

UK Lathkill, Sparton

Daddy Longlegs

UK Sparton

FOAM BODIES (see pages 83 and 84)

McMURRAY ANT BODIES

Balsa wood coloured red and black.

US AA.

MOE BLANKS

Ready-made Mother of Epoxy heads on a hook. All you need do is dress up the body. Available in two shapes: Diamond (amber, lime, clear) Teardrop (yellow, amber, clear)

AUS Alpine; *US* Cabela; *INT* Orvis.

SPONGE BODIES

US Cabela.

BODY WRAPPINGS

ANTRON BODYWOOL

A Lureflash product that has gained worldwide acceptability. Parallel strands of trilobal Antron yarn sold on a card and with many other applications apart from making bodies. Colours: fl. white, fl. pink, fl lime, fl. orange, fl. yellow, light brown, dark brown, dark green, blue, grey, purple, black, red, claret, cream, golden yellow, olive,

Fibres and winging materials: (from left) Z-Lon (Blue Ribbon), Nymph Rope (x 2), Sea Fibre, Polar Aire (olive and red) and below, Z-Lon (John Betts).

ginger, amber, medium olive, green highlander, peach.

UK Rooksbury, Saville, Sportfish, Watercraft; *US* Bailey, River Edge.

ARIZONA SPARKLE YARN

A sparkle leech-type yarn which, when teased out, creates an iridescent body. Colours: amber/olive, black, black/blue, black/red, blue, brown/copper, chartreuse, chestnut, chestnut/olive, dark brown, green, green/black, green/chartreuse, hot pink, olive, olive/brown, orange, red, rust, rust/brown, rust/olive, silver, violet, white, yellow, black/violet, yellow/green.

US Marriott

AUNT LYDIA'S SPARKLE YARN

This rug yarn has been used for years because its three trilobal strands separate easily. Useful for caddis pupa imitations. It is stiff enough to be used in crab flies such as the Brown Permit Crab and Ghost Crab, and it holds its shape well. Colours: black, yellow, purple, red, orange, burnt orange, rust, tan, brown, dark brown, kelly green, white, light yellow, gold, dark gold, insect green, olive, blue, light blue, grey, cream, dark tan.

US Hunter, Marriott.

BERLIN WOOL

For modern and classic salmon flies. Sold on the card. The most popular colours are: black, light blue, medium blue, royal blue, fiery brown, brown, claret, light claret, dark claret, medium green light green, olive green, magenta, orange, light orange, reddish orange, dark orange, purple, scarlet red, white, yellow, lemon yellow, golden yellow, bright yellow.

UK Slater.

BILL'S BODI-BRAID

A wide, flat-braided mylar material with pearlescent strands, which lies very flat so that it makes a good tapered body. Sold on card with 5 yards on. Colours: pearl, pearly blue, silver, gold, blue, green, red, black, lavender, teal blue, deep blue, coachman red, purple, light gold, bronze, copper.

US Marriott.

BODI-STRETCH

A very new latex body material for nymphs and stone-flies. Colours: black, brown, olive, grey, yellow, orange, amber, chartreuse, pink, clear.

US Spirit River (for local suppliers)

BODY-BRITE

A twisted core with sparsely spaced, fine Mylar strung

into it. Useful for minnows, leeches, saltwater, bass, and steelhead patterns. Colours: black, dark olive green, charcoal grey, gold, purple, silver, red, burgundy, pearl.

US Blue Ribbon.

BODY-FLEX

Soft, transparent, flexible, it comes on a thin sheet for cutting into strips and winding. Colours: clear, yellow, orange, claret, olive, light brown

UK Niche, Saville, McHardy, Watercraft.

BODY GLASS

The Orvis equivalent of Nymph Rib, Nymph Glass, etc.

US MM; *INT* Orvis.

BODY STRETCH

In strips of $1/4$", translucent and stretchy material. Colours: black, brown, cinnamon, clear, fl. yellow, olive, orange, pink, yellow.

UK Sportfish, Anglian.

BODYGILLS

Looks like a short-fibred synthetic moleskin, but the backing is very fine foam and strengthened with an open weave net. For cutting into strips and wrapping like chenille.

UK Niche.

BUGSKIN

A strong, flexible, leather-like material, created by Chuck Furimsky. Compresses and ties in easily, conforming to the shape of the underbody. The material is porous and absorbent and seems to create a more life-like effect than some impermeable synthetic products. Bugskin is useful for subsurface nymph, stonefly and crayfish patterns, but absorbs floatant well too. The material is sold in 3in x 5in patches, with full tying instructions including tying photographs.

Naturals:
Black, mottled brown, brown, tan, cream, olive, red, gray, buckskin medium brown, yellow, caddis green, tangerine, light brown, light olive.

Flash Naturals:
Bright gold, matt gold, bright silver, pewter, platinum, copper, green, pink, blue.

Pearlized Naturals:
Black silver, brown gold, bronze, mustard, copper, rusty, olive, peacock, lead.

Wild Naturals:
Rainbow trout, speckled leech.

US Hunter, Cabela, Gorilla.

BURLAP

Used for segmented bodies on stoneflies, caddis larvae and steelhead flies. Colours: natural, bleached, black, brown.

US Marriott, MM.

CANADIAN SERIES MOHAIR (Leech Yarn)

An old standby for tying leeches and other shaggy bodied flies. Colours: Canada blood, Canadian brown, pond olive, spectrumized brown, black, olive, grey.

US Bailey, Marriott, River Edge, BR, MM.

CLARK'S TYING YARN

A slightly coarser Z-lon like material but good for emerger shucks and wings on dry flies.

AUS Alpine; *US* Marriott.

DAN BAILEY BODY FUR

Fibres of ³/4" strung together for wrapping bodies especially streamer and saltwater patterns. Shaping is by cutting. Colours: white, eggshell, sulphur, cream, ginger, tan, light dun, medium dun, dark dun, pink, orange, fire orange, red, red brown, brown, light olive, dark olive, green, wood duck, blue, black, fl. yellow, fl. chartreuse, fl. pink, fl. orange.

US Bailey.

DIAMOND BRAID

A popular material for bonefish, permit and general saltwater work, as well as for streamers. It covers quickly, ties easily and has lots of reflective colour. A flat diamond braid is available for bodies needing less bulk. Colours: silver, gold, copper, red, blue, green, pearl, purple, olive, lime, yellow, orange, pink, light blue, dark blue, crimson, brown olive. See also under Spooled Materials.

US Kaufmann.

FLAT BRAID

Similar to Diamond Braid but much smaller, narrower and flat. Colours: pearl, silver, gold.

US Kaufmann.

FLEXI FLOSS

From Orvis, a floss substitute that won't fray. Stretches extensively, so it makes really tight and smooth bodies, and the colours remain absolutely fast. Comes with some 70 strands 3.5" long: white, lemon yellow, fl. chartreuse, lime green, dark green, black, brown, orange, red.

US Marriott; *INT* Orvis.

FLOSS FLEX (also sold as 'Spandex')

Looks and feels like floss, but is a stretchy, Lycra-like material. Colours: white, black, fuchsia, orange, chartreuse, yellow, brown, lime green, blue, purple and red.

US Blue Ribbon Flies.

477 KILLER BUG YARN

Designed to replace the no longer made Chadwick 477 wool used by Frank Sawyer.

UK Niche, Saville, Lathkill, Slater, Norris, Watercraft.

FRITZ / GLISSEN GLASS

Mother of pearl material with pearl fibres which pulsate with the movement of the water. Also comes in Translucent and Micro ('Mini Fritz') forms. Colours: black, yellow, orange, red, pearl black, olive, green, brown, blue, white, white, lime green.

UK Niche, Saville, Slater, Sportfish, Walker, McHardy, Watercraft.

FURRY LEAD / FLUFFY LEAD

Lead wire, fine dubbing and tinsel all on the one thread. Suitable for nymphs and wet flies. Colours: white, black, pink, yellow, red, blue, dun, grey, olive, brown.

AUS Alpine; *US* Marriott.

FUZZY LEECH YARN

Very hairy yarn, allowing a scruffy 'buggy' effect to be wound directly onto a hook, without dubbing. Suits leech, dragonfly and stonefly nymphs and large streamer, patterns. Scruffiness is enhanced by teasing. Sold in five yard lengths, in 20 colours: olive, rust, dark brown, brown, grey brown, black, grey, purple, red, orange, chartreuse, lavender, white, fl. yellow, shrimp pink, fl. pink, sea green, yellow, highlander green and fuchsia.

GER Brinkhoff; *US* Cabela, Kaufmann; *INT* Orvis.

GORDON GRIFFITHS' WOOL YARN

A wool that can hold its vibrant colours underwater, in two-ply wrap that can be easily separated for thinner applications. Its most valuable colours are the fluorescent ones: red, orange, yellow, green, pink.

US Hunter.

LATEX

For segmented bodies on caddis larvae it makes a neat tapered wet looking body. Available as thin or heavy in: cream, green, charcoal.

AUS Alpine; *GER* Brinkhoff; *UK* Saville, Slater, Walker, Norris, McHardy, Watercraft; *US* Marriott, Kaufmann, Hook & Hackle.

LIFE-FLEX

Lifelike rubber skirting and winging material that is very durable. Available in: beige, black, brown, cinnamon, clear, dark olive green, fl. blue, fl. yellow, grey, insect green, light olive green, orange, purple, red, rust, tan, white, yellow.

US Marriott, Blue Ribbon.

McFLYFOAM MATERIAL

Resilient and sponge-like, this is not a foam but a combed-out yarn that is good for sculpted patterns like Woolheads. Its spongy texture allows it to be spun packed or clipped like a deerhair for surface poppers. Egg flies can be made with this material as well.

Colours: bright red, red, deep red, orange, dark orange, burnt orange, golden tangerine, early girl, yellow, chartreuse, Kelly green, caddis green, watermelon, pink, ripple, strawberry, cerise, purple, january, late pink, fudge, McRoe, late McRoe, white, light olive, golden olive, brown, light pink, black, gold, cream.

US Marriott.

LIQUI-LACE POLYMORPHIC GLITTER

Latex-like material with glitter granules embedded that reflect light at different angles and give a spectacular sheen. It can be wound alone or over a dubbed body. Colours: clear, sand, olive, white, gold, red, smoke.

US Custom Aquatics, Marriott

MAGIC GLASS

This is Veniard's version of 'half round' stretchy plastic monofilament, used for ribbing and wound bodies. The colours are meant to be long lasting as the pigments are added during extrusion. Comes in 14 colours: clear, black, red, yellow, shrimp pink, blue dun, orange, fl. yellow, brown, green, light olive, claret, medium olive, dark olive.

GER Brinkhoff; *UK* Sparton, Rooksbury, Niche, Saville, Lathkill, Slater, Sportfish, Anglian, Norris.

MARBLED LATEX

Marbled throughout to break up the solid colour, these thin durable sheets are ideal for scuds (shrimps), nymphs or larvae. Colours: light brown, grey, olive, yellow.

AUS Alpine; *US* Marriott; *UK* Niche

Dubbing bristles from Lureflash (top right), Minnow Body (x 2) from Hedron (above left), Mylar Piping (x 2) from Veniard, Holographic Tubing from Umpqua (middle column), Sparkle Yarn from Umpqua (right column).

MOHLON WOOL

A fuzzy yarn arising from a blend of Mohair and Orlon giving really 'buggy nymphs'.

AUS Alpine.

NYMPH GLASS

Thin stretchable ribbing material available in: clear, black, light olive, medium olive, dark olive, green, brown orange, fl. yellow, dun, red, shrimp, yellow, claret.

UK McHardy; *US* Marriott, MM.

NYMPH RIB GLASS

Translucent stretchy plastic filament used for wound bodies or ribbing of imitative patterns, such as nymphs and shrimps. Colours: clear, black, grey, brown, red-brown, olive, green, shrimp, orange, yellow, fl. orange, fl. chartreuse.

UK Watercraft.

NYMPH RIB

From the same stable as Larva Lace but solid rather than hollow. Nymph Rib can used for wound bodies and body ribbing in a wide variety of applications: from small nymphs (stretched) to imitations of saltwater crustacea. Black, brown, clear, fl. chartreuse, green, grey, olive, orange, red/brown, shrimp, yellow, blood red.

AUS Alpine; *US* Bailey, Cabela, Gorilla, Marriott.

INT Orvis.

NYMPH ROPE

Made from strands of pure camel hair with variegated colouring. This is not the soft short underfur of the camel, but the longer hair that is more like horse tail. Twisted and wound, Nymph Rope makes very effective spiky segmented bodies for nymphs. Sold in hanks. Colours: black, brown, natural hare's ear, light tan, olive and grey.

US Montana Master.

NYMPH WRAP

Soft latex type material with translucence to show through the thread underneath. Colours: clear, yellow, orange, red, olive, brown.

UK McHardy, Watercraft.

OLIVER EDWARDS' MASTERCLASS SHADES SPARKLE YARN

Designed by Oliver to accompany the patterns in his book *Flytyers' Masterclass*, this is a soft four-ply sparkle yarn containing 33% Clear Antron. Colours: Rhyacophila green, Hydropsyche (dark), Hydropsyche (light) and Ephemera (dark mayfly), Ephemera (light mayfly), BWO nymph (light), BWO nymph (dark), brown olive (duns), sand (duns and caddis).

UK Rooksbury, Niche, Lathkill, Angling Pursuits.

OPTIMA NYMPHBODY

Flat sectioned stretchable monofilament. Colours: amber, black, brown, claret, clear, olive, dark green, grey, iron blue, red.

UK Sparton.

POLY FLASH

For winding on like chenille. The many reflective surfaces give a sparkling life-like body. Comes in pearlescent shades of: black, olive, lime, purple, royal blue, orange, pink, light blue, red, yellow, pearl.

US Marriott.

QUILL BODY

The name given to Hareline Dubbin's and D's Flyes' bleached and dyed quill stems, developed especially for tying the A.K. Best style of flies. Sold in packs of 25 quills. Colours: white, black, blue quill, baetis olive, blue wing olive, red quill, ginger quill, light Cahill, pale morning dun, melon quill and frying pan pale morning dun.

US Marriott, Cabela, AA, MM, BR.

RAZZLE-DAZZLE

A terrific fly body wrap for streamers and steelhead flies in bright brilliant colours. Pre-shape the body then tie on and wrap as if using a chenille. Width is $1/16"$ for all colours except pearl which is $1/8"$. Colours: gold, silver, bronze, copper, black, green, royal blue, red, purple, pearl.

US Rainy, Marriott.

REFLECTA FOIL

Principally used in spoons and spinners, this adhesive backed reflecting foil has several possibilities for minnow bodies and various saltwater patterns (eg. Fender flies). Sold in sheets. Colours: silver, blue, gold, green, red, copper, mother of pearl and magenta.

UK Watercraft.

SHIMMER SKIN

Crinkly pearlescent material that reflects light beautifully even under epoxy. Colours: blue, orange, green, pearl, yellow.

INT Orvis.

SUPERBUG YARN

Very imitative insect representation in a pre-dubbed

material, which is polypropylene based with a lighter surface colour intermingled on each strand. A good material for weaving. Colours: black, claret, fawn, grey dun, olive, damsel green, tups, brown.

GER Brinkhoff; *UK* Niche, Saville, McHardy, Watercraft.

SUPERFLOSS (see entry in Flosses section)

TINY MOHAIR YARN

Baby-fine in texture being 80% kid mohair and 20% nylon for strength. Good for very small fly fur dubbing. Colours: white, light tan, tan, light hare's ear, dark hare's ear, light brown, brown, dark brown, Adam's grey, iron grey, black, golden stone, golden olive, olive.

US Marriott, Rainy.

SWANNUNDAZE

Originally developed from a vinyl trim material used in automobile upholstery and marketed in gauges suited to flytying by Frank Johnson, who named it with an anagram of his daughters' names, Dawn and Suzanne. The material is a thin plastic tape with one flat side and one rounded side. To describe it as 'half round' in cross section is inaccurate. Swannundaze is available in three gauges: $1/32$", $1/16$" and $3/32$". The larger sizes are used for segmented bodies on stonefly nymphs, bonefish flies, etc. while the narrowest gauge is useful for midge pupae imitations.

One of the earliest plastic materials, Swannundaze is not now generally available but has, to a large extent, been superseded by similar, but more stretchy materials (see also Vinyl Rib).

Colours:
Standard: cream, beige, tan, ginger, medium brown, dark brown, caddis green, olive dun, dark olive, yellow, black, light transparent amber, dark transparent amber, light transparent olive, dark transparent olive, transparent brown, transparent smoke, clear, medium transparent amber, transparent pale yellow.
Extra Wide ($3/32$"): clear, transparent dark amber, transparent brown, transparent black.
Extra Narrow ($1/32$"): light transparent amber, dark transparent amber, light transparent olive, dark transparent olive, transparent brown, transparent black, clear, transparent amber, transparent pale yellow, transparent pale orange.

US Kaufmann.

SYN-SHAM

Synthetic 'shammy leather' for tying leeches, stone flies, crayfish and similar patterns. More durable than natural suedes, Syn-Sham is also produced to a controlled thickness and is very supple and easy to tie with. Colours:

natural, kelp green, black, muskrat grey, hare's ear, sand, palomino, earthworm, brown, blue dun and larva white.

US Intertac (for local suppliers).

UNI WOOL YARN

Very similar to Berlin Wool, very soft and easy to use. Colours: chartreuse, fl. yellow, green highlander, chinese red, black, light pink, fl. orange.

US Hunter.

V-RIB

A thin ($3/64$") transparent D-shaped vinyl fly body covering. Colours: clear, yellow, orange, amber, brown, olive, opaque black.

US Hunter, Hook & Hackle.

VINYL RIB

Like Magic Glass but finer for bodies and ribbing on hook sizes 14-20. Colours: clear, amber, red, olive, black, chartreuse, yellow, orange, grey, brown, green, rust, shrimp.

UK Lathkill; *US* Kaufmann.

VINYL ROUND RIB

Translucent perfectly round ribbing with just the right amount of stretch. For woven bodies, ribbing and segmented bodies. Colours: Clear, orange, brown, red, green, olive, black, amber, rust, shrimp, fl. chartreuse.

UK Lathkill.

CHENILLES

Chenille (french for 'caterpillar') generically covers various yarns (eg. cotton, silk or rayon) radiating short fibres at right angles to the longitudinal axis. They were traditionally constructed with the short radiating fibres trapped between twisted core strands. Now a chenille-type yarn has been created by electrostatically 'flocking' fine synthetic fibres onto a single strand core, pre-coated in a tough adhesive. This is variously sold as Suede Chenille, Ultra Chenille, Vernille, etc.

Gauges run from 'micro-chenilles' (almost synthetic herls) to 'jumbo chenilles' (with a half inch pile). They can be mottled or variegated, incorporate strands of tinsel or Mylar-type materials, be entirely made of tinsel or have a tinsel or wire core (see Dubbing Brushes). Widely available.

AUS Alpine; *GER* Brinkhoff; *JAP* Sawada; *UK* Rooksbury, Niche, Saville, Lathkill, Sportfish, Anglian, Sparton, Walker, Norris, McHardy, Watercraft; *US* Marriott, Hunter, Cabela, AA, Bailey, Gorilla, Kaufmann; *INT* Orvis.

BRAZILIAN VELOUR

A velour that has a subtle glowing sheen all round the outside. Can be used for dry fly bodies (after applying Scotch Guard) or untreated for emerger or nymph bodies. Colours: (Regular) black, light gold, medium gold, dark gold, brown, light tan, light grey, medium. grey, dark grey, charcoal grey, dark forest, olive, dark olive, golden olive, peacock olive, red, crimson, yellow, orange, tangerine. (Exotic) claret, light damsel blue, dark damsel blue, light smokey, dark smokey, light salmon, dark salmon, light mint, dark mint, royal blue.

US BT, MM, River Edge.

CACTUS / CRYSTAL CHENILLE

A translucent synthetic which is very shiny and furry. Colours: olive, red, pink, pearl, yellow, hot orange, bright green, purple, dark olive, fl. fuchsia, root beer, chocolate brown.

AUS Alpine, *UK* Saville, Lathkill, Sportfish , Anglian; *US* Marriott, BR, BT, MM, River Edge.

EASY DUB MICRO CHENILLE

An easy way to produce the appearance of a fine dubbed body, without having to dub fur onto a thread. Colours can be blended by twisting two or more different shades together. Sold in 1.5m lengths per packet. Colours: blue dun, red, iron blue, claret, light olive, orange, rust, dark olive, yellow, grey, cinnamon, medium olive, black, brown, chartreuse.

UK Walker, Rooksbury, Niche, Lathkill, Anglian, Norris.

DYED RAINBOW CHENILLE

Dyed over multi-coloured tinsel giving dark, muted metallic colours.

US Marriott.

ESTAZ

Some say this is the best value in flashy chenilles with its very strong core and long fibres for fine attracting flash.

US Marriott, Hunter, AA, Kaufmann, Hook & Hackle, MM.

GLO-BRIGHT CHENILLE

A combination of regular and crystal chenille giving a more substantial body with flash.

US Marriott, Kaufmann.

GLO-BRITE FLUORESCENT SUEDE CHENILLE

Colours: neon-magenta, pink, crimson, scarlet, fire orange, hot orange, amber, chrome yellow, yellow, phosphor yellow, lime green, green, blue, purple, white.

UK Rooksbury, Niche, Sportfish.

ICE CHENILLE

Translucent and sparkly, available in medium and large.

AUS Alpine, *US* Marriott, Hunter, Cabela, Kaufmann.

JUMBO CHENILLE

For very large lures and Muddler heads instead of deer hair. Colours: black,white.

UK Saville.

KRYSTAL FLASH CHENILLE

Either a solid tinsel chenille or a pearl tinsel dyed for more subtle flash.

US Marriott.

MAGIC DUBBING

Micro-chenille used for Palomino Midges and extended bodies in small sizes, as well as a body material. It has a fine diameter core with dubbing wound in and it comes in: medium brown, mahogany, chartreuse, medium olive, light brown, pale morning, black, medium dun, dark dun, chocolate brown, light olive, olive brown, sand, yellow, rust, pale yellow, orange, red, insect green.

US Marriott, Hunter.

MARABOU CHENILLE

From Benecchi in Italy, a material that winds a very mobile thorax or body. Colours: white, black, sage, dark orange, pin, cocoa brown, chartreuse, hot orange, fl. white.

UK Lathkill.

PEARL CHENILLE

Chenille with pearlescent tones giving iridescence and shimmer. In medium and large sizes.

US Marriott.

POLY CHENILLE

A polypropylene chenille that is used for detached bodies. The Norwegian flytyer, Staffan Lindstrome, makes a remarkably realistic high floating cranefly imitation using a poly chenille body, a parachute hackle and legs made from synthetic paintbrush fibres.

NOR Rakkelhanen.

SPARKLE CHENILLE

Regular chenille with a silver tinsel core coming in fine, medium and large sizes.

UK Saville, Lathkill; *US* Marriott.

SUEDE CHENILLE

AUS Alpine; *UK* Niche, Saville, Lathkill, McHardy.

SPECKLED CHENILLE

Variegated chenille with alternating bands of colours. Many combinations offered.

AUS Alpine; *JAP* Sawada, *UK* Niche, Saville, *US* Marriott, Cabela.

SUPER CHENILLE

Perfect colours for Superbuggers or Marabou Muddlers arrived at by mixing tinsel or pearl chenille with rayon chenille colours: pearl/black, pearl/peacock, pearl/brown, pearl/wine, silver/black, gold/ black, pearl/black/burnt orange, copper/gold/black, red/blue/black, pear/fl. pink/fl. green, fl. fire orange, fl. red

US Marriott.

TINSEL CHENILLE

For very flashy bodies (see also Krystal Flash Chenille).

AUS Alpine; *UK* Lathkill; *US* Marriott, Cabela.

ULTRA FINE EASY DUB MICROCHENILLE

Half the diameter of Easy Dub Microchenille, the Ultra Fine version is useful for small flies and, particularly, for woven body techniques. Sold in dispensers of four colour ranges each containing 75cm each of five different colours: olives, browns, bright colours, greys & duns.

UK Walker, Rooksbury, Niche, Lathkill, Anglian.

ULTRA CHENILLE

A high-density plush, small diameter chenille for San Juan Worms, coming in Micro, Standard, and Medium sizes. Colours: fl. red, fl. yellow, fl. orange, fl. chartreuse, fl. pink, fl. cerise, dark olive, white, cream, yellow, orange, light grey, tan, worm brown, tobacco brown, golden brown, wine, red, light olive, caddis green, dark brown, kingfisher blue, olive, purple, black, dark grey.

US Marriott, Cabela.

VERNILLE

A 'floc chenille' (see also Suede Chenille), used for larger-bodied flies. Available as a set of six colours in a dispenser from Orvis, or in single colours: red, black, chocolate brown, olive, tan and insect green.

US Hunter; *INT* Orvis.

VERNILLE SUEDE CHENILLE Extra Fine

About 1mm in diameter and half the size of Suede Chenille. Can be twisted together for colour blends or speckled effect. Colours: black, white, claret, orange, red, olive, dark olive, yellow.

UK Niche.

EGGS

EGG HEADS

Ready-made imitation fish eggs requiring no tying, being simply threaded onto a hook - singly or in clusters - and there you have it! Try them also as eyes on unweighted seatrout flies, secured to the hook shank with a drop of cyanoacrylate glue. Available in sizes 3mm, 5mm, 10mm. Colours: yellow, orange, pink, red, black, tan.

UK Watercraft.

GLO-BUG YARN

A synthetic material used to imitate salmon or trout eggs or to form bodies for a very flashy range of Coho patterns. Heavy serrated shears are recommended for trimming the material! Colours: flame, gold nugget, salmon egg, peachy king, white, cerise, chartreuse, baby pink, light roe, dark roe, egg, Alaskan roe, apricot supreme, deep dark red, cream delight, steelhead orange.

AUS Alpine; *UK* Angling Pursuits; *US* Hunter, Cabela, AA, Kaufmann, MM, River Edge; *INT* Orvis.

KRYSTAL EGGS

Pre-formed eggs made of Krystal Flash and egg yarn. Colours: white, cheese, hot pink, salmon egg, peach, fl. chartreuse.

GER Brinkhoff; *US* Kaufmann, Hook & Hackle.

KRYSTAL GLO-BALLS

The easy way to tie Globugs is to put a hook through the centre of one of these sparkly egg balls and superglue it to the hook. Colours: bubble gum, pink, chartreuse, orange, cheese and red.

US Marriott, Cabela.

MEG-A-EGG

Eggs with added sparkle from crystal chenille filaments available six to a pack with diameters of 5mm, 7mm, 9mm. Available in: pink, orange, peach, chartreuse.

US Marriott.

EYES

BEAD CHAIN

Apart from tethering bath and sink plugs, a simple and effective material for eyes, adding weight to the front of

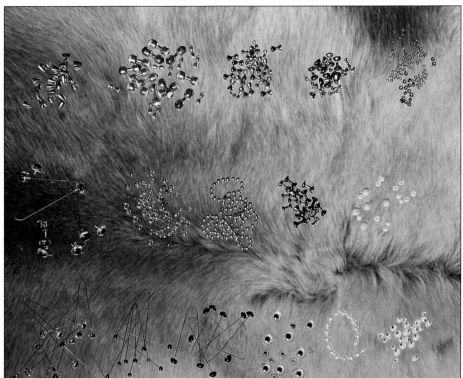

LEFT Various forms of eyes and beads: including Dazl-eyes, Crystal eyes, Pearlescent bead chain, Black eyes, Bead eyes, Chain eyes, Lumi beads, Dumbell eyes, Living eyes, Glass beads and Bullet head beads

the fly, found in at least three gauges, in a silver (chromium) finish, but also in 'gold'. Pairs of beads are cut from the chain and the resulting 'dumbbell' is bound on with figure-of-eight wraps. Twisting can be prevented by cyanoacrylate or epoxy glue reinforcement, or by using a loop eye hook provided the link between the beads is long enough to straddle the loop of the eye.

AUS Alpine; *GER* Brinkhoff; *UK* Niche, Lathkill, Sportfish, Sparton, Walker, Watercraft; *US* Marriott, Montana Master, Hunter, Bailey, Kaufmann, BR; *INT* Orvis.

BOOBY EYE NETTING

A white stretchable material for enmeshing suspender balls. Useful for emerger nymphs, etc

UK Rooksbury.

BLACK EYES

Round, black glass eyes mounted on soft flexible wire stems, for use on Mice, Shrimps, Crayfish, Bass and Saltwater patterns. Sold in packs of five pairs, in 3mm and 5mm sizes.

GER Brinkhoff.

BRITE EYES

Individually machined bar bell eyes that are non-toxic and environmentally friendly, but add weight to the fly. They come as small, medium or large and in either a

silver or black nickel finish.

US Whitetail, Gorilla.

CRYSTAL EYES

Coloured glass taxidermy eyes, mounted on soft wire stems, that can be bent to the desired position after tying on. Used for streamers and realistic bait fish imitations, the glass adds forward weight to the fly, producing a slight diving action when retrieved. Available in sizes: 5mm, 6mm, 7mm and 8mm.

GER Brinkhoff.

DAZL EYES

Quality 'dumb-bell' type of eyes with beautiful finish and machined to a perfectly symmetrical shape from a non-toxic metal. Ideal for all patterns requiring such weighted eyes, such as Nobblers, weighted streamers and bass and saltwater patterns. Available in five sizes. Nymph, Mini, Extra Small, Small and Medium, in either 'brass' or 'nickel' finish.

US Whitetail, Marriott, River Edge; *UK* Anglian.

DOLL EYES / AUDIBLE EYES

Black pupil rolls around over yellow or white background in diameters of 3mm, 4mm, 7mm, 10mm.

AUS Alpine; *GER* Brinkhoff; *US* Marriott, Hunter, Cabela, Kaufmann; *UK* Lathkill.

EPOXY EYES

Self-adhesive eyes handmade in epoxy in silver/black and red/black.

UK Rooksbury; *US* Hunter, Bailey, River Edge, BR.

FIBRE OPTIC EYES

A very heavy gauge fluorescent nylon monofilament, emitting a strong glow from the cut end, catching available light and using internal reflection. Eyes are formed by melting the material on a hot light bulb or in a flame, taking care not to char it. The melted end can then be flattened by pushing it against a piece of glass or polished metal surface. Sold in short lengths. Available in lime green (2mm and 1mm dia.), blue and yellow (1mm dia. only).

UK McHardy.

FISH SCALE POWDER

Mixed with epoxy for iridescent heads, eyes, and bodies.

US Fly & Field.

GLASS EYES

Black pupil with clear or amber background on a long wire stem. Six in a pack at diameters of 3mm, 5mm, 7mm.

US Marriott, Montana Master.

HOLOGRAM EYES

Three dimensional eyes suitable for epoxy flies. Colours: yellow, red, silver. See also Molded Eyes.

UK Lathkill; *US* Marriott

HOURGLASS EYES

Machined as opposed to cast, Hourglass Eyes are perfectly symmetrical. They centre themselves on the hook making the fly ride correctly. Available in brass or nickel in packs of 24 and in five sizes (micro, mini, extra small, small, medium)

US Marriott

IMITATION JUNGLE COCK EYES

A number of manmade alternatives to the real thing exist, eg. plastic, paint on feather. But it has to be said that none are as good as the natural.

GER Brinkhoff; *UK* Slater; *US* Marriott, Cabela, Bailey, Hook & Hackle.

ITALIAN BEAD EYES

Drilled especially to be used as the head on a Bead Head pattern. Three sizes 2.7mm, 3.2mm, 3.8mm. Colours: gold, silver, copper black.

US Bailey.

LEAD EYES

To add weight and jigging motion to the fly. Available in standard lead, non-toxic lead and plated lead.

US Marriott, Montana Master.

LEAD DUMBELL EYES

UK Sportfish, Anglian.

MOLDED EYES / 3-D HOLOGRAM EYES

Add sparkle and colour and three-dimensional realism. Waterproofed and self-sticking these are arguably the best eyes around for the tyer. There are three sizes $1/4$", $5/16$", $3/8$" and three proven colours: silver, red, chartreuse.

GER Brinkhoff; *US* Cabela, Kaufmann; *INT* Orvis.

MONO NYMPH EYES

Used for eyes on damsel and dragonfly nymphs, coloured black in four sizes (extra small, small, medium, large)

US Marriott, BR.

OPTIC EYES

Plastic bobble eyes with a mobile black pupil inside, especially useful for large buoyant patterns, where prominent eyes are required (Mice, Muddlers, Bass Bugs, etc.) There is no stem or other means of attachment and so they must be glued to built-up thread heads, or into 'sockets' burnt into spun deer hair. Available in various sizes, with white or yellow background.

UK Sportfish, Niche, Saville, McHardy; *US* Marriott, Bailey.

ORVIS DEEPWATER EYES

Dumb-bell shaped brass eyes in nickel, black and gold plate (much brighter than brass and will not tarnish) coming in packs of 25: small, medium or large.

US Marriott, *INT* Orvis.

ORVIS PRE-PAINTED EYES

Add realism without having to paint tiny dots on small surfaces. Cast metal dumb-bells decorated with pre-painted eyes in a durable polymer epoxy finish. With 89% the weight of lead, but ecologically sound as they contain no lead, nickel or cadmium. Available in a variety of sizes and colours, they suit many streamer patterns and especially large saltwater baitfish imitations. Colours: black on pearl, black on red, black on yellow. Diameters: $1/8$", $5/32$", $3/16$", $7/32$", $1/4$".

Sold in packs of 10.

INT Orvis.

PEARL PLASTIC EYES

Highly reflective plastic eyes which have to be glued in place. Durability improves if the eyes and head of the fly are encapsulated in epoxy. Available in packs of 10 eyes, in sizes: 5mm and 8mm.

US Marriott.

PEARLESCENT BEAD CHAIN

Pearlescent plastic beads fused onto a thin string core. Lighter than metallic bead chain, it has similar uses. The beads can be coloured with waterproof markers, or painted with a pupil to improve the eye effect. Most commonly found in 3mm dia. size. Colours: pink, blue, orange, green and pearl.

UK Saville.

PLASTIC BEAD CHAIN EYES

Not so weighty as Pearlescent Bead Chains and they come in pearl, dyed pink, dyed blue, dyed orange, dyed green, black, light brown, light olive, green, purple, mother of pearl at a diameter of 4mm.

US Marriott.

REAL EYES

From Spirit River, these hour-glass shaped eyes have a stepped depression aiding tying.

US Hunter, Cabela, Marriott, AA, River Edge.

SALTWATER EYES

Black or gold-plated (bright non-tarnish) solid brass eyes designed for saltwater use, available in packs of 25, in sizes: small ($^1/8$" x $^1/4$"), medium ($^5/32$" x $^9/32$"), large ($^7/32$" x $^3/8$").
Also available is a saltwater assortment, containing 100 beads in a four compartment box.

INT Orvis.

SOLID EYES

Solid plastic-stemmed eyes with a black pupil on a gold, orange, yellow or white background in diameters of 4.5mm, 6mm, 7.5mm.

US Marriott, Montana Master.

STICK-ON EYES

Peeled from a sheet and stuck on, they benefit from an epoxy or varnish overcoat

AUS Alpine; *UK* Lathkill; *US* Marriott..

STICK-ON PRISMATIC EYES / TAPE EYES

Adhesively backed in silver, gold, and aqua at diameters of $^7/32$", $^9/32$", $^3/8$".

GER Brinkhoff; *UK* Lathkill, Anglian; *US* Marriott, Cabela, AA, Kaufmann, RE; *INT* Orvis

FIBRES

ANTRON

This tri-lobal DuPont manufactured yarn is available quite widely today and in numerous colours and presentations and mixes. In its pure and raw white state it is available from some sources, eg. Blue Ribbon Flies.

AUS Alpine; *GER* Brinkhoff; *UK* Sparton, AA, *US* Marriott, MM.

ANTRON SPARKLE YARN

Antron spun into a yarn with an interwoven tinsel strand giving a sparkly frosty effect. This versatile material can be used as a dubbing, or wound directly onto the hook shank and then brushed out, to create a hairy effect. It can, just as easily, be tied in as a wing material in its own right or as a supplement to other wing materials.
Sold in 2m lengths, in the following colours: amber/olive, black/violet, chestnut, green/black, olive/brown, rust/brown, white, black, blue, chestnut/olive, green/chartreuse, orange, rust/olive, yellow, black/blue, brown/copper, dark brown, hot pink, red, silver, yellow green, black/red, chartreuse, green, olive, rust, violet.

US Cabela, Kaufmann.

CLEAR ANTRON

Its name refers not to its clarity but is a registered marketing trade name. An excellent material when blended with other dubbings, if translucency and sparkle are required. It can also be used to great effect in spinner wings and on emerger patterns (described by Gary LaFontaine, in his book *Caddisflies,* for the wings and shucks of emerging and diving caddis). In large hatches of caddis, when the trout refuse ordinary artificials, an Elk Hair Caddis with a little Antron added under the wing, fished just below the surface film, can produce spectacular takes.

UK Niche, Saville, Lathkill, *US* Fly-Rite, Hunter.

CRIMPED NYLON

Long translucent strands of crimped (crinkled) nylon, used mainly in large saltwater patterns. This is still used by some saltwater tyers, but has largely been superceded in the Hedron stable by Supreme Hair (see Wings section). Its diameter is 0.006". Colours: black, white, chartreuse, blue, purple, orange, red, green, yellow, pink.

US Hedron (for local suppliers).

DARLON

A trilobal nylon a little softer than Z-lon, promoted by Darrel Sickmon under the name of D's Flyes, and distributed to the trade by Hareline Dubbin. Used for wings and shucks in imitative patterns (duns, spinners, midges, etc.) and as a wing material in larger streamer and attractor flies. Colours: white, pearl, black, light dun, medium dun, olive, dark green, light green, tan, gold, shrimp orange, dark brown, rust brown, bright red, orange, purple, yellow, light pink, royal blue.
Fluorescent colours: hot pink, orange, amber, dark dun, claret, green, chartreuse, light olive.

US Bailey, Kaufmann, MM.

GHOST FIBRE

Long-fibred (30 cm) ultra fine polypropylene material with great potential for streamer wings, or as trailing tapered tails, which becomes translucent in water, making it ideal for small bait fish imitations - as demonstrated by Roman Moser. It can also be used for 'loop-wing' patterns and for other applications where a polypropylene yarn wing might be used. It can be used as a substitute for polar bear, or chopped up as a dubbing material. Colours: white, cream, yellow, light violet, orange, red, wine, blue dun, pink, dark violet, dark green, olive, dark brown, chartreuse.

GER Brinkhoff; *UK* Angling Pursuits.

HI-VIS

Similar in texture to Ghost Fibre, this is a versatile material being used from small spinner wings to large saltwater flies. It can also be chopped up to make a passable seal's fur substitute. Sold in packs of 4" fibres as 'Hi-Vis', it is also available in 8" lengths as 'Wing Fur' and 10" lengths as 'Sea Fibres'. Colours: beige, red, brown, lavender, royal blue, grey, black, sulphur, light dun, orange, white, pink, red brown, blue, mint, medium dun, yellow, wood duck, dark olive, cream, forest green, rust, lime, claret, purple, dark brown, turquoise, navy blue, steel blue, kelly green and chartreuse.

AUS Alpine; *US* Bailey, Marriott, Hunter, AA.

PERMATRON

A long hank of Antron fibre with a permanent wave that can be used for a variety of applications: wings, wound bodies, tails, shell backs. It can also be cut up to add a spiky, sparkle effect to other dubbing materials. Colours: white, ghost pink, sand, yellow, orange, red, blue, chartreuse, grass green, light green, green, dark olive, gold, light brown, root beer, dark brown, grey, black, purple, burnt orange, pale yellow, cream, rust and claret.

US Marriott.

PLUSHILLE

Effectively a Chenille with an extremely long 'pile' coming as ribbon-like strips of long transverse fibres,

Ghost fibre in various colours, with a big game fly made from it.

joined down the centre by a line of stitching. The material is tied in by this line of stitching, which acts like the 'core' strands of a true Chenille, and the Plushille is then twisted before winding onto the hook shank. After winding, the pile of the material can be modelled, with scissors, to create fish shapes, as frequently demonstrated by the Austrian flytyer Roman Moser. Coloured with Pantone pen and used in conjunction with wire stemmed glass taxidermy eyes, it can be used for most realistic minnow imitations. The finished texture is soft and pliable, while retaining its shape. Plushille is actually a mixture of crinkly, moderately soft fibres and flashy strands that give it glitter and sparkle. Sold in single colour 60cm strips, with full tying instructions. Colours: white, yellow, orange, pink, red, brown, olive, blue, grey, black.

GER Brinkhoff.

POLYPROPYLENE YARN / POLY YARN

A smooth textured yarn that is now available under a number of names. Its uses are growing along with its popularity. Less dense than water, polypropylene is particularly suited to dry fly applications. Siliconization of the yarn makes it even more water repellent than standard polypropylene. The Niche Products material is available only in white, pale grey, dark brown and black, though other sources have wider ranges of colours.

AUS Alpine; *UK* Niche, Saville, Lathkill, Sportfish, Walker, McHardy; *US* Fly-Rite, Marriott, Hunter, Cabela, BR.

SPARKLE YARN

This is a coloured yarn, criss-crossed with fine silver metallic filaments, which give a double ribbed effect. Colours: orange, pink, cream, red, green, lime, blue, white and yellow.

UK McHardy, Watercraft; *US* River Edge.

Z-LON

Developed for flyting by John Betts, Z-lon can be used for all kinds of wings, from tiny spent-wing spinners, to large streamers. In its crinkle form it can be chopped up to make an excellent seal's fur substitute, having a very similar denier to the real thing. Available in 'straight' or 'crinkle' forms, in 19 colours: white, black, light dun, medium dun, dark dun, cream, ginger, brown, olive, dark olive, olive brown, red, pink, yellow, light blue, blue, green, orange, purple.

US Blue Ribbon, Bailey, Kaufmann, BR, MM, River Edges; *INT* Orvis

FOAMS

BOOBY EYES

High density cylindrical ethafoam with 20 eyes per pack in sizes: small, medium and large. Colours: red, yellow, white, black, green, orange.

UK Rooksbury, Niche, Saville, Sportfish, Watercraft.

DAMSEL & DRAGON FLY FOAM

Damsel and dragonfly bodies are easily made using this close cell blue coloured foam, with the body segmentation being achieved by using black thread or permanent marker pen.

AUS Alpine; *US* Rainy, Cabela.

EDGEWATER FOAM

Using a high-quality closed-cell foam superior to cork or balsa, this company produces a whole range of foam components for flytyers including:

Terrestrial Bodies
for hoppers, beetles, crickets, cicadas. Colours: perch, white, yellow, black, chartreuse.

Pencil Poppers
Colours: black, yellow, chartreuse, white, blue, purple.

Divers
for both freshwater and saltwater. Colours: black, white, chartreuse, yellow, blue, purple.

AUS Alpine; *US* Marriott, Hunter.

FLOAT FOAM

Rainy's Float Foam is a buoyant synthetic body material, that was developed by the American flytyer Rainy Riding, to overcome her frustration at tying terrestrial patterns that would not float. Float Foam is very easy to work with, extremely durable and especially suited to such patterns as ants, beetles, hoppers, dragonflies, etc. Colours: white, yellow, black, orange; in three sizes: small ($1/8$"), medium ($3/16$"), large ($1/4$"). Each pack contains a 60cm strip and tying instructions for seven Rainy fly patterns.

US Rainy, Marriott, Cabela, Bailey, Whitetail, Blue Ribbon, River Edge, Montana Master.

FLY BODY FOAM

From Benecchi in Italy. A 2mm sheet, 12x20cm, in black, green, white, yellow.

UK Sportfish.

FLY FOAM

Closed-cell polyethylene foam developed by Jim Smithers buoyant patterns. Colours: brown, tan, white, black, yellow, orange, and green.

US Cabela.

FOAM ANT BODIES

AUS Alpine; *US* AA, Blue Ribbon.

FOAM BEETLE BODIES

AUS Alpine

FOAM BODIES

Closed cell polyethylene foam material available in cylindrical or extruded form, in several diameters and in a limited range of colours.

It is very buoyant and particularly lends itself to large fly patterns which would otherwise be difficult to keep afloat (eg. Bass Bugs, Damsel and Dragonflies) and for ants, mayflies, craneflies, etc. Colours: white, blue, grey, small and medium. The white ones accept waterproof marker pen colouring.

INT Orvis

FOAM FROG BODIES

AUS Alpine.

FOAM POPPER BODIES

Already slotted for ease of placement on the hook. Only acrylic paints should be used on these bodies.

AUS Alpine; *US* Marriott, Cabela.

FOAM SPIDER AND ANT BODIES

Colours: black, white, green, yellow, red, brown, grey, orange, tan.

US Marriott.

FURRY FOAM

A flexible sheet with a soft foam centre and fuzzy on the outside. For very fuzzy nymphs in: grey, cream, red, fl. chartreuse, yellow, orange, rust, light olive, dark olive, green, moss green, dark grey, tan, brown, dark brown, black, pink, fl. yellow, fl. orange.

GER Brinkhoff; *UK* Lathkill, Sparton, Watercraft; *US* Marriott, Cabela, Whitetail, Hook & Hackle, Blue Ribbon, Montana Master.

INTERTAC / LARVA LACE FOAM SHEETS

A complete line of foams designed for the convenience of the tyer . The pre-sliced widths and thicknesses have been specifically designed for varying underbody or body build-up requirements. The line comprises Open Cell Sliced (black, white, blue), Closed Cell Sliced (white, black, olive, grey, yellow, orange, green), Closed Cell Sheet (white, black, olive, grey, yellow, orange,

green, blue). The open cell is for wet flies, the closed for dries.

US Marriott, Gorilla, River Edge, BR.

L&L FLY FOAM

An extremely dense closed-cell foam for dry flies available in: brown, tan, white, black, yellow, orange and green.

US Marriott.

L&L STRETCH FOAM

Has great stretching ability to make tight, seamless, soft bodies. Matches the underside of insects, but can also be coloured with waterproof marker pens. Colours: cream , light olive, light red brown, tan.

US Marriott

METALLIC BEETLE BODIES

Pre-cut strips of a plastic foam sheet with a metallic finish on either side, which can be used for tying buoyant imitations of beetles that have iridescent colouring. The material is very easy to tie in, requiring only legs to complete a realistic beetle imitation. Sold in packs of four 6" long strips. Colours: brass, olive, copper and peacock.

Also available as 'Quicksight Beetle Bodies': as above, but with a bright fluorescent spot on the back of each beetle. Sold in packs of four strips (sufficient for 24 beetles), with tying instructions.

US Marriott, Blue Ribbon; *INT* Orvis.

McFLYFOAM

For both wet and dry flies, this material can be used as a synthetic substitute for wool on wool heads but also its spongy texture allows it to be spun, packed, or clipped like deer hair for surface poppers. Egg flies can be made with this too. Colours: brite red, red.deep red, orange, dark, orange, golden, tangerine, early girl, yellow, chartreuse, Kelly green, caddis green, iliamna pink, ripple, strawberry, pink, cerise, purple, January, late pink, McRoe, watermelon, late McRoe, light yellow, grey, brown, white, fudge, burnt orange, copper, grey olive, light olive, golden olive, black, gold, cream.

US Marriott

ORVIS QUICK-SIGHT ANT BODIES

With a white head they are easier to see in the water. They come in small, medium and large sizes. Colours: black or cinnamon.

US Marriott, Blue Ribbon; *INT* Orvis.

POLYCELON

A high quality micro-pore closed-cell foam for dry flies and emergers from Traun River Products. Colours: white, yellow, orange, olive/grey, black, brown, green.

GER Brinkhoff; *UK* Niche; *US* Blue Ribbon.

POLYETHYLENE FOAM

Polyethylene foam is 'blown' in a range of cell sizes and marketed under various brand names, by the companies that make it and also sold under several 'house names' by various flytying suppliers. Much tougher and more resilient than Polystyrene foam, it resists crushing better and is not dissolved by the solvents used in many floatant preparations. Widely available.

UK Saville.

POLYSTYRENE BALLS

These were used for John Goddard's famous Suspender Buzzer, which floats with its head just in the surface film and the body hanging down underwater. These balls are also used for the eyes on Booby flies. They are normally attached by being wrapped in a small patch of nylon stocking material, which is drawn tight and tied to the hook. Sold at most fly stores in small packs of mixed sizes, polystyrene balls are also available from pet shops as the filling for bean bags.

AUS Alpine; *UK* Rooksbury, Saville, Sparton, Walker, McHardy.

SCINTILLA FLY BUOY BODY FOAM

Smooth textured, thin, closed-cell foam sheet, just $1/16$" thick. For ants, hoppers and beetles, it can also be used to add buoyancy to other patterns. Colour range is referenced, as with other Kenn Ligas products, to the Borger Colour System (BCS): dark green (BCS8), grey (BCS110), insect green (BCS18), real white (BCS107), bluish green (BCS139), medium brown (BCS99), smokey tan (BCS55), real yellow (BCS52), ant black (BCS110), Danube blue (BCS140), peachy (BCS72) and burnt orange (BCS71). Note: bluish green (BCS139) is to be discontinued and replaced by red.

US Marriott, Bailey, AA.

UNDER BODY FOAM

An open cell (absorbent) foam used for quickly building bulk and shape to underbodies of large nymphs, terrestrial imitations, etc. Colours: black, brown, white, and green.

US Rainy.

LEGS

ANT LEGS / BEETLE LEGS

Braided thread coated in lacquer. More durable than deer hair or hackle, these synthetic fibres are used to imitate the legs of beetles, ants, etc. Available in black and brown in 1m lengths.

INT Orvis.

DADDY LONGLEGS (Crane Fly) PRE-TIED LEGS

UK Saville, Lathkill.

ENRICO'S SQUID TENTACLES

It is argued that tentacles on a squid pattern are as important as wings on a mayfly one. This is a braided white polypropylene cord which has good light-reflecting qualities and life-like movement.

US Marriott

FIRE TIP SILI LEGS

The same as Speckle Flake Legs but with two toning. Colours: black/red, clear/fl.orange, camel/ orange, purple/hot pink, black/purple.

US Marriott

FROG LEGS

Flat frogs legs for Poly Frog bodies and Bass bugs.

AUS Alpine.

HOPPER LEGS

To save the frustration of tying knotted legs these are pre-knotted legs available in dyed yellow turkey round wing, black turkey round wing, and natural pheasant.

UK Saville, Lathkill; *US* Rainy.

RUBBER LEGS (RUBBER HACKLE) / RAINY'S ROUND RUBBER LEGS

This is round section elastic filament, used for legs, antennae and other appendages of many bass patterns and in such flies as the Girdle Bug and Bitch Creek Nymph. Available in fine, small, medium and large gauges. Packs contain 40 x 30cm strands. Colours: black, white, grey, yellow, neon yellow, orange, neon orange, chartreuse, light green, neon green, bright red and brown.

AUS Alpine; *GER* Brinkhoff; *UK* Rooksbury, Saville, Lathkill, Watercraft *US* Rainy, Marriott, Hunter, Cabela, Bailey, Gorilla, BR, River Edge.

SILI LEGS

'Sili' stands for Silicone Flake Rubber Legs (Spandex). They are the same as Speckle-Flake Legs but in solid colours: white, yellow, orange, red, hot pink, purple, blue, brown, black, hot lime, green, hot chartreuse.

GER Brinkhoff; *US* Marriott, BR, River Edge.

From left: a selection of Hot Tails (Avro), Fibre Optic Super Hair (purples), and Ultra Hair.

SPECKLE-FLAKE LEGS (SPANDEX)

The material is naturally soft and wiggly. Packs have 5 bands of 20 legs each 20" long. The first colour is the leg colour and the second the colour of the flake. Available in: red/blue, purple/blue, black/blue, black/red, clear/silver, chartreuse/silver, white/silver, blue/silver, brown/orange, pumpkin/black, smoke blue/black, orange/black, smoke/black, olive/black, lime/black, chartreuse /black, brown/black, pumpkin/green, orange/black.

US Marriott, Cabela, Kaufmann.

OPTICS

BRIGHTON FLASH

Appears virtually identical to Ripple Flash, but is available in pink and blue, as well as in gold and silver.

US Bailey.

DRF FLUORESCENT MATERIALS

Produced by Danville. Colours: neon magenta, phosphor yellow, arc chrome (orange), signal green, fire orange (scarlet), electron white, horizon blue, sunrise pink (shell).

Also available:

DRF Floss; **DRF Wool**; **DRF Chenille**; **DRF Tow** (a thick woolly yarn for Baby Doll lures, or can be cut up for dubbing); **DRF Filaments** (nylon monofilament dyed fluorescent).

UK Saville.

EDGE BRIGHT

Plastic sheets that, when sliced into thin strips, glow on the cut side. When wrapped on the hook the glow is evident and flashy. Available in: neon red, orange, green, yellow, peach, chartreuse, black, clear, purple.

UK Slater; *US* Marriott.

EVERGLOW FLASH

Glow-in-the-dark material useful for winging. Available in: green, orange, red, white, yellow.

US Marriott.

EVERGLOW TUBING

Tubing that glows in the dark when activated by light. Useful for coloured water or late night fishing. Comes as small, medium or large in: white, orange, yellow, red.

US Marriott, Hunter.

FIRE FLY PRODUCTS

Welsh-based company, Avro Products, markets a collection of luminous products, including flydressing materials.

The Avro Firefly range includes various beads, plastic flexible sheet, miniature 'light' capsules, paints and 'grubs' moulded in soft luminous plastic. These materials can be incorporated into flies and lures intended for night fishing, for use at great depth, or in other conditions of low light (eg. ice fishing). The manufacturer recommends that these materials are used with restraint as lures don't have to shine like beacons. The materials are 'charged' by ultra violet light and will glow brighter after exposure. The following products are available:

Double-sided Strip: For bodies, butts, tags and strips in wings on salmon and seatrout flies.

Lureflash Reflecta Foil (left), Avro Kaleidoscope (right), Lumi material (below)

Lumi Beads: Particularly good for seatrout fly eyes on unweighted streamers, they can also be slipped onto the hook as a bead head, or slid onto the leader before knotting on the fly. Colours: orange and green, in 4mm and 6mm (packs of 15).

Adhesive backed Sheet: For punching out dots to enhance spinners and spoons and for similar applications, though generally too bulky for flytying.

Lumi Paints: Small bottles of luminous lacquer in: green, yellow, orange, red or blue.

Lights: Small glass capsules containing luminous material, which provide an intense glow. Supplied with shrink tube for attachment to hook shanks. Supplied in packets of two or five. Colours: yellow, orange, green, blue, red, and white.

Holographic Sheet: Two designs of holographic reflective sheet (6cm x 15cm) that can be cut into strips for bodies, wing or tail filaments. Not luminous.

Super Wings: Transparent elastic 'rubber' wings, containing particles of glitter. Super Wings can be used as a substitute for feather slip wings. Available in several colours.

Hot Tail: A crimped synthetic fibre (8") offered in unusual, contrasting two colour combinations. Suitable for saltwater and pike streamers. Colours: white/red, white/green, yellow/green, yellow/fl. red, chartreuse/red, hot pink/purple.

UK Sportfish, Walker.

FLUORESCENT TWINKLE BODYWRAP

A Lureflash product that is essentially Fishscale Bodywrap but in neon fluorescent colours. Colours: white, orange, yellow, lime, pink.

UK Watercraft.

FLUORESCENT WOOL

Colours: white, scarlet, hot orange, yellow, green, blue, pink, grey.

AUS Alpine; *UK* Lathkill, Saville, Walker, Norris, McHardy.

GLO-IN-THE-DARK PEARL PIPING

Diagonally braided piping with alternating white Everglo and translucent Pearl strands. Good in daylight but really comes alive during low light and dark conditions. Sizes: medium or large.

US Kaufmann.

HOLOGRAPHIC FLY FIBRE

A tinsel streamer wing and skirt material from Hedron with 10" long $1/16$" wide strands reflecting holographic images that give a three dimensional effect, glowing with strong prismatic colours like a diamond. Its use in trout flies is probably limited to ribbing or adding a few

strands to the wing of a streamer. For large saltwater attractors, however, it has fantastic possibilities. Sold in packaged hanks. Colours: silver/silver, silver/gold, silver/green, silver/red. Umpqua market a similar material, spooled as a tinsel.

AUS Alpine; *GER* Brinkhoff; *UK* Lathkill; *US* Marriott, Hunter, Cabela, Blue Ribbon.

HOLOGRAPHIC FLASH

A tinsel 7.5" long that mimics the scale shimmering qualities of baitfish. Comes in two widths: Regular $1/32$", Mini $1/69$". Colours: red, black, chartreuse, gold, lime, minnow blue, aqua blue, peacock black, natural, silver, pink, purple.

US Marriott, Kaufmann, MM; *UK* Anglian.

HOLOGRAPHIC TINSEL

A long 10" tinsel that shimmers with 'life'. Designed for streamers and saltwater flies.

US Marriott, *INT* Orvis.

HOLOGRAPHIC TUBING (AURORA)

Braided holographic Mylar tubing, that throws off rays of colour when turned in the light. Its uses are as limitless as for conventional Mylar tubings: streamer and tube fly bodies, etc. Sold in packaged one-yard lengths and available in: iridescent peacock, iridescent gold, iridescent silver, reddish pink, aquatic blue, pearl pink and minnow blue.

GER Brinkhoff; *US* Marriott, Kaufmann, River Edge, MM.

LUMINOUS BODY WRAP

A Benecchi product on a spool (1mm width).

UK Sportfish.

PRISM LITE

Adhesive material on a sheet, with prismatic light effects. This can be used for the bodies of baitfish.

US Montana Master.

RE-FLASH TUBING

A product from D's Flyes, for streamer, saltwater and minnow bodies. Colours: pearl, black, olive, red, orange, purple, chartreuse, pink, blue, brown, yellow.

US AA, MM.

RIPPLE FLASH

A mobile tinsel with extra flash from the inbuilt hologram effect resulting in a constant light movement along its length. For tailing, winging and ribbing. Available in silver and gold.

UK Lathkill, Slater, Sportfish, Anglian.

STAR FLASH

A holographic wing material with reflective properties much like that of a prism. Narrow and soft like Flashabou. Colours: gold, silver, red

US Kaufmann.

PIPINGS

CORSAIR

A tubular nylon mesh popularised by Jack Gartside. Made from very tough nylon in a loose weave, materials show through nicely for baitfish or eel imitations. It can be twisted or pulled into many useful shapes. Comes in three sizes: $1/3$" white, $1/4$" white, silver/white, $1/2$" white, translucent silver, gold, gold/black.

US Hunter.

EZ BODY BRAID

Looks not unlike Corsair, but is softer, and also comes in a pearlescent form. Available in small, medium and large sizes in black, silver, white and pearl.

UK Anglian; *US* Blue Ribbon; *INT* Orvis

FISHSCALE BODY TUBE

A woven tube of pearlescent material, similar to Lureflash Mobile, which can be used as a sleeve body on tube flies, or wound onto a hook shank to produce a fatter body. Easier to use than Mylar tubing as it does not unravel so readily at the cut end. Available in three gauges (small, medium, large) in 22 colours: mother of pearl, red, rainbow black, rainbow yellow, rainbow blue, rainbow pink, blue pearl, orange pearl, pink pearl, yellow pearl, purple pearl, black, black pearl, copper, black & silver, silver, black & gold, gold, salmon pearl, shrimp pearl, green pearl, multi pearl.

AUS Alpine; *UK* Saville, McHardy, Watercraft; *US* Marriott, MM.

FISHSCALE BODY WRAP

Fine diameter tube for wrapping bodies of flies, tubes or Waddingtons, in similar colourations to Fishscale Body Tube.

UK McHardy, Watercraft, Niche.

FLASHABOU TUBING

Flashabou woven into tubing, similar to but limper than Mylar tubing. Creates realistic fishscale effect on minnow flies, streamers and tube flies. Comes as 'small' or 'medium' in colours: silver, gold, green, copper, blue,

red, black.

GER Brinkhoff; *US* Marriott.

FLASHABOU MINNOW BODY

This is one of the best Mylar tubings, in bright non-tarnish colours. The woven Mylar gives an excellent impression of fish scales for use in Zonkers and as a sleeve for tube fly patterns. Small, medium and large gauges in colours: silvertone, goldtone, greentone, pearl, coppertone, bluetone, blacktone.

GER Brinkhoff; *US* Marriott, Hunter, Kaufmann.

FROST BITE

A braided, clear material that can be used for nymphs, steelhead and salmon fly bodies.

US Hareline (contact for local suppliers)

LOUPER TUBING

Used to make Louper flies, it is used in association with Gold, Silver or Copper heads, in 4mm or 3mm sizes. A clear soft tubing cut into 12mm lengths (4mm bore) or 10mm lengths (3mm bore) and then sliced lengthwise to obtain a half-tube scoop, which is impaled on a 2X long-shank barbless hook to sit behind the Gold head. The Louper's scoop causes the fly to swim in an agitated, wriggling fashion. Comes with instructions.

UK Saville.

MYLAR CORD TUBING

The traditional hollow-bodied braided Mylar material for flies such as Zonkers. Comes as small, medium or large, in gold, silver and pearl. Other colours: black, fl. yellow, chartreuse, light blue, dark blue, pink, purple, orange, lavender, olive, green, yellow.

AUS Alpine; *UK* Sparton, Niche, Lathkill, Slater, Sportfish, Anglian, Sparton, Walker, McHardy; *US* Marriott, Hunter, Bailey, Kaufmann, Hook & Hackle.

OPAL-LIFE BODY BRAID

A braided-body tubing for streamer, baitfish and salt-water patterns with a beautiful scaley appearance. The clear material glistens green until moved up towards the light when it takes on a pinkish hue.

UK Anglian, Lathkill; *US* Small Fry.

PEARLESCENT TUBING

Luminescent, semi-transparent tubing for Zonkers, bait-fish and tube flies, available in diameters of $1/8$", $3/16$", $1/4$". Colours: black, red, yellow, dark blue, light blue, pink, olive, lime, orange, purple.

GER Brinkhoff; *UK* Niche, Lathkill, Slater; *US* Marriott, Kaufmann, Hook & Hackle.

POLYFLASH

From Turrall, this is a loose woven tubing made of semi-translucent coloured tinsel. Colours: chartreuse, pearl, red, yellow.

UK and *US*: available from all Turrall stockists. In case of difficulty contact Turrall direct. *US* MM.

SECOND SKIN

A very fine diameter stocking-like tubing. Used with a highly visible material as a core running inside this tube, the material gives a very lifelike appearance of scaling and segmentation. Second Skin can be used to make very convincing imitations of sand eels, needle fish and even ragworm. It can also be used for wing cases, as a body wrap, for trailing shucks and other applications.

A good way to store this material is to slip it onto a drinking straw rather like a stocking on a leg. Any desired core material can be threaded easily down the bore of the straw, which can then be pulled out of the Second Skin, leaving the core in place. Sold in approx. one metre lengths, with tying instructions. Colours: white, yellow, dun, cream, wood duck, red, chartreuse, black, green, blue, olive, dark brown, light dun, warm grey.

US Marriott, AA.

VELVET TUBING

Discovered by Page Rogers and used in her Cinder Worm and Sand Eel patterns. After removing the core, the material is very easy to work with, either wrapped or used as a tail for saltwater, bass or pike flies. After being cut to length, the tubing should be glued to prevent unraveling - two recommended glues are Goop and Barge Cement. Colours: black, red, and white. The white dyes easily, and the material has a very snakey look in the water.

US Hunter.

Tails: (top row from left)Tails, Microfibetts, Fibett Tails; (middle row) Betts tailing fibres; (bottom) mongoose guard hairs.

SPOOLED MATERIALS

ANTRON SPARKLE YARN

Just what it says it is, on a spool for instant wind-on bodies. Nice and hairy for a 'buggy' glistening look. Comes in 37 colours.

UK Sparton.

ANTRON YARN

Antron yarn is supplied on the spool or on the card.

US Kaufmann, *INT* Orvis.

BOREALIS BACK

Very thin plastic ribbon, with one pearlescent side. Body wrap, shell backing or wing casing for shrimps, nymphs, etc. Comes on bobbins, in: white, yellow, pink, mauve, light blue, light orange, light green purple.

US Marriott, Montana Master.

DIAMOND BRAID

Used on steelhead and saltwater flies and does not tarnish. Gives a brighter more tapered appearance to Mylar bodies. Colours: pearlescent, silver, gold, copper, pink, royal blue, bronze, lime green, purple, red, black, multi-colour, pearl yellow, peacock blue, light blue, chartreuse.

US Marriott, Kaufmann.

GLITTER BODY

Floss and tinsel combined, for shiny bodies on streamers and saltwater flies. Does not sparkle quite as much as Diamond Braid. Colours: pearl, silver, copper, gold, pink, royal blue, red, green, peacock, rainbow, purple, black

US Marriott

HAIR HACKLE

Super-thin thread with long flowing fibres protruding from the core that can be wound to give a hackle effect. It can be used in patterns for large saltwater attractors. Also sold on cards and available in: light dun, medium dun, dark dun, slate grey, black, white, black, white, cream, brown, dark brown, olive brown, rust, dark red brown, tan, pale warm grey, yellow brown.

US Marriott.

MIDGE METALLICS

Crinkled, thin, strong metallic fibre (on a sewing machine bobbin) for bodies, tails and wing-flash. Colours: purple, pink, red, pearl, silver, gold, blue, copper, black, multi, emerald, brass.

UK Lathkill; *US* Marriott.

RED COACHMAN TINSEL

Red tinsel spooled for any Royal pattern.

US Marriott

WRAP-A-DUB

Pre-spun acrylic fibres on a core thread giving extremely neat bodies. Colours: creamy grey, tan, yellow olive, slate, red brown, caddis green, olive brown, greyish tan, medium grey, cream, chocolate brown, dark olive.

UK Lathkill; *US* Marriott.

TAILS

DELTA FLEXI-TAILS

The original soft plastic flexible tails, as used on the Waggle-Lure. Colours: black, fl. orange, fl. yellow, lime green, white, lumi-glo.

UK Saville.

FIBETT TAILS

Synthetic nylon hairs replicating the tapering, fine-pointed form of natural animal hairs. Originally manufactured for artists' paint brushes, the potential as a tail material was quickly spotted by such inventive tyers as John Betts. Sold in commercial quantities in several base thicknesses in white, gold and brown, this material is available repackaged for flytying in convenient small swatches (the fibres fused together at their butts) and in a number of dyed colours: black, white, olive, dark dun, light dun, ginger. The white can be coloured easily with waterproof marker pen.

US Kaufmann, RE; *UK* Anglian; *INT* Orvis.

LUREFLASH TWISTER TAILS

Soft plastic tails either large (2") or small (1.5"). Colours: black, white, orange, lime, fl. yellow, glitter clear.

UK Saville.

MICROFIBETTS

Popularized by John Betts, these are fine-tapered nylon filaments, originally developed as a synthetic substitute for expensive natural hairs for artist's brushes. Used almost exclusively to imitate the tails of Ephemerid duns and spinners, Microfibetts are longer and more durable than hackle fibres and more translucent than natural guard hairs. They dye easily and can be coloured with waterproof marking pen. Colours: white, brown, dark dun, light dun, ginger, red brown, yellow, cream, olive, tan, black, light blue dun, dark blue dun.

AUS Alpine; *GER* Brinkhoff; *UK* Lathkill, Sportfish, Angling Pursuits; *US* Marriott, Hunter, Cabela, Bailey, Kaufmann, Hook & Hackle, River Edge, MM; *INT* Orvis.

SPINNER TAILS

Very fine synthetic barred tail fibres, which make good shrimp antennae too. Colours: blue dun, red game, cream, olive, white, black.

UK Niche.

SUPER THIN TAILS

Super-thin Microfibetts (about 40% thinner) which are excellent for tiny flies and Spring Creek patterns. Available in: white, ginger, olive, dark olive, red, brown, light dun.

US Marriott.

TAILS (see also Super Thin Tails)

Similar to Microfibetts but 40% thinner, designed for fly sizes 18-28. Colours: white, ginger, olive, dark olive, red brown, light dun.

US Whitetail.

WAGGLE / TWISTER TAILS

Flexible tails of the translucent rubber-like Plastisol material used so extensively by American freshwater bass fishers. These tails waggle and move seductively when pulled through the water. Waggle tails are attached by threading the hook through the centre of the tail (as if baiting with a real worm). In order to keep the tail in place, the hook shank is usually first covered with a layer of tying thread and coated with a cyanoacrylate glue. Carefully trap the head end of the Waggle Tail with further turns of thread. Attach a hackle or wing for extra security. The tails are used in the Waggle Tail range of flies and also very effective 'Muddlerized', with a spun deer hair head. Available in small (12") and medium (22"). Colours: black, white, fl. pink, fl. yellow, orange, red, green, chartreuse, yellow, clear and blue sparkle.

UK Sparton, Saville; *US* River Edge.

TUBINGS

LARVA LACE

Thin, translucent plastic tube, developed to provide realistic wound and woven bodies and ribbings on nymph imitations, etc. The standard material can be stretched to reduce its diameter, making it suitable for a wide range of fly sizes. Larva Lace can be coloured with waterproof marker pens, while other effects can be achieved by threading floss or tinsel through its hollow bore, prior to winding. Colours: black, brown, clear, fluorescent chartreuse, fl. orange, fl. red, green, grey, olive, orange, red/brown, shrimp, yellow and blood red.

AUS Alpine; *UK* Rooksbury, Niche, McHardy, Watercraft; *US* Marriott, MM, River Edge, Hunter, Cabela, AA, Bailey, Kaufmann.

LARVA LACE MIDGE

A finer gauge of the preceding material, for tying smaller sized-flies.

US Marriott, Cabela, Bailey, Kaufmann, MM, River Edge; *UK* Niche.

LIQUI LACE

Soft, flexible plastic tubing, used as a body and ribbing material. The 'unique' claim of this product is that coloured liquids can be more easily sucked up the tube before it is wrapped and tied off. This alters the refractive properties of the tube as well as its density, allowing further subtleties in larval and nymphal imitations. This product is associated with Mike Tucker and his Liqui-Flies concept.

Midge Lace (sizes 18-26): clear, black, olive, white, fl. red, chartreuse, orange, fl. orange, dun, pheasant tail brown.
Medium Lace (sizes 8-18): clear, black, gold, dark olive, red, brown, orange.
Woolybugger Lace (size 8 only): clear, black, olive, purple, gold, neon green.
Iridescent Lace (sizes 8-18): red, green, violet. A Pantone marker pen can be applied to these to create different colours.

US Custom Aquatics, Marriott, MM, River Edge.

POLYTHENE BUZZER TUBING

Extremely fine diameter clear tubing which makes excellent buzzer nymph bodies. Colour is achieved by inserting a thin metallic tinsel or fibre into the tube. Size 1mm for size 12 hooks, and 0.063mm for 14-16 hooks.

UK Saville.

ULTRA LACE TUBING

A very thin soft tubing useful for inserting other materials inside for subtle body effects on small flies. Colours: grey, yellow, brown, orange, lime, olive, red, clear, black.

UK Sparton, Rooksbury, Lathkill, Slater, Sportfish, Anglian, Walker, Norris.

WINGS

AIRE-FLOW CUT WINGS / PERFECT CUT WINGS

Pre-cut wings made from a buoyant, veined material. Made by Rocky Mountain Dubbing and distributed by Spirit River. Mayfly, stonefly/caddis, hopper, and cut-your-own provided. Colours: *Mayfly*: tan, creamy, white, medium, olive, speckled olive, speckled grey, yellow. *Stonefly/caddis*: black, brown, speckled tan, olive, speckled olive, speckled grey, yellow. *Hopper*: mottled olive, mottled brown.

US BT, Montana Master, Blue Ribbon

ANGEL HAIR

Finely shredded Mylar which can also be used for dubbing as well as winging material. Colours: gold, blue, grey, yellow, turquoise, orange, dark blue, copper, dark brown, light brown, brown, dark orange, dark red, burgundy, chartreuse, red, lime, bright blue, green, purple, bronze, silver, fuchsia, black, pink, dark green, pearl/blue, pearl/green, pearl/gold.

US Anglers Choice.

BIG FLY FIBRE

Synthetic hair wing material (formerly called Hairbou), with a good underwater action, principally used for large saltwater flies. Available 'straight' or 'crinkly' with a fibre length of about 10".
Colours: black, brown, honey, silver grey, copper, white, yellow, green, blue, red, gold, orange, purple, TB.blue, hot pink, lavender.

GER Brinkhoff; *UK* Lathkill; *US* Hunter, River Edge, Cabela; *INT* Orvis.

CELO-Z WING

Clear, cellophane-like wing material designed for spinners.

US Cabela, AA, Blue Ribbon, MM.

CRAFT HAIR

Finely textured hair for use on streamers and saltwater patterns available in: white, black, red, pink, kelly green, yellow, light blue, dark blue, tan, grey, flame red.

US Marriott, Kaufmann.

CRYSTAL FLASH

Crinkly filaments that flash many tiny points of light. Use sparingly in small bunches to give 'life'.
Colours: silver, gold, red, royal blue, pearl, pearl blue, peacock, lime green, fl. pink, fl. yellow.

UK Sparton; *US* AA; *AUS* Alpine.

CRYSTAL HAIR

The Lureflash development from earlier Flashabou types of flat Mylar strand. This material consists of twisted individual strands, that give an enhanced sparkle effect. It can be used for tails and wings of flashy, streamer flies, either on its own or blended with other hair wing materials. Particularly suited to baitfish imitations.
Various colours, including: peacock, gold, olive, dark purple, copper, silver, blue pearl, hot orange, black, light blue, hot yellow, pink pearl, green, mother of pearl, smolt blue, pearl mix, grey ghost, royal blue, lime, purple pearl, red, wine and root beer.

UK Rooksbury, Niche, Lathkill, Sportfish, Walker, Norris, McHardy, Watercraft.

CRYSTAL TWIST

Fine strands of twisted mylar which come in 7" hanks of approx. 900 strands per packet. Colours: black, olive, gold, copper, purple, silver, red, pink, pearl, lime.

US Montana Master.

DAN BAILEY HI-VIS FLOATER

Treated with water repellent coating this makes good dry fly winging material. Colours: the same 26 as for Dan Bailey Body Fur (see page 73)

US Bailey.

DAN BAILEY RAINBOW THREAD

Strands of 10" polypropylene, finer than Krystal Flash. Colours: pearl, white, multi, olive, black, yellow, pink, purple, aquamarine, green, metallic blue, red, gold, silver copper.

US Bailey.

DAN BAILEY WING FIBRE

Strung winging material with fibres 7" long for large saltwater, bass, or trout flies. Colours: same 26 as for Dan Bailey Body Fur (see page 73)

US Bailey.

DUN WING (see under Winging, page 101)

There is a product known as Roman Moser's Dun Wing, from Traun River Products, consisting of wing shapes printed on a fine fabric for cutting out. Davy Wotton's Dun Wing is a fine synthetic yarn.

EVETT'S WING MATERIAL

Intended to accurately reproduce natural mayfly wings. Very durable. Comes with tying instructions, 12 wings to a pack and in four sizes: XS (20-22); S (16-18); M (12-14) and L (8-10).

US Marriott; *INT* Orvis.

Types of foam for the flytyer, including:Rainy's Float Foam (in tubular form),
Rainy's Float Foam and Rainy's Underbody (left).

FANTASTIC WING

Synthetic wing material from Mustad (relevant for larger imitative patterns, such as stoneflies, caddis flies and grasshoppers). Has the appearance of a fine woven fabric, decorated with four different mottled designs. The open weave, pervious to air, should help avoid the leader spinning effects sometimes encountered with sheet-wing materials during casting. Sold in packs of the four different mottled colours that cover most imitative needs. *GER* Brinkhoff.

FIRE FLY

A Hedron material of bonded metallic nylon with an outstanding realistic life-like motion. Gives the maximum of flexibility, strength, flash and colour. The hanks are a foot long with 450 strands per hank. Colour: Royal Blue, Chartreuse, White, Gold, Copper, Red, Silver, Pink, Lavender, Gree, Black, Peacock, Bronze, Grey, Purple.
US Marriott, Hunter, Cabela; *GER* Brinkhoff.

FISHAIR

Very durable, translucent synthetic hair for streamers, especially saltwater, used on its own or combined with other fibres. The untapered fibres give the wing a rather hard trailing edge, less subtle than one with a natural hair. Available in 70 denier gauge, 6" and 10", and in 24 denier, 4" long. The widest colour range is available in the 'standard' 70 denier, 6" material and includes: polar bear, natural white, fl. yellow, fl. tangerine, fl. dayglo yellow, mustard yellow, fl. dayglo chartreuse, fl. lime green, emerald green, moss green, sky blue, silver blue, royal blue, peacock, purple, nugget gold, squirrel brown, natural brown, fl. day-glo orange, feather red, burgundy red, fl. dark. pink, fl. pink, mouse grey, natural black, olive green, pale pink.

US Marriott, Hunter, Cabela, Bailey, Kaufmann, BR, MM, RE; *AUS* Alpine.; *INT* Orvis.

FLASHABOU

Flashabou was the first of the soft, mobile, synthetic tinsel materials, sold in hanks and intended to be tied in bunches as 'wings' on streamer patterns.

The name derives from its flashiness and supposed similarity to Marabou. Flashabou's gaudiness makes it particularly suited to saltwater and pike patterns.

Colours: silver, gold, kelly green, pearl, copper, mint, electric blue, lime green, dark blue, red, black, purple, fuchsia, light blue, yellow bronze, pink, grape, purple chub, fountain blue, ocean blue, bull frog, rainbow, salt & pepper, June bug, perch.

Also available in the following colours dyed over pearl: black, fl. yellow, chartreuse, light blue, dark blue, pink, purple, orange, lavender, olive, yellow, peacock.

Saltwater Flashabou

Heavier, wider gauged Flashabou, some 10" for large saltwater patterns and jigs.

Colours: silver, gold, pearl copper, dark blue, red, black, purple, salt & pepper. Also available in dyed pearl colours: chartreuse, dark blue, pink.

Glow-in-the-Dark Flashabou

Luminous Flashabou, for use at night, very deep fishing, ice fishing jigs, etc. Colours: white, pink, yellow, orange, and green.

Flashabou Accent

Similar to Crystal Hair, but from the Flashabou stable. Colours: silver, gold, green, pearl, copper, electric blue, dark blue, red, black, fuchsia, rainbow. Also in pearl, over-dyed in the following colours: black, fl. yellow, chartreuse, light blue, dark blue, pink, purple, orange,

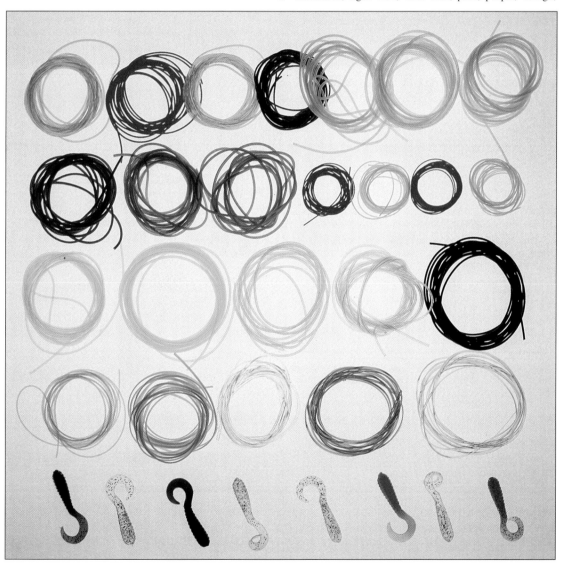

Ligni Lace, Larva Lace, Nymph Rib and Waggle Tails.

olive, yellow, peacock.

UK Lathkill; *US* Marriott, Hunter, Cabela, Bailey, Kaufmann, Hook & Hackle, Blue Ribbon, River Edge; *AUS* Alpine; *GER* Brinkhoff; *INT* Orvis.

FLASHIBOU

To be known as 'Maraglit' from 1997. A Lureflash product of flat metallic winging material which is very similar to the company's Mobile product (see page 97), but without the micro monofilament support strands. Colours: gold, silver, copper, bronze, black, gun metal, red, blue, green, purple, green & pearl, gold & pearl, silver & pearl, black & pearl, red & pearl, mother of pearl, multi-mix, rainbow, magenta.

UK Saville, Lathkill, Norris, Watercraft.

FLY FILM

Looks rather like hand-painted raffia (raffene), of varying width, which can be used for wings, shellbacks, wing cases, etc. Sold in strips of about 2m, with tying instructions. Colours: clear, mottled black, mottled silver/black, mottled brown, dark dun, mottled light dun, tan and mottled hopper yellow.

US Cabela, Whitetail, River Edge.

FLY FUR

A synthetic fur with mobile action like Marabou, but offering the bulky appearance of wool, with lots of sparkle. Useful for wings on streamers and saltwater patterns. It has an almost natural 'underfur', which can be combed out to give a lighter, less bulky effect. Colours: white, black, brown, auburn, blonde, red, green, grey, tan, lime, light blue, orange, royal blue, light pink, dark pink, rust, light gold, lavender and chartreuse.

US Blue Ribbon, Hunter; *INT* Orvis.

GLIMMER

Flowing thin material for saltwater and streamer flies. Each strand has a large spectrum of colours that flash in the water and the light. Adds more bulk to the fly without adding more bulk to the tie-in area. Reacts well to epoxy covering. Colours: chartreuse, orange, pearl, gold, yellow, pink, rainbow, translucent rainbow, purple.

INT Orvis.

HI-VIS (see Hi-Vis fibre, page 82)

HOLOGRAPHIC SPARKLE

A fine fibred material in hank form for adding flash to wings and tails.

UK Sportfish.

KRINKLE FLASH

Fine hair-like mylar tinsel reinforced with nylon. Can be used as a tail material or ribbing as well as for wings. **Holographic Krinkle Flash** has a holographic flash material mixed within the mylar. The hanks come 7" long.
Colours: amethyst, brass.bronze, chartreuse, copper, electric blue, fuchsia, gold, green, pearl, pewter, purple, red, royal blue, sea foam, silver, sky blue. Holographic colours: amethyst, bronze, chartreuse, gold, pearl, sky blue.

US Marriott

KRYSTAL FLASH

The American product comprising very fine twisted Mylar type strands, with tiny reflective bubbles along its length. Used on its own, it creates a spectacularly sparkly wing for various attractor patterns. A few strands combined with other winging materials, show through as pin-prick sparks of light. Krystal Flash and other twisted strand materials have extensively superceded the flat stranded Flashabou-type material, and this one is available in a wide range of 'metallic' and 'pearlescent' colours:
Solid: silver, gold, red.
Pearlescent: pearl, pink, hot yellow, purple, mixed colours, pearl blue, black, hot orange, peacock, lime, green, olive, smolt blue, grey ghost, dark purple, root beer.
Fluorescent: orange, shrimp pink, cerise, chartreuse, fire orange.

US Marriott, Hunter, Bailey, Gorilla, Kaufmann, Hook & Hackle, Blue Ribbon, MM, River Edge; *UK* Lathkill; *GER* Brinkhoff; *INT* Orvis.

LACE WING

A thin, soft-textured, yet durable, 'lace' winging material, that makes most realistic insect wings. The sheet has fine perforations to counteract leader twist when casting. Most types of insect wing shape can be cut from this material, which is easily tied in. Sold in 3" square sheets, in the following colours: natural, black, green and brown.

UK Rooksbury, Sportfish, Walker, McHardy, Watercraft; *AUS* Alpine.

LAZER LIGHT

(see entry in Dubbing section, page 56)

McFLYLON FLY MATERIAL

Crafted from combed polyfibre with crinkle texturing this material is intended for wings, parachute posts and dubbing blends - for fresh and saltwater fishing. Colours: white, black, yellow, chartreuse, green, bug juice olive, purple, red, pink, silver, copper, blue.

US Gorilla.

MICROWEB

A fine-lacquered, synthetic mesh. It can be folded and cut to shape to make symmetrical wings for imitative fly patterns. A special loop knot is recommended for tying in Microweb, which is fully described in the accompanying instructions. Sold in packs of ten strips of either mixed or single colours: white, slate, cricket black, light dun, yellow sally, Cahill cream, chocolate brown, olive, medium olive, metallic mixed and speckled mixed.

US Marriott, Hook & Hackle; *AUS* Alpine; *GER* Brinkhoff.

MOBILE

Lureflash's versatile metallised plastic material for wings, with incredible mobility in the water. Can also be used as ribbing or body material. Colours: copper, lime gold, rainbow green, silver, pearl mix, mother of pearl.

Luminous Mobile

Activated by light and shines phosphorescent at night or deep down in the water. Colours: lime, orange, yellow, red, white.

Twinkle Mobile

Myriad pearl flecks to give added attraction. Available in: hot orange, rainbow black, claret, cream, bronze, light brown, black, grey, dark green, red, purple, blue, ginger, light blue, salmon, aquamarine, olive, fl. white, fl. orange, fl. lime, fl. pink, fl. yellow, lum. white, Lum. green, Lum. red, Lum. yellow.

Translucent Mobile

Comes in black, blue, aqua-green, olive, fiery brown, dark brown, dark green, red, dark olive, golden yellow, fl. yellow, fl. pink, fl. white, fl. red.

UK Rooksbury, Niche, Saville, Lathkill, Slater, Sportfish, Anglian, Sparton, Walker, McHardy, Watercraft.

MOTION

A new mylar, flashabou-style material from Spirit River, in hanks 14" long. Colours: *Glass*: brown pearl, olive pearl, grey pearl, orange pearl, purple pearl, pink pearl, black pearl, pearl, blue pearl, green pearl, red pearl. *Solid*: gold, white gold, silver, red. *Glow-in-the-dark*: fl. pink, fl. green, fl. yellow.

US Spirit River (contact for local suppliers)

MOTTLED WING MATERIAL

Mottled coloured sheets from which shapes are cut as desired. Colours: brown, tan, grey.

US Montana Master; *INT* Orvis.

MYSTIC WINGING FIBRE

A long, fine synthetic hair with very fine pearlescent fila-ments. Colours: black, white, orange, red, fl. yellow, fl. chartreuse, fl. orange.

UK Niche, Sportfish.

NEER HAIR

A hank of long fine sparkling synthetic fibres suitable for wings. It can also be spun, stacked or twisted for body wrapping. Colours: smoke, white, light blue, black, olive.

UK Lathkill; *US* Marriott.

OCEAN HAIR

Similar to Ultra Hair (page 101) but shorter (6-7") and available in: black, green, fl. white, root beer, blue, purple, fl. pink, chartreuse, orange, red, yellow, fl. fuchsia.

US Marriott.

ORGANZA

Available through most material shops, with various subtle variants some of which make excellent dry fly dun and spinner wings.

UK Lathkill.

ORGANZA WING MATERIAL

For hundreds of years, Japanese weavers have produced a unique fabric known as silk organza, often used in wedding dresses. Tyers use it for mayfly wings. Mustad have discovered a synthetic substitute which has the transparency of genuine organza, is more durable and retains its shape after being chewed by fish. It can be easily coloured with waterproof markers and cut to any required shape. Sold in large sheets.

GER Brinkhoff.

POLAR AIRE

A shiny synthetic substitute for Polar Bear which comes in long hanks ready to clip or pull loose fibres. Also used for parachute posts, Wulff-style flies, and spinner wings. It can be coloured with waterproof marker pen. Available in colours: black, polar white, golden yellow, purple, red, fl. chartreuse, fl. hot pink, fl. orange, brown, silver grey, burnt orange, royal blue, fl. pink, shrimp pink.

US Marriott, Cabela, Montana Master.

POLYFLUFF

Used for the wings of dry flies, from small spinner repre-sentations to the Wulff series, as it is very translucent and highly visible at distance. Try it for parachute wing 'posts' and strike indicators too. A good calf tail substi-tute with high floatability. Bright white in its natural form, as often supplied, but is available dyed in six colours: clear, wood duck, light dun, medium dun, dark dun, and brown.

US Marriott.

POLYGARN

One of the best dry fly wing and body materials. Popular in Scandinavia for many years for the famous Rakkelhanen Caddis. Serious caddis fishermen, will want this in their stock of materials. Sold in lengths of about 1m. Colours: rust, dark brown, light ginger, olive, light brown, dark blue dun, grey olive dirty yellow and greeny dun.

NOR Rakkelhanen, Bergqvist; *SWE* Bergqvist.

POLY WING

A white material from Benecchi for parachutes, spent wings, duns and spinners.

IT Benecchi (contact for local suppliers)

REFLECTIONS

A braided synthetic with very high reflective qualities which is stiff enough to use as winging material whilst remaining highly mobile. Probably best coated with epoxy for maximum benefit. Colours: pink/red, blue/pink, rainbow, lilac/rainbow, gold/pink, purple/green, blue/green.

US Marriott, Montana Master; *AUS* Alpine.

SALTWATER HAIR

A brushed wool patch adding pulsating action to salt-water streamers. Colours: white, red, yellow, tidal blue, marine blue, hot orange, pink, tan, lime green, purple, root beer, chartreuse.

US Marriott.

SCINTILLA WING FILM

Originally developed for imitating spinner wings, this material also makes excellent shell backs on shrimps. If cut and bent to the 'tent roof' shape of an adult caddis wing, this film can be used for unbelievably effective 'diving' caddis patterns. The film is transparent, with an iridescent sheen. It is fairly durable and resistant to tearing. The crinkly texture gives a good impression of the reflection and segmentation of a natural insect wing. Supplied in packs of three sheets with tying instructions.

US Marriott, Bailey, Gorilla, Montana Master.

SEA FIBRES

Also known as Enrico's Sea Fibres, this is used for tying large saltwater patterns (up to 10"). Particularly notable for making large lures that are light and easy to cast long distances. Colours: red, lavender, royal blue, grey, black, orange, white, pink, blue, dark grey, yellow, tan, dark olive, lime, purple, steel blue, kelly green, and chartreuse. Also available in shorter length fibres for trout and bass flies, in which form it is marketed as Hi-Vis.

US Hunter.

SEA FLASH

Very long (about 21") soft, supple strands of lightly

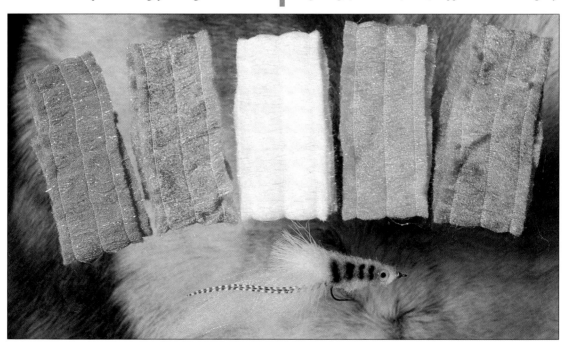

Plushille in various colours, showing the lines of stitching and a fly made from it.

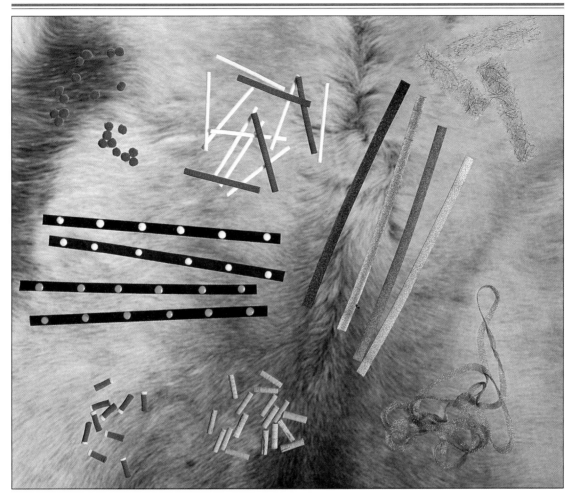

Body materials (clockwise from top left): eggs, foam bodies, caddis cases, metallic beetle bodies, Second Skin, cork bodies, Quick-sight any bodies, Quick-sight beetle bodies.

crimped Mylar used mainly for saltwater, bass and pike patterns. Colours: champagne/gold, silver, brass, iridescent pearl.

US Montana Master.

SHIMAZAKI FLY WING

An interesting material enabling extremely realistic imitation of insect wings. The colours and vein patterns are actually sandwiched between two very thin plastic films. The colour range available not only mimics natural insect wings, but also includes imitations of commonly used feathers and furs.

One drawback of this and indeed any impervious sheet material used for winging, is that it can cause leader 'spin' during casting. This is more problematical with large upwing patterns, such as mayflies and less so with flat-winged imitations, such as sedges. Supplied with tying instructions.

Colours: clear vein, light grey, medium grey, cree, pale yellow, dirty yellow, hopper yellow, march brown, speck brown, dark brown, stonefly, sandy dun, speckle grey, dark grey.

US Marriott, Kaufmann, BR; *GER* Brinkhoff.

SHIMAZAKI AIR THRU WING

Similar to Fly Wing, but the wings are air permeable to help avoid the problem of leader twist during casting. Comes with detailed instructions in: light grey, medium grey, dark grey, pale yellow, white, dirty yellow, bronze dun.

US Marriott; *AUS* Alpine; *GER* Brinkhoff.

SOFT WING

New from Benecchi, a very soft, synthetic winging material for producing diaphanous dry fly wings. Very strong and can be stretched by hand for softer, gauzier effects. Colours: white, cream, dun, dark dun.

IT Benecchi (contact for local suppliers)

SPARKLE WING

This material is very translucent, crinkly and floats well. It can be used to imitate insect wings and nymphal shucks. A pearl version of Lacewing. Colours: olive pearl, pink pearl, red pearl, kingfisher blue pearl, yellow pearl, mauve pearl, mother of pearl.

UK Watercraft; *US* Montana Master.

SPECTRA HAIR

This appears to be very similar to Ultra Hair but comes from the Umpqua stable.

US Montana Master.

SPINNER GLASS

Designed for spent spinner wings and available in: cream, white, pale watery dun, medium dun.

US Marriott, Blue Ribbon, Montana Master.

STREAMER HAIR

Also known as Shetland Streamer Wool or Streamer Wool. Natural wool 6-8" long of very fine texture, giving a Marabou-like action. Colours: white, red, purple, kelly green, light olive, rust, dark brown, fl. orange, fl. chartreuse, fl. pink, fl. yellow, yellow, silver grey, black, salt blue, fl. blue, brown, olive.

US Marriott, Kaufmann; *AUS* Alpine.

SUPER HAIR

An amazing fibre for hair wing and streamers. Considerably finer than most other synthetic hairs, this material is very mobile. It is also very translucent and 'collects' light, which is emitted from the cut ends of the fibres. The fineness makes it very nice to tie with.

The hair is 10-11" long and is sold in quarter ounce packs. Colours: black, brown, dark brown, white, olive, sea foam green, green, bright green, grey, smoke, yellow, dark purple, burnt orange, purple, chartreuse, red, dark blue, pink, peach, lavender, light blue and green chartreuse.

US Hunter, Cabela, Whitetail, Hook & Hackle, Bailey, MM; *AUS* Alpine; *INT* Orvis.

SUPREME HAIR

A slightly limper version of Crimped Nylon produced by Hedron. Diameter: 0.004". Colours: black, brown, white, yellow, orange, red, olive, pink, purple, lavender, green, light green, blue, light blue, chartreuse, smoke grey, shrimp, fuchsia.

GER Brinkhoff; *US* Blue Ribbon.

SUSSEX META-FLASH

Another thin and colourful long-flowing winging fibre.

JAP Sawada.

SYNTHETIC LIVING FIBRE (SLF)

Comes in hank form (see page 61)

TEAR-DROP WING MATERIAL

Translucent with mottled markings this is ideal for fly wings. Doubling or tripling the material allows several wings to be cut out at the same time. The wings are shaped by using wing burners, wing cutters or scissors.

US Rainy.

TIEWELL SPARKLE FLASH

Multi-coloured, extra strong, flat Mylar strands supported by nylon filaments. There is little need to blend colours for baitfish patterns, as the strands closely match the reflective sparkle of moving fish. Colours: natural pearl, yellow pearl, blue pearl, green pearl, rainbow pearl, pink pearl, gold, silver, copper, gun metal, metallic rainbow, graphite, pale blue rainbow, aqua rainbow, emerald rainbow, purple rainbow, red rainbow, dark blue rainbow, pink rainbow, multi rainbow.

US Marriott, Hunter, Cabela, AA; *AUS* Alpine.

TRASHABOU

Perhaps not for the purist but an amusing name for cut-up trash or grocery bags (which come in various colours) for a cheap and quick, mobile, plastic material for winging or for skirts. Norm Bartlett has popularised the idea with his 'T.B.' series of flies.

TWINKLE

A stranded pearlescent material used for flashy hair wings on streamer patterns. The material can also be used for wound bodies and tails. In Twinkle, the flat iridescent strand is supported by being loosely woven with very fine monofilaments (cf. the Flashabou, Krystal Hair types).

In 1993, three UK trout records were held by fish caught on flies tied with Twinkle. Colours: fl. white, fl. pink, fl. lime, fl. orange, fl. yellow, light brown, dark brown, dark green, blue, grey dun, purple, black, claret, cream, ginger, light blue, salmon pink, aquamarine, olive, rainbow, dark blue, hot orange, magenta, pastel pink, rainbow black. Also luminous colours: white, red, yellow, lime, orange.

UK Rooksbury, Niche, Lathkill, Sparton, Walker, McHardy, Watercraft; *AUS* Alpine.

ULTRA HAIR

A synthetic hair which is crimped every $1/4$" making it stiffer than some winging materials. It comes in two styles:

(1) in the USA:
12" long, designed for very big saltwater streamer patterns. Colours: white, dark blue, light blue, red, fl. chartreuse, green, yellow, orange, black, amber, olive, silver, root beer, pink, purple, chartreuse.

US Marriott, Hunter, Blue Ribbon, MM.

(2) in the UK
Distributed by Lureflash in 7" hanks and used for shrimp feelers, winging, etc. Colours: black, white, orange, yellow, lime, red, pink, blue.

UK Sportfish, McHardy, Watercraft.

WASP WING

A crinkled pearlescent sheet material, that gives the impression of the veins and segmentation of the natural insect wing. Used in conjunction with other modern materials, such as Rainy's Float Foam and Crystal Hair, one can achieve very convincing imitations of ants, stoneflies, beetles, etc. Sold in two sheet packs.

UK Rooksbury, McHardy, Watercraft.

WIDOW'S WEB

Long (9") semi-translucent fibres giving great undulating movement in vibrant colours: blue, royal blue, yellow, pink, chartreuse, red, lime, lavender, black, grey.

US Marriott; *INT* Orvis.

WINGING / DUN WING

Davy Wotton's highly water repellent material with similar properties to CDC. Colours: BWO, dunny olive, dark grey dun, olive dun, danica yellow olive, pale grey dun, spinner-light fawn.

UK Lathkill, Angling Pursuits; *US* Fly & Field.

WING-IT

Artificial hair that can be used for the wings of 'no hackle' flies, spinners, stoneflies, midges and soft-wing streamers. Marketed by the Norwegian flytyer Staffan Lindstrom, the material is believed to be only available in Scandinavia.

NOR Rakkelhanen, Bergqvist; *SWE* Bergqvist.

WYNGS

Popularised by John Betts, this winging material is sold in sheets printed with various sizes and shapes of wing outline. Wyngs can be used for most flat wing and down wing imitations (stoneflies, caddis flies, etc.). The wings, which can be cut to shape or burned with wing burners, are totally waterproof and extremely tough. The opaque material can be coloured with waterproof marker pen. Sold in packs of four sheets, each of which provides more than 30 wings.

US Marriott; *AUS* Alpine.

ZING

Resembles a sort of ultra-fine, transparent, synthetic raffia - or simply wrapping paper for gifts! Another John Betts 'discovery', Zing is fairly strong across the grain, but splits quite easily longitudinally, enabling the appropriate wing width to be obtained.

This tendency to split has an important side benefit, since it reduces the propensity for wings made from Zing to act as tiny propellers, causing leader twist during casting. When split thus it makes the sound when cast that gives it its name. Zing is easy to work with and can be used in a host of imitative applications.

It can be easily coloured with waterproof marking pen (even at the streamside when the hatch has been identified) and is sold with illustrated tying instructions and suggestions provided by John Betts.

US Marriott, Kaufmann.

Threads, Tinsels & Flosses

Contents

Contents of this Section:	page
Sources and suppliers	103
Tying Threads	104
Flosses	108
Lurexes	109
Pearls and Optics	110
Metallics	111
Dubbing Waxes	113

THERE ARE many threads available today and they have many differing properties. The tyer will want to use the one most suited to the task in hand. In this respect, thickness, stretchability, the material the thread is made of, whether it is pre-waxed or unwaxed, whether in a flat or round profile on the hook - these will be some of the considerations. Many threads today are either nylon (eg. Danville Flymaster) or polyester (eg. Uni-thread). But extra strong threads like Kevlar are effectively as tough as carbon fibre. Thicker threads are described by lower numbers (eg. 3/0) and thinner threads by lower numbers (eg. 12/0). Silk floss is still available, but most modern flosses are made of synthetic materials such as rayon, dacron, nylon and polyester. Stretchy flosses, such as those made of lycra (which holds up track-suit trousers) are also now available. These new materials may not please the purist but they do come in vivid colours - indeed as fluorescents. Rayon and acetate flosses tend to fray easily, but they are very shiny.

LEFT *Lureflash Chenilles, Fritz, Fishscale Bodytube and Sparkle Yarn.*

SOURCES & SUPPLIERS

ANGLER'S CHOICE
US Angler's Choice, Blue Ribbon.

BENECCHI
UK Lathkill, Sportfish; *US* Whitetail, Hunter; *INT* Orvis.

DANVILLE
AUS Alpine; *GER* Brinkhoff; *JAP* Sawada; UK Angling Pursuits, Lathkill, Saville, Sportfish, Danville; *US* Marriott, Hook & Hackle, Kaufmann, Whitetail, Hook & Hackle, Hunter, Cabela, Gorilla, Blue Ribbon ; *INT* Orvis.

DATAM PRODUCTS
UK Saville, Niche, McHardy, Norris, Rooksbury, Sportfish, Walker.

DYNACORD
UK Niche; *US* Whitetail.

GORDON GRIFFITHS
UK Niche, Norris, Rooksbury; *US* Hunter, Marriott.

GSB THREAD
US Marriott.

GUDEBROD
AUS Alpine; *US* Marriott, Whitetail, Cabela, Bailey.

INTERTAC
US Marriott, Cabela, Gorilla.

JAPANESE SILK FLOSS
US Marriott

KREINIK MANUFACTURING CO. INC.
US Whitetail

HOLOGRAPHIC TINSEL
GER Brinkhoff; *UK* Lathkill, Sportfish; *US* Marriott, Cabela.

LAGARTUN
AUS Alpine; *NOR* Bergqvist; *SWE* Bergqvist; *UK* Sportfish, Lathkill; *US* Marriott, Hook & Hackle, Hunter, Blue Ribbon.

LUREFLASH
UK Watercraft, Saville, McHardy, Walker, Anglian.

MOSER
GER Brinkhoff; *UK* Angling Pursuits, Lathkill, Niche.

ORVIS
INT Orvis

PAC
US Marriott, Blue Ribbon.

PEARSALL
UK Lathkill, Niche, Saville, McHardy, Norris, Rooksbury, Sportfish; *US* Marriott, Hook & Hackle, Hunter, Blue Ribbon.

SPARTON
UK Sparton, Saville, McHardy, Walker.

SUSSEX
JAP Sawada.

THOMPSON
GER Brinkhoff; *US* Marriott.

TIEWELL
AUS Alpine; US Marriott.

UNI-PRODUCTS
JAP Sawada; *UK* Lathkill, Angling Pursuits, Niche, Saville, McHardy, Rooksbury, Anglian; *US* Marriott, Whitetail, Hook & Hackle, AA, Cabela, Gorilla, Bailey, BR, MM, RE.

VENIARD
UK Niche, Saville, Rooksbury, Sportfish, Lathkill, Walker.

WAPSI
US Marriott.

TYING THREADS

BENECCHI

MULTISTRAND
Ultrafine XXF
Equivalent to 12/0, the thread is formed by several thinner ones that make it up to a breaking load of 450 grammes. It comes unwaxed in: black, orange, red, chocolate, tobacco, brown, dark brown, green, dark dun, light dun, sandy, white, yellow, dark green, opal, dark blue, emerald, pink, magenta, blue.

Superfine XF
Equivalent to 10/0 with a breaking load of 750 grammes. Unwaxed in: black, red, wine, tobacco, brown, dark brown, green, dark dun, light dun, sandy, white, yellow, dark green, pink, magenta, blue, olive, dark tobacco, light tobacco, copper.

Fine F
Equivalent to 8/0 with a breaking load of about 1 kilogram. Unwaxed in the same 25 colours as the Superfine.

TWISTED THREADS
Strong Fine F
Strong, fine thread for the tyer looking for a 900 grammes breaking load with a diameter of 10/0. Colours: black, orange, red, wine, tobacco, brown, dark brown, green, dark dun, light dun, sandy, white, yellow, dark green, olive, dark tobacco, light sandy, light tobacco, copper, tan.

Strong Medium M A
A special type of unwaxed thread with a very strong, twisted, round section. Equivalent to 6/0 and can be used for rod building. Colours: black, red, wine, dark brown, green, dark dun, light dun, white, yellow, pink, light sandy, violet.

Superstrong L
An unwaxed thread for big flies, bass bugs, tarpon flies etc. Breaking load is 2,000 grammes - equivalent to 4/0. Colours: black, red, wine, tobacco, dark dun, light dun, dark tobacco, light tobacco, tan, mustard yellow, ivory, light wine.

Natural Kevlar
Softer than some Kevlar threads, it makes strong knots and takes glue well. Colour: yellow.

DANVILLE
Often referred to as Flymaster Threads.

Waxed 6/0
Colours: black, white, red, yellow, coffee, olive, grey, orange, eggshell, wine, beige, maize, tobacco, light olive, fl. red, fl. orange, fl. yellow, fl. green, fire orange, fl. blue.

Monocord 3/0
A strong thread that is flatter than many to prevent build-up on hooks and makes smooth bodies. Colours: black, white, red, yellow, grey, light orange, burnt orange, beige, tobacco, blue, dark brown, charcoal, green, maize, olive, coffee, silver, worm green.

Monocord A&B threads
Waxed and thicker threads for handling thicker materials and larger flies. 'A' comes in: black, white, red, yellow, tobacco, worm green, grey, light orange, burnt orange, coffee. 'B' comes in: black, white, red, yellow.

Nymo

An 'A' size thread that is as strong as any available. As strong as Kevlar but does not cut materials or groove bobbins. Colours: white, black, beige, yellow, orange, red, gold, light green, moss green, blue, brown.

Flymaster+

Very strong and durable, this is about an 'A' size. Colours: black, white, red, yellow, coffee, olive, grey, orange, eggshell, wine, beige, maize, tobacco, light olive, fl. red, fl. yellow, fl. orange, fl. green, fire orange.

Spiderweb Fine 1

2/0 white thread.

Flat Waxed Nylon

A 210 denier thread about size 'A' used on saltwater and other large flies for quick head build-up. Colours: black, white, yellow, red, grey, tobacco, olive, fl. red, fl. yellow, fl. orange, fl. green, fire orange, fl. white, fl. blue, fl. pink.

Stretch Nylon

Available in fluorescent shades of red, yellow, orange, green, fire orange, white, blue, pink and natural.

DYNACORD

Super Thread

Very strong German thread that requires a stabbing movement with the scissors to cut under tension. Chris Helm, of Whitetail Fly Tieing Supplies, describes this as 'the finest thread for deer hair work and applications where a strong thread is required.' Does not dull scissors and has no memory. Colours: grey, black, white, red, green, orange, brown.

Midge Thread

A 50 denier midge thread regarded by some as stronger than Kevlar. The white takes waterproof pens well for colour choice.

GEL-SPUN POLYPROPYLENE THREAD (GSP)

Has a breaking strength of 7.5 lbs and is almost impossible to break. It is about 6/0 in diameter but has the characteristics of 8/0, so few wraps are needed to secure materials. Colours: white, black, dark olive, light brown, dark brown, yellow, cream, orange, red, light olive, silver grey.

GORDON GRIFFITHS

Sheer Ultrafine

At 14/0 this is an extremely fine single ply, slightly waxed, thread which has great strength. Ideal for midges and Clyde-style flies. Colours: black, white, primrose, brown, orange, red, claret, grey, dun, cinnamon, green.

Wisp Microfine

At 8/0 very fine and strong for tying the smallest of flies. Available waxed or unwaxed. Colours: black, white, red, claret, brown, grey, yellow, olive, dun, cinnamon.

Cobweb Superfine

Fine and strong at 6/0, either waxed or unwaxed. Colours: black, white, brown, beige, cream, yellow, orange, red, claret, grey, olive, green, purple.

Cobweb 2

Thicker than Cobweb Superfine for lures and large nymphs, available in: black, white, fl. green, fl. yellow, fl. orange, fl. red, fl. pink.

GUDEBROD

BCS Thread

Colour matched to the Borger Colour System in 3/0, 6/0, 8/0 and 10/0. The spools for this thread need the Gudebrod flytying bobbin or the Griffin multi-thread adjustable bobbin, but this is now also available in standard spools of 100 yards.

3/0 colours: bright green (BCS 19), olive green (BCS 30), white (BCS 107), fl. orange (BCS F77), orange (BCS 77), light pink (BCS 79), fl. red (BCS F85), red (BCS 85), fl. chartreuse (BCS F21), dark yellow (BCS 45), dark rusty brown (BCS 65), medium brown (BCS 103), dark blue grey (BCS 113) black (BCS 118).

6/0 colours: light olive green BCS 20), dark olive green (BCS 33), blue (BCS 136), white (BCS 107), orange (BCS 77), dark yellow (BCS 45), light yellow (BCS 39), tan (BCS 94) light rusty brown (BCS 63), dark rusty brown (BCS 65), brown (BCS 98), light grey (BCS 105), dark grey (BCS 119), black (BCS 118), fl. scarlet (BCS F81), red (BCS 85).

8/0 colours: light olive green (BCS 20), dark olive green (BCS 33), white (BCS 107), dark yellow (BCS 45), light yellow (BCS 39), tan (BCS 94), light rusty brown (BCS 63), dark rusty brown (BCS 65), brown (BCS 98), light grey (BCS 105), dark grey (BCS 119), black (BCS 118).

10/0 colours: white (BCS 107), green (BCS 21), rusty brown (BCS 66), light olive green (BCS 20), grey (BCS 108), yellow (BCS 42), black (BCS 118).

6/0 Waxed Thread

Colours: black, light olive, dark olive, light yellow, dark yellow, light rusty brown, dark rusty brown, light grey, dark grey, hot orange, red, tan.

Kevlar Thread

Colours: yellow, orange, red, light green, olive, brown, black.

G Thread

Colours: black, white, red, light olive, dark green, dark yellow, light brown, pink, bright green, rusty brown, grey, fl. chartreuse, fl. red, fl. orange.

INTER-TAC

Mono Thread

From the Larva Lace stable of Phil Camera, a special translucent nylon thread with good strength and invisible qualities. About 8/0 and available in thin and ultrathin. Shades: light, dark smoke.

LUREFLASH

Supergrip

A general purpose tying thread in which the thread fibres are constructed to maintain a circular cross section. Pre-waxed in: black, insect green, insect brown, white, grey, red, claret, olive, grey dun, cream, yellow, light blue, dark blue.

Micro-Grip

A very fine thread for tiny dry flies and small midges. Pre-waxed in: black, grey, bottle green, brown, blue dun, claret, olive.

Multi-strand

A general purpose thread with no twist that will lay flat on a hook shank. Pre-waxed in: black, red, bottle green, brown, blue dun, claret, orange, primrose, olive, white.

Lure-Grip

Half as thick again as Multi-Strand, for lures and muddlers. Black only.

Kevlar Thread

Will not accept dye, but can be coloured with permanent marker pen. Colour: natural cream.

ROMAN MOSER

Power Silk

From Roman Moser, a Kevlar-type thread which can be used from midge to streamer and saltwater flies. Its breaking strength is 4lbs and needs cutting under tension. Best used with a ceramic bobbin holder. Colour can be changed by using Color-It, but it is available in 6 colours: yellow, red, brown, grey, olive, black.

ORVIS

Ultrafine

12/0 multi-stranded thread, unwaxed, in: black, orange, red, chocolate, tobacco dark brown, green, dark dun, light dun, white, yellow, dark blue.

8/0 Microfil

Pre-waxed polyester with diameter of 8/0 but strength rated at 6/0. Does not stretch as much as nylon and has a slightly rougher finish. Colours: black, white, brown, camel, tan, olive, dun, red, orange, primrose, dark grey, grey, fine orange, yellow, rusty brown.

Prewaxed 6/0

Winds flat to reduce bulk. Colours: white, yellow, tan, fire orange, black, light orange, cream, red, grey, claret, pale yellow, light tan, brown, olive, hot pink, chartreuse.

Prewaxed 3/0

Monocord

Colours: black, red, grey, yellow, green, brown, white, orange, blue, tan, olive.

Pre-waxed Kevlar

Colours: yellow, black, red, orange, olive, brown.

'A' Pre-waxed thread

Stronger than Monocord and with greater bulk. Colours: red, white, black, yellow.

PAC

8/0 Uni-Thread

Very strong for its size and can be used on small flies. Pre-waxed in: black, red, dark brown, rusty dun, olive, iron grey, camel, orange, grey, tan, fl. orange, fire orange, yellow, rusty brown, light Cahill, purple, olive dun.

6/0 Uni-Thread

Continuous polyester monofilament with semi-bonding, rather than twisting of the filaments. Colours: white, black, red, olive, yellow, grey, orange, wine, camel, tan, green, pink, light blue, royal blue, doctor blue, iron grey, rusty dun, dark brown, light Cahill, fire orange, rusty brown, purple, olive dun.

3/0 Uni-Thread

Colours: white, black, red, brown, olive, orange, light Cahill, yellow, green, light blue, fl. chartreuse, grey, iron grey, wine, dark brown, tan.

PEARSALL'S PURE SILKS

Gossamer

The original extra fine tying thread, specified for many traditional patterns. Gossamer has very little stretch and has largely been superceded by thinner, stronger, synthetic threads, except where authenticity is deemed important. Sold on 45m spools.

Colours: black, white, highland green, olive green, hot orange, lemon yellow, scarlet, brown, gold, claret, primrose yellow, purple.

Naples

Thicker than Gossamer and used for tying larger sized flies, especially salmon patterns. Naples has almost entirely been superceded by stronger, thinner synthetic threads. It is mostly used these days by traditionalists seeking 'authentic' reproduction of old patterns. Available now only in black and scarlet.

SPARTON

These threads are normally supplied pre-waxed, but can be obtained unwaxed as well.

Sparton Professional

Fairly thin but very strong and copes with Muddler heads well. Colours: black, white Greenwell yellow, orange, red, medium olive, pale green, buff, brown, bottle green, blue dun, iron blue, sky blue, olive dun, purple.

Sparton Micro

Very thin for making really small heads on flies. Intended for small-winged flies and micro ties. Colours: yellow, black, white, brown, olive, bottle green, red, buff, blue dun, iron blue.

Sparton Macro

Very, very strong. Colours: black, white, olive, brown, red, purple, yellow, orange.

THOMPSON

Monobond Kits

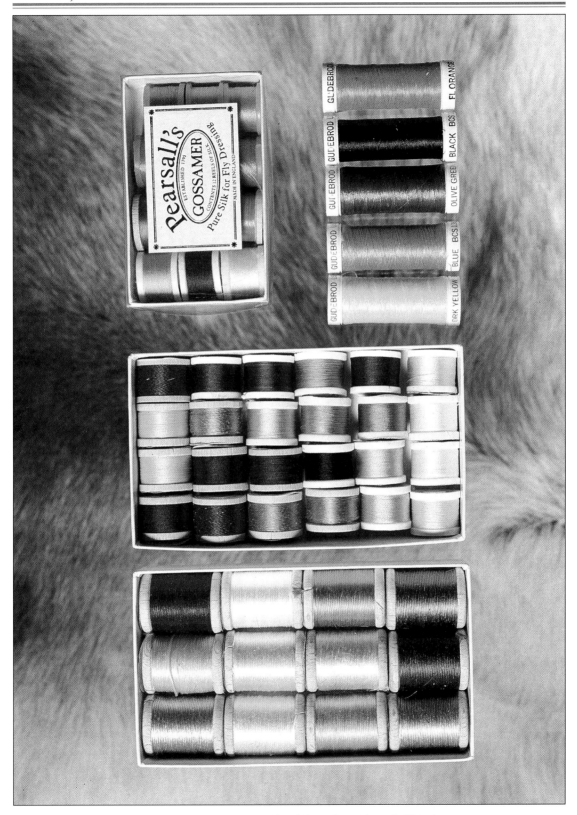

Pearsall's silks and Gudebrod threads (on long bobbins).

A dozen sewing bobbin spools with an assortment of colours in each kit.

6/0 Monobond
3/0 Monobond
Monobond Super Strength

UNI-PRODUCTS

This has become a popular thread with flytyers all over the world. The super fine, yet strong thread. It is constructed of semi-bonded filaments. These are not twisted and so lie flat on the hook shank, giving less build up, hence smaller more compact heads and bodies. Spools are labelled with all the information required by the flytyer (i.e. product name, colour, size, quantity, waxed or un-waxed). The Uni-Products range has grown significantly over recent years.

2/0 Poly II
A two-ply polyester thread, twisted and un-waxed. This is a heavy gauge, traditional tying thread for large bass and saltwater patterns. Available in 50 and 100-yard spools.
Colours: black, eggshell, green, grey, dark brown, olive, orange, royal blue, red, tan, wine, yellow.

3/0 Kevlar
This is an extremely strong thread, useful for tying large saltwater patterns. Sold in 50-yard spools: 'waxed' or 'un-waxed'.
Colour: natural (pale yellow).

3/0 Mono-thread
A multi-filament nylon thread, used for tying large flies, where strength and rapid build-up are needed. Also useful for spinning deer hair, where a thicker thread has less tendency to cut through the hair being spun. Sold in 50-yard and 100-yard spools, in both waxed and un-waxed forms.
Colours: black, brown, fluorescent chartreuse, green, grey, iron blue, dark, brown, light blue, light Cahill, olive, orange, pink, red, tan, white, wine, yellow.

Uni-cord
A very strong thread for large deer hair flies and bass bugs, etc. Sold on 50-yard spools.
Colours: black, brown, green, orange, pink, white.

6/0 Uni-thread
Uni-thread is made from continuous polyester filaments, slightly bonded. This thread ties flat on the hook and is used as a general tying thread. Sold in 50-yard and 200-yard spools, waxed or un-waxed.
Colours: black, camel, blue, green, grey, iron grey, dark brown, light blue, light Cahill, olive dun, olive, orange, pink, purple, royal blue, rusty dun, red, fire orange, rusty brown, tan, white, wine, yellow.

8/0 Uni-thread
Continuous polyester filaments, slightly bonded, ties flat on the hook and very strong for its diameter. Ideal for small dry flies. Sold as 50 and 200-yard spools, waxed and un-waxed.
Colours: black, camel, fl. orange, grey, iron grey, dark

brown, light blue, light Cahill, olive dun, olive, orange, pink, purple, royal blue, rusty dun, red, fire orange, rusty brown, tan, white, wine, yellow.

Size 'A' Mono-thread
This is similar to the 3/0 Mono-thread, but a heavier gauge and much stronger. Useful for larger flies and particularly for spinning deer hair, where firm pressures are needed to compress and flare the hair, while the thicker gauge reduces the tendency for the thread to cut into the hair bundle. Sold on 50-yard and 100-yard spools, waxed and un-waxed.
Colours: black, brown, chartreuse, green, grey, dark brown, light blue, orange, pink, primrose, red, white, wine, yellow.

FLOSSES
(including synthetic)

ANGLER'S CHOICE

Superfloss
Made from Lycra so has immense stretch properties.
Colours: red, bright pink, fuchsia, orange, bright orange, shrimp, yellow, chartreuse, purple, pale olive, black, brown, light brown, olive, light olive, lime green, bright green, burgundy, grey, white, blue, turquoise.

BENECCHI

Poly Floss (small)
Colours: white, bone white, black, dark dun, dun, medium dun, light dun, sandy dun, beige, dark chocolate, cocoa brown, medium brown, tan, light grey olive, pinkish tan, sand, tannish yellow, cream, bordeaux, red, fire red, dark orange, orange, yellow, sulphur, orange tan, coffee, forest green, moss green, sage, emerald, pink, light pink, fuchsia, purple, blue night, electric blue, greenish opal, opal, light purple, light blue.

Poly Floss (medium) Colours: black, light dun, blue night, electric blue, fire red, yellow, greenish opal, opal, fuchsia, light purple, light blue, emerald.

DANVILLE

Four strand rayon floss
Good for tapered, flat or rounded bodies. It is made flat so unravelling is not necessary, but single strands can be used. Colours: white, black, yellow, orange, burnt orange, grey, tobacco, scarlet, worm green, chartreuse, olive, peacock, kelly green, insect green, copenhagen blue, cream, pale yellow, yellow, charcoal, silver grey, beige, ginger, gold, coffee, dark brown, wine, dark red, apple green, moss green. forest green, purple, pink, coral, rust, powder blue, soldier blue, turquoise, peach, hot pink, fuchsia, navy, lilac, royal blue, seal brown, hunter green, lavender.

Acetate Floss

Acetone put on this hardens the body. Colours: white, black, yellow, orange, burnt orange, grey, tobacco, scarlet, worm green, chartreuse, olive, peacock, kelly green, insect green, Copenhagen blue, cream, pale yellow, yellow, charcoal, silver grey, beige, ginger, gold, coffee, dark brown, wine, dark red, apple green, forest green.

GORDON GRIFFITHS FLOSS

Shiny rayon floss in: black, white, claret, red, magenta, hot orange, primrose, olive, blue, brown, green.

KREINIK 100% silk floss.

JAPANESE SILK FLOSS

100% pure silk, single stranded, with outstanding sheen. Colours: pink, green, light blue, blue, dark blue, lemon, yellow, gold, light orange, orange, dark orange, purple, black, red, scarlet, crimson, dark crimson, cinnamon, green olive, golden olive, lilac, claret, fl.green.

LAGARTUN

French Silk Floss Single line strand floss. Colours: natural white, fl. white, black, cornflower blue, azure, pale blue, blue rat blue, green highlander, olive, lemon yellow, rusty rat yellow, burnt orange, red, burgundy, lilac, paler green.

LUREFLASH

Rayon Floss Colours: black, white, grey dun, brown, yellow, golden yellow, pink, red, orange, olive, cream, dark green, lime, claret, purple, dark brown, blue, kingfisher blue.

Acetate Floss Similar to Rayon Floss but when wound on a body and acetate solvent is applied it will mould to any shape. Colours: black, white, brown, red, yellow, claret.

Midge Floss Fine untwisted floss for tiny insect bodies.

ORVIS

Flexifloss

Another Lycra material in: white, lemon, yellow, fl. chartreuse, lime green, dark green, blue, black, brown, gold, orange, red, fl. pink.

PAC

Uni-Floss Single strand nylon floss. Colours: white, bright yellow, rusty orange, orange, Italian blue, doctor blue, purple, dark blue, black, tan, beige, golden brown, brown, dark brown, red, wine, grey pink, charcoal, emerald green, olive, dark green, burnt orange, rust, cream, royal blue, light green, dark rust, green highlander.

PEARSALLS

Stout / Tag Floss Body Silk

Described in Pearsall's 1884 price list as 'The old large make, suitable for ancient needlework, eastern embroidery and ecclesiastical vestments'. Used as body floss for traditional salmon flies. Colours: black, white, highland green, olive green, hot orange, lemon yellow, scarlet, brown, gold, claret, primrose yellow, purple, royal blue, Cambridge blue, silver, yellow.

Marabou

Traditional floss silk for trout flies, comprising two twisted strands that can be split for tying smaller flies. Colours: black, white, highland green, olive green, hot orange, lemon yellow, scarlet, brown.

SUSSEX

Silk Floss

Classic silk floss

THOMPSON KITS

An assortment of different coloured flosses on sewing bobbins in a plastic container.

Monobond Floss

Thompson Poly Floss

Polycryolin Kit

UNI-PRODUCTS

Uni-Floss

Made from nylon and rayon, this is a strong and shiny one-strand floss. Sold on 15-yard and 80-yard spools. Colours: dark blue, beige, black, bright orange, brown, bright yellow, charcoal, cream, doc blue, emerald green, golden brown, green highlander, grey, dark brown, dark green, combo, dark rust, light blue, light green, olive, orange, pink, purple, royal blue, red, rust orange, rust, tan, white, wine.

Nylon Stretch

Used mainly for the tags and butts of streamers and Atlantic salmon flies. Sold on 30-yard spools. Colours: black, chartreuse, chinese red, fuchsia, green, hot-pink, combo, orange, white, yellow.

LUREXES

DANVILLE

Flat Mylar Tinsel

In silver one side, gold the other. Sizes 10-18.

Oval Mylar Tinsel

Gold or silver in sizes 10, 14, 16, 18.

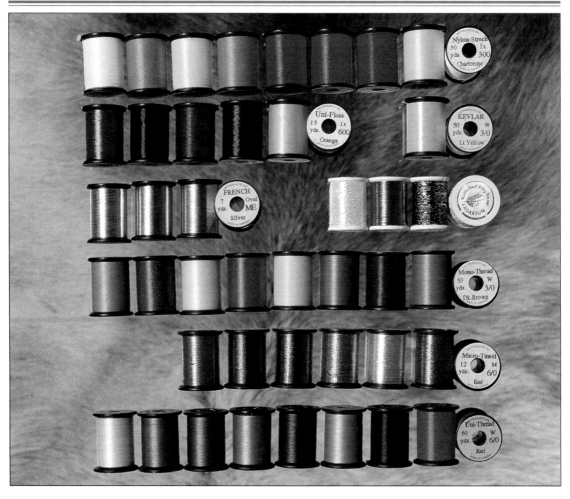

ABOVE A colourful selection of threads, flosses and metallics.

GORDON GRIFFITHS

Lurex Tinsel Silver or deep gold. Also comes gold one side and silver the other as **Double Lurex Tinsel**.

LUREFLASH

Fine in: silver, green, purple, gold, red, black, blue, magenta, bronze, gun metal, copper.
Medium in: silver, gold, copper.
Wide in: silver, gold, copper.

SPARTON

Superfine Nymph In gold or silver.
Medium For wet flies in: gold, silver copper, red, blue, fushsis, lilac, black, green, bronze gun metal.
Wide For lures in: gold, silver, copper and dual sided gold/silver. Also in pearl.
Super Hard Dual/Usage For salmon flies.

UNI-PRODUCTS

Tinsel Mylar

A flat gold on one side and silver on the other Mylar tinsel, 0.002" thick, in sizes: 10, 12, 14, 16.

PEARLS & OPTICS

BENECCHI

Iridescent Thread
The base colour is highlighted with iridescent 'spots' which add subtle light-attracting properties. For, bodies, ribbing and thoraxes. Colours: olive, light olive, rainbow, white, blue, fuchsia, light pink, orange, peach, yellow, hot orange, red, dark fuchsia, pink, purple, dark red, light lilac, lilac, violet, dark violet, dark blue, indigo, turquoise, sapphire.
Poly Floss Fluo Extra Small
Colours: white, chartreuse, green, orange, hot pink, fuchsia.
Poly Floss Fluo Small
Colours: same as for Extra Small (above).

Fluorescent Thread

A fine but strong thread for ribbing, tags, heads or even complete bodies. Colours: lime green, orange, red, green, fuchsia, yellow, pink, light red, hot orange, salmon orange, orangish yellow.

DANVILLE

Depth Ray Floss

Fluorescent material available in: red, yellow, orange, green, fire orange, white, blue, pink, natural.

DATAM PRODUCTS

Glo-Brite Fluorescent Floss

Colours: Neon magenta, Glo-Brite pink, Glo-Brite crimson, Glo-Brite scarlet, fire orange, Glo-Brite hot orange, Glo-Brite orange, Glo-Brite amber, Glo-Brite chrome yellow, Glo-Brite yellow, phosphor yellow, Glo-Brite lime green, Glo-Brite green, Glo-Brite blue, Glo-Brite purple, Glo-Brite white.

GORDON GRIFFITHS

Supearl

Very fine pearlescent flat thread for use as ribbing or, taking a bunch of filaments, tails or breathers.

Superglo Fluorescent Floss

Intensely fluorescent floss that should be used sparingly for thoraxes, butts or tags. Colours: signal green, fire orange, neon magenta, phosphor yellow, Arc chrome.

HOLOGRAPHIC TINSEL

Utilises light refracting qualities that add shimmering effects. Available as a spooled thread in gold and silver at two widths $1/32"$ and $1/69"$ often described as medium and small.

LUREFLASH

Chameleon Tying Thread Changes colour when exposed to ultra-violet light.
Luminous Tying Thread Thread which glows in the dark.
Fluorescent Tying Thread Strong synthetic waxed thread with enough stretch to grip materials. Colours: white, lime, orange, red, yellow.
Prismatic Tinsel Metallic tinsel with an almost holographic effect.
Glow Floss Very bright fluorescent floss for bodies, tags and tails. Colours: red, yellow, lime, pink, orange, white, green highlander.
Pearl Tinsel Pearlised plastic tinsel in a mother of pearl oyster colour in fine, medium and wide widths.
Fine Round Pearl Tinsel For ribbing.
Deep Ray Wool Colours: white, lime, orange, red, yellow.

PAC

Neon 1/0 Spooled fluorescent 1/0 thread in neon shades of: yellow, orange, chartreuse, green, red, burnt orange.

SPARTON

Sparton Fluo Thicker than many fluorescent threads. Colours: red, yellow, white, orange, green, magenta.

TIEWELL

Sparkle Flash Pearl Thread

Made of Tiewell Sparkle Flash this is more than just a tying thread as it adds a shiny translucency to the pattern. Colours: pearl, gold pearl, light olive pearl, dark olive pearl, lime green pearl, caddis green pearl, peacock pearl, tan pearl, charcoal pearl, pale yellow pearl, dark chocolate pearl, brassie, bonefish copper, burnt orange pearl, pink pearl, red pearl, orange pearl, purple pearl, blue pearl.

UNI-PRODUCTS

1/0 Neo Fluorescent

A very bright neon thread in 2-ply, twisted. This makes beautifully coloured heads. 50-yard spools.
Colours: bright orange, chartreuse, green, combo, orange, red, yellow.

Uni-Yarn Fluorescent

A small diameter yarn in brilliant fluorescent colours.
Colours: chartreuse, chinese red, green highlander, combo, light pink, orange, yellow.

Uni-Glo

A flat, luminous material, that glows in the dark.
Sold on 14-yard spools.
Colours: pearl, green, combo, orange, pink, yellow.

METALLICS

BENECCHI

Metallized Thread

Can be used straight from the bobbin holder. A nylon core totally covered by thin metallic plate. Colours: silver, gold, copper.

DANVILLE

Flat Tinsel
Flat Embossed Tinsel
Oval Tinsel
Twist

GORDON GRIFFITHS

Glitterbody Braided thread with attractive flash in 13 colours: white pearl, black pearl, silver pearl, green pearl, silver, gold, copper, red, green, olive, teal blue, kingfisher blue, purple.

Nymph Wire A fine wire in red, olive green and pink.

Metallised Thread Comes three-stranded in silver and gold and single stranded in: silver, gold, yellow gold, red, green, blue, copper.

Embossed Metallic In silver or gold, medium or broad.

Metallic Tinsel Very bright and soft and does not cut thread when tying down. Fine, medium or broad in: copper, silver, gold.

Oval Thread Used as an over-ribbing. Fine, medium or broad, in silver or gold.

KREINIK

Manufacture braids for flytyers under the name Hi-Luster. The company's products come on a long thin spool and a multi-thread bobbin is needed to use them.

High Lustre Braids in fine, medium and heavy.

Metallic Wrapping Thread

Metallic Flash

Tyers Ribbon

LAGARTUN

Oval X-Strong Core Synthetic core for strength. Available in fine, small, medium and large in either silver or gold - and in ruby, chartreuse or mauve in medium only.

Oval Silk Core Very fine diameter for size 12 and under flies, in silver and gold.

Round Tinsel For tags on flies, fine or medium in gold or silver.

Flat Tinsel Very manageable with enough springiness to prevent crumpling - small or medium in silver or gold.

Poly Oval Tinsel X-Strong The winding on the synthetic core is itself synthetic but contains precious metals (eg. silver) and is varnished to maintain brightness.

Small: copper, coral/rose, gold, silver, peacock pearl.

Medium: gold, silver, pearl, copper.

Large: gold, silver, pearl, salmon pearl.

Poly Oval Tinsel Similar to X-Strong but without the strong synthetic core. Colours: platinum, black, gold, silver, copper, pearl.

Flat Lying Tinsel gold or silver, in medium, large or XS large.

Flat Embossed silver or gold.

Poly Torsade Highly regarded as a body material in rainbow or green.

Plisse Embossed with striations to look like an oval tinsel. Gives the effect of an oval tinsel without the bulk. Only in medium in gold, copper, silver.

LUREFLASH

Dual Tinsel

Dark gold one side, silver the other in fine, medium and wide widths.

Embossed Metallic Tinsel gold or silver in fine, medium or wide.

Oval Tinsel gold or silver in fine, medium or wide.

Oval Flat Worm Tinsel Gilt Colour or Silver Plate - fine, medium or wide.

Round Tinsel
Fine: gold, pink, red, silver, rainbow, green, blue, copper
Medium: gold, silver

Copper Wire Fine, medium, wide.

Coloured Copper Wire Fine or medium in red or green.

Gold Coloured Wire (brass) Fine, medium or wide.

Silver Wire Fine, medium or wide.

SPARTON

Oval Gold, Silver (medium, fine), Copper (medium).

Copper Wire Fine, thick

Silver & Gold Wire Medium at 006 in.

THOMPSON

Tinsel Kit on sewing bobbins.

UNI-PRODUCTS

Axel Flash

A woven flashing material on spools and hanks. Great for streamer bodies and ribbing.

Colours: black, copper, fuchsia, green, gold, combo, pearl, purple, rainbow, royal blue, red, silver black, silver.

Micro-Tinsel

The size of 6/0 thread, this round tinsel can be used for neatly wrapped tags on smaller salmon flies or for ribbing small dry or wet fly patterns. Sold on 12-yard spools.

Colours: bronze, blue, copper, green, gold.

Also available in 3/0 gauge. Colours: grey, combo, multi-colour, old gold, pink, purple, red, silver.

French Flat Embossed

An extremely high quality varnished metallic tinsel, that won't tarnish. Available in wire and oval tinsel, in: X-Small, Small, Medium and Large.

Flat embossed tinsel: size 12 gold, silver.

Flat embossed tinsel: size 17 gold, silver, copper.

VENIARD

Made in Europe, these high quality traditional metallic tinsels are available in gold and silver.

Flat: in sizes Nos 1 to 7.

Embossed Flat: in sizes Nos 3 & 5 only.

Solid Wire: in sizes Nos 25, 26 & 27.

Oval: sizes Nos 14 to 19.

Round Thread: sizes Nos 20 & 21 only.

Lace Twist: sizes Nos 20 & 21 only.

FLATS
1. 0.012" (0.30mm)
2. 0.015" (0.40mm)
3. 0.023" (0.60mm)
4. 0.030" (0.80mm)
5. 0.040" (1.00mm)
6. 0.043" (1.10mm)
7. 0.048" (1.20mm)

OVALS
14. 0.020" (0.50mm)
15. 0.022" (0.55mm)
16. 0.030" (0.80mm)
17. 0.035" (0.90mm)
18. 0.040" (1.00mm)
19. 0.058" (1.50mm)

ROUND THREADS
20. 0.007" (0.20mm)
21. 0.010" (0.25mm)

LACE TWIST
22. 0.016" (0.40mm)
23. 0.020" (0.50mm)
24. 0.022" (0.55mm)
25. 0.007" (0.185mm)
26. 0.006" (0.155mm)
27. 0.005" (0.125mm)

Fine Lead Wire 0.37mm
Medium Lead Wire 0.60mm
Fine Copper Wire 0.125mm
Very Heavy Copper Wire (plain) 0.40mm
Very Heavy Copper Wire (tinned) 0.40mm

WAPSI

French tinsel
Flat, oval or embossed in silver or gold. In sizes: small, medium, large.

DUBBING WAXES

The days of blocks of Beeswax or Cobbler's Wax on the tying table are passing. The modern tyer has a terrific range of waxes to choose from, most encased in lipstick-style containers. Among the products offered are:

BT's
Fairly new in the market place from Al and Gretchen Beatty of Montana, but has rapidly gained a strong following. It really stays on the thread and not on the hands. Comes as Tacky and Super Tacky.

UK Sportfish, Lathkill, Rooksbury, Niche; *US* BT, MM, RE, Marriott.

JOHN BETTS WAX
Both soft and hard formulas are sold in push-up dispensers. The soft pink wax has the most general applicability for tying a wide range of fly sizes. The red-dotted harder wax works better with heavier fibres, or where sparse amounts are needed.

US Marriott.

COBBLERS WAX
Called for in older fly patterns when tying with silk to obtain the correct colour change, eg. when applied to primrose yellow gossamer tying silk for the body of the Greenwell's Glory. If not stored in an airtight container, or kept in conditions that are too warm, cobbler's wax has a tendency to dry out and become brittle.

UK Anglian, McHardy, Lathkill, Rooksbury, Niche.

DILLY WAX
A clear liquid wax that can be used for flydressing as a dubbing wax, but is also recommended as a leader and fly line dressing and as a fly floatant. Dilly wax is sold in small plastic, squeeze tubes, with screw tops.

UK Niche, Rooksbury, Angling Pursuits; *US* Flyrite.

DOIRON'S PROFESSIONAL FLY TYING DUBBING WAX
This wax is extremely tacky, giving good adhesion to spiky and unmanageable dubbing. Unlike some other sticky waxes, this one does not tend to ball up on the thread and it is very easy to use.

AUS Alpine; *US* Marriott; *INT* Orvis.

GEHRKE FLY MAKER'S WAX
UK Walker, Sportfish, Sparton; *US* Marriott, Bailey, BR, Hook & Hackle

LLP FINGER WAX
US Marriott.

LOON'S HIGH-TAC AND LOW-TAC WAX
Also appears under the name of 'Swax'.

GER Brinkhoff; *UK* Slater; US Marriott, Bailey, AA, Hunter.

LUREFLASH FLY TYING WAX
A medium-soft wax.

UK Watercraft.

LUREFLASH LIQUID WAX
Supplied in a bottle.

UK Watercraft.

ORVIS QUICK DUB DUBBING WAX
A softish wax with good tackiness that does not ball up or flake.

INT Orvis.

RAINY'S DUBBING MOISTENER
Finger bowls that save finger licking. Filing clerks are familiar with the principle involved.

US Marriott, Rainy, Blue Ribbon.

SCIENTIFIC ANGLERS DUBBING STICK
AUS Alpine; *UK* Sportfish, Saville; *US* Blue Ribbon.

SPARTON SUPER STICKY WAX
UK Sparton.

SUPERIOR WAX
A half ounce tube of wax very similar to the old Wonder Wax, having high tackiness, low build and neutral buoyancy.

US Hunter, Marriott.

THERMOWAX
JAP Sawada.

VENIARD'S FLY TYERS WAX
The traditional piece of wax.

JAP Sawada; *UK* Walker, Niche, Slater, Sparton, McHardy, Saville, Norris.

VENIARD'S LIQUID WAX
Contained in a bottle.

JAP Sawada; *UK* McHardy, Walker, Lathkill, Niche, Sparton, Saville, Norris; *US* Hunter.

WAPSI
Listed as Regular, Super Sticky, Premium and Professional but especially as **Premium Dubbing Wax** ('Super Sticky' formula)

UK Sportfish, Lathkill; *US* Marriott, Hook & Hackle, Kaufmann.

WILSON'S WAX
From Creek Company

US Marriott.

Cements, Epoxies & Varnishes

CEMENTS AND VARNISHES used in flytying have come along way in recent years. In some parts of the world purists take the view that glue should never be used in fly dressing and would refer dismissively to such work as 'Insect Modelling', while in other areas the liberal application of glues and varnishes as undercoating procedures are the norm to more securely fix materials. Set out in this section are a selection of cements and varnishes available today.

Apart from those offered through flytying retailers, many flytyers today look along the nail varnish shelves in stores and opt for top coat products such as Revlon's Top Speed or Sally Hansen's Hard as Nails.

ANGLER'S CORNER HEAD CEMENT

Faster than most other brands so it needs thinning more often. However, it is highly regarded in the US and produces a high gloss with just a couple of coats. It comes as a wet or dry head cement and in a range of coloured cements: black, yellow, red, white, blue, fl. orange, fl. hot pink, fl. chartreuse, fl. neon red, fl. fire orange, pearl.

US Hunter, Marriott.

ARON ALPHA GLUE

A superglue that the Edgewater Company found in extensive tests forms the strongest bond with stainless steel. Very useful for saltwater popper construction.

US Hunter, Marriott.

CELLIRE

The original Veniard celluloid varnish. Unitit is the thinner provided for this product. Colours: clear, white, red, black, yellow.

UK Anglian, Saville, Niche, Rooksbury, Lathkill,Walker; *AUS* Alpine; *US* Hunter

CRYSTAL CLEAR EPOXY

This is very clear epoxy that gives an almost glass bead finish to fly heads, both for durability and 'display' fly purposes. It gives a really professional finishing touch to exhibition grade tying and is particularly effective on salmon and steelhead patterns and saltwater lures.

US Kaufmann.

DAVE'S FLEXAMENT

Clear, flexible tying cement, that has many applications beyond that of ordinary cellulose varnish. It can be used for consolidating underbodies and for coating delicate body materials (eg. quill) to improve durability. While remaining flexible after it has dried, Flexament can be used for reinforcing and stiffening feathers, for wings and wing cases and for 'repairing' split jungle cock nail feathers. It can also be used for coating whip finishes, but gives a rather matt finish. Kept well thinned, Flexament has good penetration of thread wraps and fibres. It is sold in one ounce square bottles, with a special sealed screw top. A thinner is available, similarly packaged.

US Marriott, Hook & Hackle, AA, Cabela, River Edge, Blue Ribbon, MM, Hunter; *INT* Orvis.

DELTA BOND

Instant super glue adhesive. A fast acting glue from Loctite and designed for anglers. Ideal for bonding flylines, it can be used for flytying.

UK Niche.

DEVCON 2 TON EPOXY

Used for saltwater and epoxy head patterns. This is a slower drying (approximately 20 minutes at room temperature), but stronger epoxy than Devcon's '5-Minute' Epoxy, which is too fast for many applications. If one ties a lot of epoxy head flies, a rotary drying device is a worthwhile accessory. These can be had purpose made, or made from modified spit turning drives, from barbecue suppliers.

UK Sportfish.

DEVCON 5 MINUTE EPOXY

Quick setting, two part epoxy resin. Used for various epoxy patterns, such as shrimps Mother of Epoxy flies, etc.
Widely available in model shops.

UK Anglian, Lathkill, Sportfish; *US* E.A.T.; Hunter; *AUS* Alpine.

DURO QUICK GEL NO RUN SUPER GLUE

An essential material for use in making flies with Rainy's Float Foam, apart from its more general uses. Comes in a tube.

US Whitetail.

ENRICO'S SUPER SET EPOXY : ONE-MINUTE EPOXY

A clear drying one minute curing time epoxy. Because of its speed, good for underlay before putting on an overcoat of another epoxy,for final touch-up work, or filling small gaps.

US Enrico.

EPOXY PAINT

Produces a nearly indestructible finish to flies. White is used as a primer for the fluorescent colours,and a clear overcoat is put over the lot as an outer skin. Can be used for creating eyes as well. Colours: red, yellow, black, white, clear.

US Marriott, Kaufmann.

FEATHER GLUE

Davy Wotton's product which is clear,flexible,and dries in seconds.

US Fly & Field.

FEATHER WELD

Lureflash's new product competes with Floo Gloo. Claims to reduce brittleness. A thinner is provided.

UK Watercraft.

FLASHABOU FLAKES LACQUER

A hard, fast-drying cement mixed with flakes of Flashabou. Comes with a brush applicator and is used on popper bodies and streamer heads to give a scaley appearance. Gold and silver.

US Marriott.

FLEX-LOC HEAD CEMENT

From the Larva Lace stable of Inter-Tac and specially formulated for use with synthetic materials. Dries quickly,has good flexibility,and can be applied safely to monofilament and fishing knots, as well as synthetics. It can be thinned with methyl ethyl keytone.

AUS Alpine; *US* Whitetail, Cabela.

FLOO GLOO

A clear flexible lacquer, that can be applied to feathers to bond the individual fibres together. Applied to feather 'slip' wings, Floo Goo prevents them from splitting and maintains their shape, even after catching several fish. Floo Glue is unaffected by water and solvent type floatants. Sold in 15ml applicator bottles. A thinner is also available.

UK Anglian, Saville, Niche, Rooksbury, Lathkill, Sportfish.

FLY-RITE NON-TOXIC HEAD CEMENT

Dries clear and flexible, never thickens, and does not need to be thinned. It has an ethyl alcohol base.

US Fly-Rite, Whitetail.

FRITZ VON SCHLEGELL HEAD CEMENT

Comes with a built-in applicator brush in a spill-proof bottle. One of the earliest of the american cement products to be seen in Britain.

US Marriott, E.A.T.; *UK* Sparton.

GRIFFIN HEAD CEMENT

Griff's Multi-coat
A thicker cement designed for heavy build-up and glossy heads. Good where multiple coats are required on saltwater flies.

Griff's Thin - specially formulated for deep penetration and fast drying. One on the quickest penetrating cements.

Griff's Thinners - allow customizing of cement thickness to personal taste.
US Marriott, Hunter.

GUDEBROD HEAD CEMENT

US Marriott, Cabela; *UK* Rooksbury

HARD AS NAILS

A clear nail varnish top coat reinforced with nylon.

UK Sportfish.

HOUSE OF HARROP FLY TYING CEMENT

A high performance cement bearing the name of innovative tyer Rene Harrop. Fairly new, but gaining a good reputation quickly.

US Marriott.

HUMBROL SUPERFAST CLEAR EPOXY RESIN

Good for clear lure heads,sandeel lures and fry encapsulation of eyes.

UK Niche

LOON HARD BODY EPOXY KIT

A non-toxic alternative to lead weighting on flies. Two equal parts of epoxy putties are combined and moulded onto the hook. It sets in half an hour and is 75% the density of lead.

US Marriott, Cabela; *GER* Brinkhoff.

LOON HARD HEAD FLY FINISH

Water based coloured head lacquer for hard glossy heads and bodies. Colours: yellow, red, orange, blue, black

US Cabela, AA, Bailey; *GER* Brinkhoff.

LOON HEAD CEMENT SYSTEM

A needle tip applicator allows great accuracy when using this flexible polyurethane cement. Solvents are fast drying and low in toxicity. Comes with 18 gauge and smaller 20 gauge needles for finer work.

US Marriott, Cabela, MM, Bailey; *GER* Brinkhoff.

LOON HEAD FINISH SYSTEM

Comes with an 18 gauge needle applicator,is non-penetrating and viscous for a high gloss head build-up.

US Marriott, Cabela; *GER* Brinkhoff.

LOON HYDROSTOP NEW FLY TREATMENT

Not a cement or varnish,but used at the end of tying a dry fly. A fly soaked after tying in this silicone mixture becomes permanently treated with a water resistant coating.

US Marriott, Cabela, Bailey.

LOON SOFT BODY EPOXY KIT

A two part epoxy for building larger soft body flies. It comes in two speeds : Fast Cure which gels in 5 minutes and sets in 25; Slow Cure which gels in 25 minutes and sets in an hour and a half. Both remain flexible after curing and will not harden, discolour, or crack in sunlight. Slow Cure is colourless and clear,while Fast Cure is tinted slightly yellow. Good for Bonefish and Permit patterns.

US Marriott, Cabela, Kaufmann; *GER* Brinkhoff.

LOON WATER BASE HEAD CEMENT SYSTEM

Fast drying and quick penetrating,a non-flammable polyurethane emulsion that contains no toluene. It dries completely clear giving a tough and waterproof finish. This is an ideal choice when tying plastic bodied flies that are attacked by solvent based products.

US Marriott, AA, Cabela, Hunter, Bailey; *GER* Brinkhoff.

LOON WATER BASE HEAD FINISH

Has the same general properties of the Head Cement,but contains more solids for faster head or body build-up.

US AA, Cabela; *GER* Brinkhoff.

LUREFLASH VARNISH

Colours: clear, black, red, white.

UK Saville, Watercraft.

ORVIS HIGH GLOSS HEAD CEMENT

This is a medium thick cement that is easy to apply and dries within minutes, giving a very high gloss finish. Sold in 1oz bottles. A thinner for this cement is also available.

INT Orvis.

PERMABOND 102 ADHESIVE

A strong cyanoacrylate glue, that can be used for bonding lead eyes to hooks, tandem hook mount construction and other applications requiring a strong quick-setting adhesive. Sold in packs of two 3gm non-spill, leak-proof plastic bottles. The makers recommend that it is stored in a refrigerator or other cool place. It is important to keep all potentially hazardous chemicals away from children. The potential for 'disaster' were a young child to get hold of a CA instant glue can be imagined!

US Marriott; *INT* Orvis.

QUICK GEL SUPER GLUE

This is an excellent all round fly tying adhesive. It hardens in a matter of seconds and, being a gel, it is rather more manageable than some of the thinner, liquid CA glues. The latter can be troublesome, seeping rapidly into feather fibres, etc. by capillary action, where often this is undesirable. Sold in a small tubes and also

A selection of dubbing waxes, cements, varnishes and glues.

available from Rainy's Flies & Supplies in a 'pen style' applicator which is particularly useful for fly tying purposes.
US Rainy, Marriott.

SILICONE

Used to form bluewater and bonefish pattern bodies.
US Kaufmann.

TUFF-FILM

A Grumbacher product which is an artist fixative used to spray feathers to make them durable.
US Whitetail, Montana Master.

WAPSI CELLULOID LACQUER

High quality lacquer in one ounce bottles. Colours: clear, black, white, yellow, red
US Hunter.

ZAP-A-GAP

A total adhesive system.

PT04 formula is a slightly thicker, gap filling, slower curing adhesive.

PT10 formula is super-thin, quick penetrating and fast drying

Zip Kicker accelerates the drying process

Flex-Zap is a no-kicker formula with flexability.

Zap-a-dap-a-doo is an all purpose adhesive and sealant that remains flexible yet bonds virtually anything.

Z-7 Debonder unglues your fingers !

Z-Poxy is a five minute quick setting epoxy.

Z-Ends are extender tips for Zap products for applications requiring pinpoint accuracy.

US Marriott, E.A.T., Cabela, Hunter, Blue Ribbon, River Edge, MM, Kaufmann; *AUS* Alpine; *UK* Niche, Lathkill; *GER* Brinkhoff; *INT* Orvis.

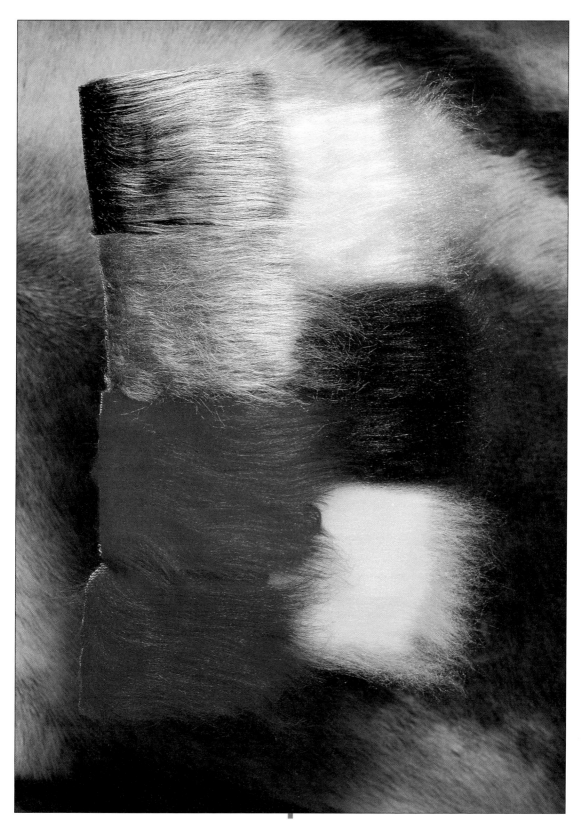

Fly Fur (Blue Ribbon Flies) and Artificial Hair (Lureflash) - manmade materials dyed in strong colours.

Dyes, Paints & Pens

DYES

MODERN FLY DRESSING materials are available in a bewildering range of colours and the flytyer of today seldom needs to dye his own materials. Nonetheless, if special colours or particular subtleties of shade are required, or if a particular material is not commonly available in dyed colours, then the modern flytyer can get great satisfaction from home dyeing.

Most natural materials do not usually need any special preparation prior to dyeing, beyond simple washing. However, some feathers and hair are naturally oily (duck plumage, bucktails, etc.) and have to be de-greased in order for a water soluble dye to penetrate properly.

Over 1994/1995 *American Angler* magazine ran an in-depth series of five articles by Dr. Ted Roubal on the subject of dyeing which are well worth consulting. In 1993 A.K. Best published his comprehensive guide: *Dyeing and bleaching natural fly-tying materials*.

BLUE RIBBON DYES

Colours: black, charcoal brown, coachman brown, yellow, orange, red, purple, dun, blue, bright green, olive, golden yellow, tan.

US Blue Ribbon.

FLYDYE DYES

All Flydye colours are sold with full user instructions. Flydye also provides a customer service, free of charge.

Questions or queries about dyeing with Flydye colours will be answered upon receipt of a stamped, self-addressed envelope.

Colours: yellow, brilliant yellow, green yellow, jungle cock yellow, brilliant orange, jungle cock orange, salmon egg, rose red, cardinal red, pink, hot pink, claret, shrimp pink, highlander green, green ghost, insect green, olive, kelly green, moss green, burnt orange, caribbean blue, turquoise blue, royal blue, purple, wood duck brown, cinnamon brown, dark cinnamon brown, chocolate brown, fiery red brown, bright rust red, grey dun, slate dun, blue dun, brown dun, black.

US Hunter.

SYNTHRAPOL

An industrial strength cleaning and wetting agent for preparing materials to be dyed.

US Hunter.

VENIARD DYES

All dyes are sold with full instructions. Veniard also produces 'Venpol', a specially designed detergent for washing materials prior to dyeing. Veniard's 'Degreaser' is sold for use on materials that have a particularly high natural fat content, such as bucktails and hackle capes.

Colours: green olive, medium brown, brown olive, golden olive, dark olive, olive dun, grey, blue dun, slate, iron blue, ginger, summer duck, fiery brown, cinnamon, dark brown, black, bright yellow, yellow (golden), hot orange, crimson, light claret, dark claret, magenta, purple, kingfisher, light blue (Cambridge), blue (Teal & Blue), dark blue, bright green, dark green, insect green, green highlander.

UK Lathkill, Saville, Niche, Sparton, McHardy, Sportfish; *US* Hunter, Kaufmann.

VENPOL

Special detergent for washing materials before dyeing.

UK Saville, Niche, Lathkill, Sparton McHardy, Sportfish.

PAINTS

ACRYLIC PAINT

Colours: clear glaze, white primer, white, yellow, red, blue, black, frog green, pearl, fl. red, fl. yellow, fl. fire orange, fl. chartreuse, fl. pink, glow-in-the-dark.

US Marriott.

ANGLER'S CORNER LURECOAT

A water-based paint for colouring flies. Colours: white, red, blue, yellow, black, fl. orange, fl. hot pink, fl.chartreuse, fl. neon red, fl. fire orange, clear overcoat.

US Marriott.

EPOXY PAINT (see *Varnish, Cements* section)

PENS

DESIGN II PERMANENT MARKERS

From the Spirit River stable, available in: gold, orange, rust, red, hot pink, lavender, olive drab, royal purple, blue green, green, moss green, olive, walnut brown, black, cool grey, warm grey.

US Marriott.

MOSER COLOR-IT PENS

Fifteen colours in a set - each divided into three colours per pen. Can be used on all synthetic wing materials, rubber and plastic.
Colours: green, insect green, olive, red, fuchsia, orange, dark brown, mid brown, light brown, dark blue, purple, light blue, black, yellow, grey.

GER Brinkhoff; *UK* Lathkill.

PANTONE PENS

Colours as carried by Kaufmann: black, brown olive, olive, reddish orange, orange, medium green, insect green, golden ginger, reddish brown, mahogany brown, tobacco brown, dark grey, medium grey, yellow, amber yellow, creamy pink, medium blue. Saville's carry almost twice as money colours.

UK Saville; *US* Kaufmann.

PRISMA COLOR PENS

Colours: crimson red, pink, yellow, ochre, chartreuse, olive, ultra marine, sepia, dark brown, light tan, black, cool grey, bronze, pumpkin, orange, French grey, peacock green, dark purple.

UK Lathkill; *US* Cabela.

WATERPROOF MARKING PENS

Complete set of fifteen colours, or individually in: rust, red, blue, moss green, olive, brown.

US Blue Ribbon.

Tools

THERE ARE so many tools and makes thereof in the marketplace that a full survey cannot be contemplated in a volume of this length primarily focused on materials. Many tools come from the Indian sub-continent and are considerably cheaper than top-of-the-range items. However, in general you get what you pay for in terms of quality and durability. Generally regarded as being the best in the field are those provided by Matarelli, Renzetti, Tiemco, Griffin, Thompson, Edgin and Dr Slick. Orvis have quality tools that they sell under their own company name.

That said, other manufacturers may produce one or two products that are simply the best around. Lawrence Waldon's Ceramiscrape Dubbing Rake is one such example. One person's accessory may be another person's vital tool, so the Accessories section (page 133) lists some other articles available to the tyer.

All the suppliers mentioned in the main sections of the book will carry a range of tools. We have restricted specific mentions in this section to items that are unique or less generally available.

Note: In the USA, what in the UK would be referred to as a Bobbin Holder is frequently called a Bobbin.

ABBY-DYNA-KING TOOLS

Make very fine hairstackers.

AUS Alpine; *UK* Lathkill, Sportfish; *US* Whitetail

A.K. BEST'S SERIES OF FLY TYING TOOLS

GER Brinkhoff; *US* Hunter.

BOBBINS

Small sewing machine bobbins are useful for re-spooling thread for use on Midge Bobbin Holders. They can be easily obtained from sewing shops, but some flytying retailers keep them in stock.

UK Lathkill

BOBBIN HOLDERS

A bobbin holder is a device that holds the spool of tying thread and allows the tier to wind the thread onto the hook accurately and under a slight, even tension.

Bad bobbin holders are troublesome and frustrating. It is worth investing in decent quality bobbin holders, with burr-free 'spigots' (thread tubes) that don't continually snag and fray one's thread.

Modern ceramic spigot bobbin holders are expensive, but are superior to other models. The ceramic tubes are far harder than even the best surgical stainless steel, which eventually becomes grooved by the fly tying thread and has to be ground back and polished from time to time. Renzetti's HT-108 has a ruby tip at the top of the tube and a plastic sleeve at the entry end for the thread protection.

The wire arms of a spigot bobbin holder need to be adjusted to accommodate the particular size of spool and provide the desired thread tension. This should be light enough to allow the thread to be drawn off easily, while still tight enough for the bobbin to hang under its own weight without unwinding.

While most bobbins are of the clip .style, other models are offered today to suit tyers' requirements

LEFT A range of bobbin holders. Top row: Sunrise, Tiemco (x 2). Bottom row: Griffin and Matarelli (x 3). Centre: Ken Newton.

Ceramic Tipped Bobbin Holders

These are standard bobbin holders, fitted with wear resistant ceramic spigot inserts, available in three sizes.

Midge

Flared Lead

For easy weighting. The only bobbin that will work in conjunction with lead spools.

US Kaufmann

Norlander Automatic Bobbin

US Kaufmann, Norlander, Marriott; *GER* Brinkhoff

BOBBIN THREADER

Makes for less strain on the eyes.

DAVY WOTTON SERIES OF TOOLS

A nicely finished range with wooden handles.

US Fly & Field, *UK* Wotton.

DR. SLICK SERIES

Particularly strong on good scissors.

AUS Alpine; *UK* Sportfish; *US* Whitetail, Marriott.

DUBBING AIDS

Ceramiscrape Dubbing Rake

Rakes and scrapers for removing dubbing from fur animal pelts have been around for some time. The Ceramiscrape, designed by Englishman, Lawrence Waldron, is in a different league entirely. Ceramiscrapes are made from zirconia ceramic, with a specially designed tooth/groove pattern diamond cut into the functional end.

A necessary part of the design is the sharpness of the teeth, which is retained almost indefinitely by the hardness of the ceramic. Adjusting the angle and firmness of the raking allows different proportions of guard hair and underfur to be obtained. The raking action also mixes the fibres together.

The Ceramiscrape is available in two models: Coarse is ideal for removing thick underfur, like that found on the body of hare, beaver or muskrat; Fine is more suited to the removal of softer fibres like rabbit, squirrel, mole and hare mask.

After using the Ceramiscrape for only a short while, one can actually determine the exact amount of dubbing needed for a particular dressing (eg. three strokes of the rake on a mole skin gives the precise amount for a size 16 Iron Blue Dun). Sold in a protective case with full instructions.

JAP Sawada; *UK* Saville, Sportfish; *US* Hunter, Fly & Field.

Dubbing Block

Used to created wired cored dubbing twists.

US Fly & Field; *UK* Wotton.

Dubbing Brush Maker

A machine for making them at home with copper wire centres.

UK Lathkill.

Dubbing Twisters

US Marriott.

Dubbing Needle

This simple tool is practically indispensable at the flytying bench. As the name suggests, dubbing needles are used to pick out dubbed fur bodies, but also perform many other picking and poking chores. Many tiers use a needle to apply varnish to the whipped head of a finished fly. It is no bad thing to have several dubbing needles, for they are notoriously easy to misplace.

Purpose-made dubbing needles are nice, but usually relatively expensive for what they are. They can be easily made by gluing stout darning needles into short bits of thin hard wood dowel with epoxy adhesive.

Dubbing Whirl

Weighted metal base with two spring arms for holding the thread, that can be spun. Quality varies greatly among those on offer. Niche, Saville, Angling Pursuits, and Rooksbury in the UK offer the original Darrel Martin dubbing whirl.

Dubbit Dubbing Tool

Three options: Standard, Hair Spin Dubbit, Loop Spin Dubbit.

AUS Alpine; *US* Kaufmann, AA, Whitetail, Bailey, Cabela; *INT* Orvis

Nicklas Dubbing Tool

Especially good for looped dubbed shaggy, buggy bodies.

US Blue Ribbon

Spinning Loop Tool

From Griffin, a unique tool which can be re-opened to add more dubbing.

US Marriott

Tiewell Dubbing Tool

AUS Alpine

EDGIN SERIES OF TOOLS

Beautiful but functional tools made in brass.

UK Sportfish; *US* Marriott, Whitetail

E-Z LEG TOOL

Designed for tying the knotted legs required for hopper, cricket and 'daddy-long-legs' patterns. Beautifully designed and simple to use, the E-Z Leg Tool is available in 'small' and 'large' sizes and is supplied with fully illustrated instructions.

E-Z BOBBIN THREADER

Rainy's bobbin threader has to be about the most durable bobbin threader obtainable. The design incorporates a spigot tube cleaner.

US Marriott, Rainy, Blue Ribbon.

GALLOWS PARACHUTE TOOL

Many vice makers provided this accessory tailor made for their vice.

GRIFFIN MULTI-BOBBIN

Accommodates thread spools such as those of Gudebrod and Kreinik.

AUS Alpine, *US* Marriott, Whitetail

GRIFFIN SERIES OF TOOLS

A very wide range of quality tools.

AUS Alpine, *GER* Brinkhoff; *UK* Lathkill, Niche, Sparton, Rooksbury; *US* Marriott, AA, Whitetail, BT, Blue Ribbon, River Edge.

GUDEDROD BOBBIN

Plastic bobbin holder for the larger Gudebrod thread spools.

US Marriott, Bailey, Cabela

HACKLE BACK

A cone that comes in two sizes and does the job of a Hackle Guard.

US Cabela, Gorilla, Blue Ribbon.

HACKLE GUARDS

Keeps hackles out of the way when finishing heads. Some come with five holes for different size hooks.

JAP Sawada; *US* Kaufmann, Bailey; *UK* Anglian, McHardy.

HACKLE PLIERS

Good hackle pliers can hold the tip of a hackle firmly, without cutting or otherwise damaging the stem of the hackle while it is being wound. The best hackle pliers will not slip under tension: the hackle stem snapping, instead. As with tweezers, hackle plier jaws should meet evenly. Thompson make a non-skid plier with rubber on both faces, which is stocked in UK by Sparton, McHardy, and Sportfish.

English

Rotary

Allows parachutes to be wrapped very close to the shank

of the hook (Griffin).

Teardrop

Soft Nose

E-Z / Ezee

Push button spring-loaded (cf. electrical clip holders).

Spinning Hackle Pliers

Hackle Grip

HAIR PACKERS, STACKERS & EVENERS

The Brassie

One of the best designed devices for packing spun deer hair really densely, for such flies as bass bugs, Muddler Minnows, G&H sedges, etc. The grooved jaws of the 'Brassie' are designed to slide along the shank of the hook, to apply pressure to both the tying thread and the spun deer hair at the same time, without damaging either. The Brassie is available in three sizes: Small, Medium and Large.

US Whitetail, Marriott, Cabela; *UK* Niche.

Hair packers

Various forms exist, but an old biro tube can achieve the same effect.

Hair stackers

Standard models conforms to the conventional design of hair stacker, having an inner tube that fits into a base. Hair is introduced, tips, down into the tube and the whole device tapped smartly on a hard surface, which causes the tips of the hair to settle evenly inside the base.

Pro-Stack

The beautifully machined Renzetti Pro-Stack incorporates two sizes of hair stacker in one tool. Renzetti also makes a 'midge' size stacker for tying flies of size 16 and smaller.

AUS Alpine; *UK* Sportfish; *US* Marriott, Hunter, Kaufmann, Blue Ribbon, AA.

HALF HITCH TOOL

US Marriott, Whitetail, E.A.T.

KEN NEWTON SERIES OF TOOLS

Ken Newton makes beautiful, well designed fly tying tools from the highest quality materials.

UK Angling Pursuits, Sportfish.

KITS

Starter kits are sometimes assembled and sold. Caution should be exercised with these to ensure that they really meet the tyer's requirements. It may be best to take advice from your local retailer and buy items individually, to be added to as needed.

IRIS TWEEZERS

Used in ophthalmic surgery, iris tweezers are possibly the finest tweezers available to the fly dresser. Made from the best surgical grade stainless steel, they have interlocking tips that enable the finest single fibre to be gripped.

INT Orvis.

LANCE

With a razor sharp edge for extremely close cutting

US Kaufmann, Cabela.

MATARELLI SERIES OF TOOLS

Californian, Franco Matarelli, makes beautiful fly tying tools from stainless steel and brass. They are widely regarded as amongst the best tools a flytyer can possess.

AUS Alpine; *UK* Lathkill, Niche, Angling Pursuits; *US* Marriott, Hunter, Kaufmann, Blue Ribbon, AA, Cabela.

MATERIAL CLIP

A rigid device that clips on the vice barrel to hold loose materials

MATERIALS SPRING

Small wire spring that can be attached in the round over the vice to hold loose materials.

PLIERS

Flat-nose pliers have many uses in tying. Go for quality,though. Tiemco DeBarb pliers are excellent.

US Marriott, *INT* Orvis.

PERRY SERIES OF TOOLS

Quality tools made of brass.

US Marriott.

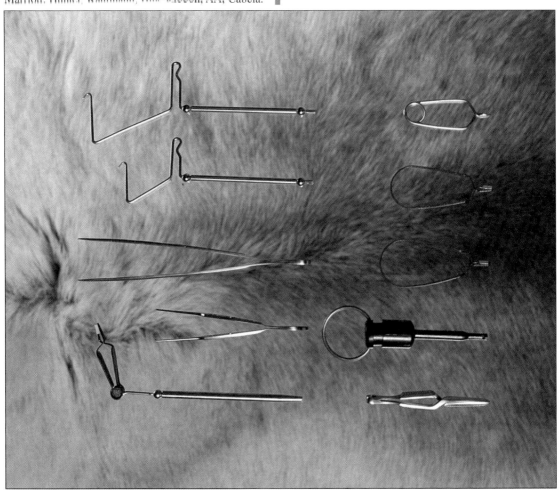

Flytying accessories (left column from top): whip finish tools (Matarelli), tweezers, hackle pliers (Tiemco); (right column from top) hackle pliers (Veniard, Tiemco, E-Z, Uni-hackle).

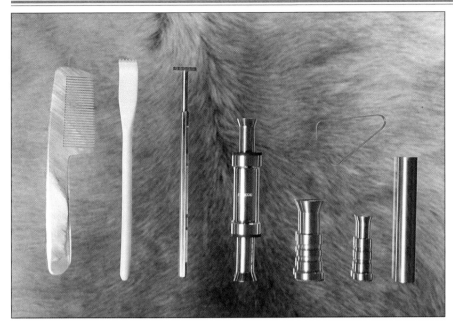

Selection of tools, including (left to right): Griffin hair comb, Cerami-scrape dubbing rake, Ken Newton dubbing rake, Renzetti Pro Stack, Ken Newton hair stackers and extension tube, and Chris Helm's Brassie hair packer.

PROFILE PLATE

A background sheet of white, grey, or green attached by an arm to the vice stem that helps the tyer sight the fly. Dyna-King and Gordon Griffiths produce two popular models.

RITE BOBBIN

A geared bobbin from Merco Products that comes as Standard, Magnum and the Shortie (not so generally available - but Lathkill Tackle in the UK stock these).

US Marriott, Whitetail, Bailey; *UK* Lathkill, Niche, Sportfish, Rooksbury.

SCISSORS

It is not realistic to expect a single pair of scissors to cope with all the cutting jobs that have to be done at the flytying bench. At least two pairs are recommended - one 'best' pair, with very fine sharp points, for precision cutting of threads, hackle fibres etc, and a second, stronger pair of scissors can be used for heavier work, such as trimming deer hair, cutting wires and quills and other duties considered too arduous for the 'best' scissors.

Tungsten carbide bladed scissors are good for finer work and a pair of serrated edge scissors as the work horse. Flush cutting, side cutters or shears are much better than scissors for cutting heavy monofilament and thin wires. Also, where any risk to one's expensive scissors is involved, it is far cheaper to replace a scalpel or craft knife blade.

SERRATED EDGE SHEARS

Useful for heavy duty cutting work.

US Hunter.

SQUIZZERS

Spring action scissors useable equally well in the right or left hand. Three profiles: Sharp Serrated, Micro Midge, Micro Fine.

US Blue Ribbon; *INT* Orvis

SUNRISE SERIES OF TYING TOOLS

A range of tools made in India.

UK Norris

TIEMCO SERIES OF TOOLS

AUS Alpine; *UK* Anglian, Lathkill, Saville, Niche, Sportfish, Rooksbury, Norris; *US* Marriott, Kaufmann, AA, BR.

THOMPSON SERIES OF TOOLS

UK Sportfish; *US* Marriott, Hunter, Kaufmann, BR.

TWEEZERS

A pair of tweezers is often useful for pulling out single fibres from feathers, selecting tiny hooks from small containers and many other little jobs for which one's fingers are too large and clumsy. The only criterion for good tweezers is that the points meet flush and evenly. Decent tweezers can be found at chemists, or in the catalogues of medical or biological instrument suppliers.

VARNISH APPLICATORS

Small glass or plastic bottles with a hollow needle for accurate application of varnish.

WHIP FINISH TOOL

These come in various styles - the most important distinction being whether they are fixed or rotate. A well designed whip finish tool allows quick and neat finishing of the fly with the proper knot. It is preferred by many professional flytyers because the job can be done much faster than by doing it solely by hand and a whip finish is neater and more secure than a series of half-hitches. The Matarelli Rotating Whip Finisher, either Standard or Long Reach, is regarded as the best there is.

WING BURNERS

For shaping wings, by heat or flame.

AUS Alpine; *GER* Brinkhoff; *JAP* Sawada; *UK* Lathkill, Niche, Rooksbury; *US* Marriott, AA.

WING CUTTERS

For cutting out pre-shaped wings.

UK Lathkill, Saville, Niche, McHardy, Slater, Sportfish Rooksbury.

Vices

WHILE FLIES can be tied without using one, a vice makes the job very much easier. Since it is usually the most expensive single item of fly dressing hardware, choosing a vice requires some care.

There are many makes and several designs of fly tying vice now available, varying greatly in degree of sophistication and price. When all is said and done, however, the principal function of a flytying vice is to hold a hook securely while a fly is being tied. Any vice that can manage this may be considered functional, at the very least.

There are three main designs for actuating the 'jaws' of a fly vice:

1) The jaws may closed by screw action. In these designs the jaws are closed either directly or by drawing the jaws into a constriction, by turning a large knurled nut.

2) The second major design uses a lever and cam arrangement which, similarly, pushes or pulls the jaws into a constriction, causing them to close.

3) In the third main type of vice, the jaws, themselves form the ends of powerful springs, held shut in their normal state under their own tension. In order to insert or release a hook, the jaws are forced apart, against the spring tension, usually by means of a lever turning a small cam.

Of the three types, the Lever/Cam and Spring/Lever types are currently easily the most popular.

The Lever/Cam actuated jaw vice is probably the most popular design today, because of its simplicity. The Thompson Model A is the archetype of this design and has been much copied by other manufacturers over the years. Veniard, Dyna-King and HMH also produce vices of the Lever/Cam type.

The American Regal was the original Spring/Lever flytying vice. It has been copied by several other manufacturers, with varying degrees of competence. The Regal design is very robust and effectively 'self sizing', requiring no time wasting adjustment to accommodate the range of hook sizes. This is an important consideration for the busy professional tier.

The choice of vice will be governed largely by the amount of tying to be done and the types of flies to be tied. Beyond the prime function of holding a hook securely, vices will usually incorporate a number features of varying usefulness. Adjustability for height, jaw angle and rotation about the axis of the hook shank are common features. As a rule of thumb: the simpler the flies to be tied, the simpler the vice that is needed. In tying complex fully dressed salmon flies, a vice that permits all sorts of adjustment and allows convenient all-round inspection is helpful. If, on the other hand, one's tying is restricted to simple nymphs and spider patterns, then a vastly adjustable and complicated vice would be rather wasted and would not warrant the extra expense.

One feature worth having is hardened tool steel jaws, which greatly extend the life of the vice. Most reputable manufacturers fit these in their better quality vices.

Vices are usually supplied either with a long stem and a C-clamp, which attaches to a table edge; or with a short stem and a heavy, free-standing

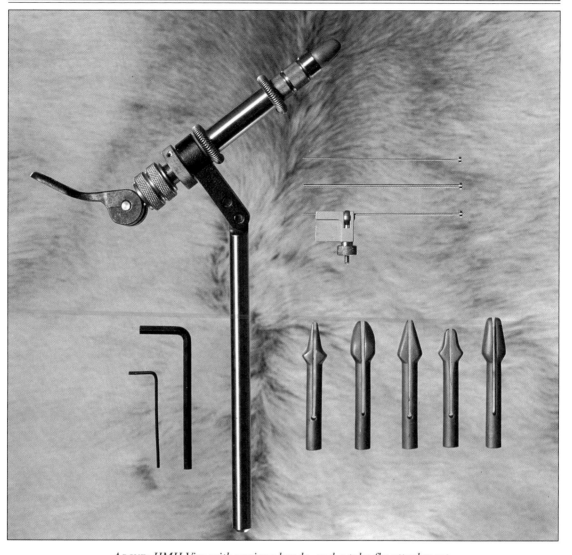

ABOVE: HMH Vise with various heads, and a tube fly attachment.

pedestal base. The latter is possibly more versatile. The most comprehensive arrangement is to have a pedestal vice and an extension adaptor (Dyna-King make an excellent example). This allows a short stemmed vice to be used with a C-clamp. These days, vice stems are almost universally ³/8" in diameter.

Many manufacturers offer a range of supplementary attachments for their vices such as third arms, parachute/gallows tools or sight boards.

Today there is a wealth of choice for the tyer buying a vice in any of the price ranges. The cheaper vices may well do all that the tier needs. Those originating from the Indian sub-continent are fairly widely available and not too expensive. Apart from the vices seen in the shops, there are also specialists who tailor make vices to exactly meet the tyer's requirements. Such precision will naturally not be cheap. Lawrence Waldon, creator of the Ceramiscrape Dubbing Rake, for example, caters for left and right handed tyers in his designs, and makes just about the neatest travel vice around.

Some of the vices available today are:

A.K.'S
The vice designed by A.K. Best
GER Brinkhoff; *US* Whitetail, Hunter.

BALLAN ROTARY VICE
US Cabela.

BANKSIDE VICE
For hand-held tying.
JAP Sawada; *UK* Saville.

BILL COE TUBE VICE

UK Saville, Sparton.

DANICA

Vices from Denmark.
Vision A The jaws are tightened by a screw.
Vision B The jaws are tightened by means of a cam.
Innovation C Can be used conventionally or rotationally.
Innovation D This is the cam model of C.

GER Brinkhoff; *UK* Rooksbury

DYNA-KING

These vices are made by Abby Precision Manufacturing Co. of California.
Sidewinder
X-1
Supreme
Monarch
Professional
Tube Fly Vice
Aristocrat
Voyager
King Prince
Squire

AUS Alpine; *GER* Brinkhoff; *JAP* Sawada; *US* Marriott, Kaufmann, Blue Ribbon, River Edge, Whitetail, Bailey, Cabela, Fly & Field; *UK* Lathkill, Watercraft, Sportfish

FLY-MATE

A Danish company producing the Concept series.
Starter and Standard

GER Brinkhoff.

GORDON GRIFFITHS
Classic Rotating

Premier
Innova A British 'Nor-vise style' vice.

UK Rooksbury.

GRIFFIN
Patriot
Superior 3AR
Superior 3ARP
2A
Superior 1A

AUS Alpine; *GER* Brinkhoff; *US* Marriott, Cabela; *UK* Lathkill, Sparton.

HMH

Originally designed by Bill Hunter, these vices passed through the hands of the API Company before coming into the hands today of Kennebec River Fly & Tackle Co. The HMH label hints of royalty at first look but actually stands for 'Hunter's Mad House'!
Premium
Standard
Sparton Nomad

UK Sparton, Sportfish; *US* Marriott, Hunter.

INTEGRA

An India-made vice.
DX360

UK Walker.

MATTHIAS ROTARY FLY VICE

A new vice with hardened/textured jaw for hook sizes 32 to 1/0. One finger rotation and easy changeover for left-handed users. Satin black with a low-glare finish. Angle adjustment allows full in-line rotation without use of extra tools.
US Matthias.

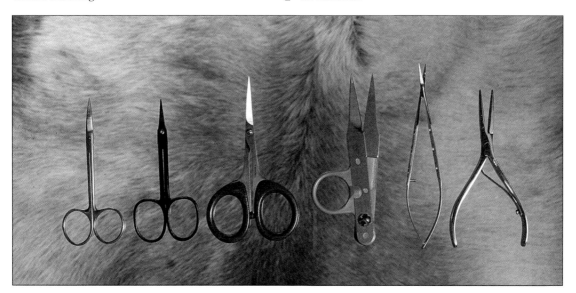

Scissors come in many shapes and sizes. These are from (left to right) Uni Products, Orvis, Tiemco, Spirit River, Iris and Orvis pliers.

MINEX BASE VISE
UK Saville, Walker.

NOR-VISE
A revolutionary style of vice where the vice does the winding rather than the hand with the bobbin. Gives terrific thread control,fast dubbing and true rotation on the same axis. Traditionalists, though, may find this concept a bridge too far for them.

CAN Country Pleasures; *US* Marriott, Norlander.

ODEHAMES
Over and under vice An English vice that has many fans. Oliver Edwards used one for years.

UK Saville, Lathkill.

ORVIS
Premier
Rotational
Intermediate

US Marriott; *INT* Orvis.

PAMOLA FLY LATHE
A unique vice that functions as as a static or in-line rotary vice. Holds hooks from 6/0 to 28. Machined from solid brass,stainless steel and teflon. The chuck and spindles are machined from molybdenum chromium tool steel. It pivots and rotates to hold hooks in any position. The spindle design allows for full rotary tying,the rotary tension is adjustable,and the Lathe easily adjusts for left or right hand use. The large diameter fly wheel and teflon bearings make for smooth rotation and sensitive feel.

US AA; *UK* Lathkill.

REGAL ENGINEERING INC.
Regal Rotary This vice uses a compression jaw style that is self adjusting and can handle hooks 6/0 to 32. Rotation is 360° and the tying angle is over 240 degrees. The mini-head handles hook sizes 14 and smaller.
Regal Standard No rotary action.
Inex An entry level vice with no rotary action.

AUS Alpine; *GER* Brinkhoff; *JAP* Sawada; *US* Marriott, Kaufmann, Hook & Hackle, Hunter, Bailey, Cabela, AA, Blue Ribbon; *INT* Orvis.

REGENT
A clone-style of the original Regal.
Standard
Rotatable

UK Sportfish, Anglian.

RENZETTI
Masters series
4000 series
3000 series
Travel vice
Traditional vice

AUS Alpine, *UK* Sportfish; *US* Marriott, Kaufmann, Hunter, Bailey Cabela, AA, BR.

SUNRISE
Indian made vices.
Rotating
Super AAA
Super AA
Eagle II

UK Norris, Saville, Lathkill; *US* Bailey, BR.

THOMPSON
Pro vice
Pro II
Model A
360 SLT vice

UK Sportfish, *US* Marriott, Kaufmann; *INT* Orvis.

VENIARD
Royal
Salmo
Prefect shadow
Croydon
Paramount
County
Super county pedestal The company's top of the range vice.

UK Norris, McHardy, Slater, Rooksbury.

WEAVER
Ultimate 1
Ultimate 2
Ultimate 3

UK Saville, Sparton, Niche, Rooksbury, Sportfish, Walker.

Accessories

APART FROM basic practical tools, flytyers (like flyfishermen) tend to be drawn magnetically towards knick-knacks and trendy new 'toys'. Thus, there is a thriving flytying accessories business. Some accessories have genuinely helpful applications, others are useful on rare occasions, and others... well... if you really think you need it you'll just have to have it - like the rest of us! Here is a selection of hopefully practical ideas.

BT's BEAD-EZY

A simple storage method for beads that allows one bead to be dispensed at a time. It comes in three sizes: small (14-18), medium (8-12), large (2-6).

US BT, Marriott.

DONOVAN OPTIVISOR

A precision binocular headband magnifier. Lenses come in power 2, 3, 4, 5, 7.

US Marriott.

DOUG BREWER'S HOT GLUE GUN

Used to make egg flies and egg-sucking leeches or to finish off heads or glue eyes.

US Marriott.

ELASTIC NECKLACE

For hanging scissors and other tools from the numerous clips thereon for ease of access. Falling over wearing this is not recommended! A Dr Slick product.

EGG GUN

A simple system for creating egg patterns in 30 seconds. From Alaska Troutfitters.

US River Edge.

FLY 'N HOOK / TACH IT

Magnetic hook and fly holders. Tach-It comes from Scherer Designs.

US Hunter, Marriott.

FUR BLENDER

No more than a small standard electric blender / mixer available from electrical goods retailers.

US Hunter, Kaufmann.

HOOK HONE

Modern hooks are generally extremely sharp. With reputable makes, it should not be necessary to try and improve on the out-of-the-box sharpness of trout sized hooks. Larger sizes for salmon, pike and saltwater may benefit from some attention before or during fishing, after they have been subjected to some wear and tear.

The hard, bony mouths of some fish will easily reject anything less than a perfectly sharp hook. The best place to sharpen hooks is at the tying bench, before applying materials, so as not to damage the finished fly and also so as not to waste time on the water. Tiemco make a ceramic hook hone, with a fine surface on one side and a heavily serrated one on the other.

US Hunter.

LAP TRAP / LAP TRAY

An apron style rubbish collector - in the pouch pocket and not on the floor.

US Marriott, Fishing for ideas.

LIGHTS

Remember voltage differences when considering purchasing lights.

Goodwin Giraffe System

A superb system, with light & magnifier combined.
US Kaufmann, Bailey ,Cabela, Goodwin.

HMH Littlelite

Sleek and unobtrusive using a 3000 hour, 10 watt halogen bulb. Casts a strong focal light, has an 18" gooseneck, weighted base and 12 volt transformer.
US Marriott.

Magni-lite

US Magni-Lite

Orvis Vise Lamp

US Marriott; *INT* Orvis

Zelco Micro Halogen Light

The first low cost,low voltage,high-tech lighting system/ Produces light equivalent to a 77 watt bulb but uses only 20 watts of low voltage electricity.
US Marriott, River Edge, Blue Ribbon.

ROUGHNECK SYSTEM

The Roughneck System is a lighting and magnifying arrangement which comes from King Tool. In terms of concept it clearly owes much to the Goodwin Giraffe system.

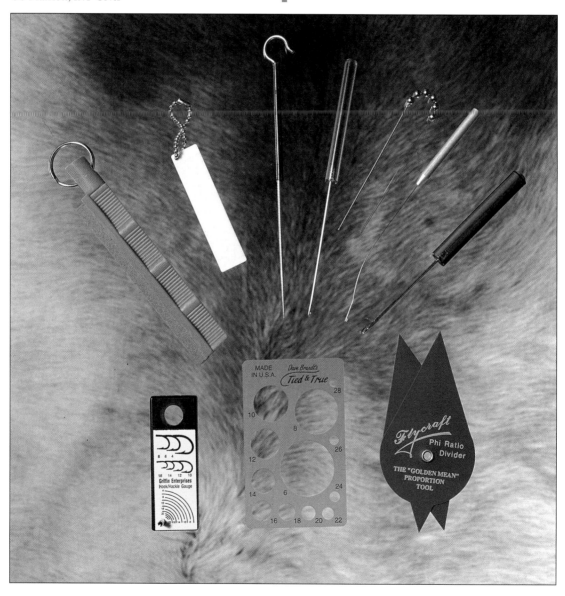

Accessories (left to right): Orvis hook hone, Tiemco hook hone, Matarelli dubbing needle, Rainy's E-Z bobbin threader, Matarelli bobbin threader and cleaner, Tiemco bobbin threader, E-Z leg tool; (bottom row) Griffin hook hackle guage, Dave Brandt's Tied & True, Flycraft Golden Mean proportion tool.

Metz saddles, showing the long length of useable hackle and the wide range of natural colours (see page 49)

MAG EYES

Worn like a sun-visor this has 2x and 4x magnification lenses, and an up and down adjust-ment knob.

US MFD Enterprises, *INT* Orvis.

MAGNIFIERS

A number of these are now available with flexible stems. Some come in combination with light systems.

Donegan Flex-a-Mag

A 4" round acrylic disk with pedestal base and flexible arm.

US Marriott

NAPTHALENE CRYSTALS

To protect natural materials when stored.

UK Lathkill

PUMICE STONE

Tiny burrs, cracks and other skin imperfections on the fingers can cause frustration when they snag on micro-fibred tying thread. One solution to the problem is to 'sand' one's rough hands with a pumice stone, widely available from pharmacies. A piece of this light, porous volcanic rock is inexpensive and will last a lifetime.

US Hunter.

SHADOW BOXES

For artistically displaying flies

CAN Artista; *US* Mountain, Sawdust, Shadow-craft, Kaufmann, Cabela.

SIZING / PROPORTION GAUGES

Fishaus Hackle Gauge
US Whitetail.

Hook and Hackle Gauge (Griffin)
Slides onto the stem of the vice and rests on the vice clamp. Hackle size is assessed by bending the 'sweet spot' of the hackle around a short pin and comparing the length of the splayed fibres against the scale printed on the background

UK Niche,Angling Pursuits, *US* AA, Bailey, Cabela, *INT* Orvis.

Tied & True Hackle Gauge
Produced by Dave Brandt from the Catskills, this neat little device helps one select the appropriate hackle for a particular hook size in the range 6 to 28. I have found that using this simple gauge has helped me to determine hackle size even before tying. With a little practice using this tool, one's ability to assess hackle size rapidly improves.

US Brandt, Marriott.

Troth Hacklemaster
US Marriott, Blue Ribbon.

Worry Wood Flytyers Gauge
US Hunter.

STATIC GUARD

Eliminates static electricity in materials. The Tote size is ideally suited to the travelling tyer.

US BT.

STORE-EZY

Clear plastic tubes, capped both ends for holding seven spools of thread or tinsel.

US BT.

TOOL CADDIES

These come in wood or hard foam.

UK Saville, Sportfish; *US* Marriott, Hunter, Cabela.

TOOL CAROUSEL

UK Saville,Sportfish; *US* Marriott.

TRAVEL TYING KITS AND BAGS

DB Dun Bag
US Marriott.

Evets Travel TY
US Marriott, Bailey.

J.W. Outfitters Kits
Master, Fly Tying or Creekside. Also the T.O.T.L. (Top of the Line), regarded by many as the outstanding carry case of them all.

US Marriott, Kaufmann, Hunter.

Mark Pack Works
US Marriott.

Orvis Flytyers Travellers Case
US Marriott; *INT* Orvis.

TRIM BAG / COLLECT ALL / WASTE TROL / TRASH TRAY

These are forms of attachment to the table below the vise to catch the rubbish before it hits the floor.

US Marriott, Bailey, Hunter, Cabela; *INT* Orvis.

TYING BOXES, TABLES AND TOPS

US D&T Enterprises (Bug Box), Gerstner, Loon, Perry Design, Pockit Sports, Roberts, Sespe, Worrywood.

Hooks

THE SUBJECT OF HOOKS is worthy of a separate volume in its own right. Hookmakers have come and gone, as have hook styles, over the years. It still remains a competitive business, as evidenced by the number of products in the market place. Hook manufacturers have caused some confusion by not standardising hook measurements - for example shank length, wire diameter, and gape.

There are the styles of hook to consider when choosing the right chassis for the particular pattern to be fished. A choice may be made between barbless or barbed hooks. Some people may opt for the latter and then seek to debarb the fly by the use of pliers. Can they be sure that such pressure has not produced micro-hairline cracks in the most critical piece of tackle that meets the fish? After all, a hook is not designed for the application of force directed in this way.

The next step on in imagination from the barbless hook has been the Bramley/Betts Tag Hook from Partridge - sometimes referred to as 'Touch And Go'. Then what is the place of stainless steel hooks? How does one weigh the advantage to the fisherman of corrosion resistance against the disadvantage this produces for a fish that escapes with such a hook in its mouth?

Some of the terminology employed is:

Gape - the distance from the point to the shank.
Throat - the distance from the point to the inside curve of the bend at its furthest point.
Shank - the straight part of the hook between the eye and the bend.
Eye - the holding circle for the leader, which can be in various forms:
 - aligned to the shank up, down, or straight.
 - shaped as a loop, taper or ball.
Spade end - an older-style flat piece of metal instead of an eye for attaching the leader to.
Points - which can be barbless, needle, spear, or hollow.
Bend - the shape of the curve between the shank and the point, which can be: Perfect, Limerick, Sproat, Sneck.

There is also the question of hook-size scales. British hookmakers have traditionally used the Redditch Scale. In the 1930s there was also in use the Pennell Scale or New Scale. Confusion may be caused when reading about an old fly pattern and in this book we have therefore used the Pennell scale for reference. The Redditch and Pennell scales relate as follows:

Redditch / Pennell	Redditch / Pennell
6/0 = 20	7 = 8
5/0 = 19	8 = 7
4/0 = 18	9 = 6
3/0 = 17	10 = 5
2/0 = 16	11 = 4
1/0 = 15	12 = 3
1 = 14	13 = 2
2 = 13	14 = 1
3 = 12	15 = 0
4 = 11	16 = 00
5 = 10	17 = 000
6 = 9	18 = 0000

The Redditch Scale is a correlation between the gape of the hook and the length of the shank. The

ABOVE: Pheasant wings (Veniard) and Partridge wings (Fishermans Feathers) - see pages 19-22

shank-length is measured from the outside of the bend up to (but not including) the eye. From gape size 18-13 the shank-length increases at a rate of $1/32$" per hook size. From gape size 12-3, there is an increase of $1/16$" per hook siz.e Above size 3 the shank length increases each time by $1/8$" up to 5/0 and $1/4$" thereafter.

Not all of the sizes in the revised Redditch Scale are made today, so usually the *odd* numbers are no longer found.

Companies making and marketing hooks today include:

AIKEN

UK McHardy.

AIRFLO

UK Norris.

ASHIMA

Made from Carbon 90 steel with chemically sharpened needle points. The splinter barb, less than 20% of the diameter of the wire, is available in a number of patterns in the series.

UK Rooksbury.

DAIICHI

High carbon steel hooks that are chemically sharpened. Mini-barbs make debarbing easier.

US Marriott, Kaufmann, Cabela, Hunter, BR, E.A.T.

DAI-RIKI

Japanese hooks of high carbon base, chemically sharpened.

US Bailey, Blue Ribbon; River Edge.

DRENNAN

UK Anglian, Walker, Saville, Sportfish, McHardy, Watercraft

EAGLE CLAW

Famous American hooks from Wright & McGill. Now with 'Lazer-Sharp' pointing. They publish a hook conversion list (below) to enable tyers to see where their product is comparable to other companies' products:

Eagle Claw	Tiemco	Daiichi	Mustad	Gamakatsu
LO5		200R		
LO54SS	811S			
LO55	2487			
LO57	3761	1550	3906	
LO58	9672			
LO59	9300	1170	94840	P-10B
LO60	5212		3399	
LO61B	100	1190	94845	
LO63	5262	1710	9671	P-102HB
LO67	808S			
L144	205BL			C-12B
L250			3407	
L281	5263	2220	79580	S-114LB

AUS Alpine; *US* Marriott, Tiemco, Hunter.

ESMOND DRURY HOOKS

Whilst there are many 'Esmond Drury style' hooks offered, the original hook is distributed solely by E. Veniard Ltd. Sue Hancock in Lincolnshire, England, who was taught to tie this special series of flies by the late Col. Drury still ties all her orders on these hooks.

UK Lathkill, Saville, Sportfish, McHardy, Watercraft, Slater.

FENWICK

Triple sharpened hooks forged and tempered from HC80 high carbon steel.

US Gorilla, Marriott.

GAMAKATSU

Produce some interesting coloured hooks - red, green, blue - along with their main series.

AUS Alpine; *US* Gorilla, Cabela, Anglers Choice.

HAYABUSA

Have introduced their Carbon 80 series of hooks to the market very recently. A number of professional tyers have been using them at shows in 1996 and have commented favourably upon them.

GER Brinkhoff; *US* Whitetail, Marriott.

KAMASAN

A subsidiary of Drennan International.

AUS Alpine; *UK* Rooksbury, Anglian, Walker, Lathkill, Saville, Sportfish, Norris, McHardy, Niche, Watercraft, Slater, Angling Pursuits.

LUREFLASH VIPER HOOKS

UK Watercraft.

MUSTAD

The famous Norwegian company that has over recent years introduced their Professional Series 80000 which have been favourably received - particularly after the addition of the barbless hooks.

AUS Alpine; *JAP* Sawada; *GER* Brinkhoff; *US* Marriott, Kaufmann, Bailey, Hunter, Cabela, AA, E.A.T., Hook & Hackle; *UK* Walker, Lathkill, Saville, Sportfish, McHardy, Niche, Watercraft.

ORVIS HOOKS

Are offered primarily through their stores, but are taken by some other retailers as well. Chemically sharpened hooks from Japan.

US Marriott; *INT* Orvis.

OWNER

The cutting points on hooks from Owner have a patented T-shaped triple edged blade led by a needle-sharp point. As the point begins to penetrate, the three cutting edges slice their way through the toughest cartilege or bone. A superb saltwater and big game fish hook. Probably none sharper or as strong.

US Marriott.

PARTRIDGE

The famous English company, based in Redditch, that sells hand-made hooks worldwide. Probably offer the widest range of hook choices, from the very small to the extremely large. They also offer an extensive barbless range and the innovative TAG hook. A number of hooks are chemically sharpened by the company's Niflor process. From 1 August 1996 Partridge became part of Mustad. It continues its Redditch operation as before.

AUS Alpine; *JAP* Sawada; *GER* Brinkhoff; *US* Marriott, Hunter, Fly & Field, Cabela, Whitetail; *UK* Walker, Lathkill, Saville, Sportfish, Norris, McHardy, Watercraft, Angling Pursuits.

SCORPION

High carbon steel hooks from Japan. Extremely sharp.

UK Lathkill.

SILKWORM GUT FOR BLIND EYE HOOKS

UK Slater; *US* Marriott.

SPRITE

A company run by a former Partridge employee that offers a limited range of hooks reminiscent of traditional styles made in Redditch. These hooks are sometimes packeted under the retailers name. Well regarded, particularly on the English still-water scene, as offering good value for money. Made from high carbon Sheffield steel wire and chemically brightened.

UK Anglian, Rooksbury, Walker, Lathkill, McHardy, Niche, Slater, Sparton.

TEENY HOOKS

Custom hooks designed by Teeny Nymph Co. and Eagle Claw. Black finish, razer sharp and very strong.

US Marriott.

TIEMCO (TMC)

Widely used, these hooks have very sharp points and the barbs are easily compressed for catch and release fishing. Have now introduced their 'Quick-Eye' hooks, in which the hook eye is open at one side so the monofilament can be slipped into the eye from behind or along the side. When the leader knot is tightened the flattened end keeps the knot from slipping off. Intended to help when age takes its toll on the eyes - and for night fishing.

AUS Alpine; *US* Marriott, Kauffman, Hunter, Blue Ribbon, Cabela, AA, River Edge; *GER* Brinkhoff; *UK* Rooksbury, Lathkill, McHardy, Niche.

TUBE FLY MATERIALS

UK Saville, Sportfish, McHardy, Niche, Slater, Sparton; *GER* Brinkhoff.

TURRALL

Made from high carbon 0.90-1.00% Sheffield steel, and they include a Keel Dry Fly hook in the series.

UK Niche.

VMC

Hooks that come from France, which are made from an exclusive bronze-plated Vanadium alloy.

US Gorilla; *UK* Saville, McHardy, Slater.

WADDINGTON SHANKS

JAP Sawada; *UK* Walker, Lathkill, Saville, Sportfish, McHardy, Niche, Watercraft, Slater.

TYPES OF HOOK

Hookmakers are constantly adding to their portfolio to meet the demands of tyers and anglers. Some examples of offerings in the market place today are:

BARBLESS HOOKS

Daiichi
1190 STANDARD DRY FLY
Round bend, standard shank length, barbless, down-eye. Bronze. Sizes 8-18.

Eagle Claw/Wright & McGill
DO64B WET FLY
Heavy wire, down-eye, barbless 'Diamond' point. Bronze. Sizes 1-8.
LO61B DRY FLY
Light wire, bronze, down-eyed and round bend. Sizes 4-18
LO64B SALMON/STEELHEAD
Bronze, non-offset and down-eyed. Sizes 8,6,4,2,1.

Kamasan
B402 BARBLESS DRY FLY
Light wire in bronze. Sizes 14-16

Partridge
CS20 MIKE WEAVER ARROWPOINT
For dry flies and smaller nymphs. The flat arrow head point provides an effective hook hold. Black finish. Sizes 10-18.
CS27 GRS ROMAN MOSER DRY FLY
For dry flies, emergers and smaller nymphs. The barbless, shaped points hold effectively. Grey Shadow finish. Sizes 10-18.
CS28 GRS ROMAN MOSER NYMPH
Heavier wire version of the CS27 GRS.
CS29-GRS ROMAN MOSER BARBLESS STREAMER Streamer hook in Grey Shadow finish. Sizes 2-8.

Tiemco
TMC 103BL
Dry fly. Down-eye, wide gape, extra fine wire. Black finish. Sizes 11-21.
TMC 109BL
Dry fly and nymph. Down-eye, wide gape, extra fine wire. 1x - 3x variable long shank. Black finish. Sizes 7-19.
TMC 205BL
Wide gape for caddis pupae, etc. Up-eye, standard wire, 5x wide, 'semi-dropped' point. Bronzed. Sizes 8-20.
TMC 206BL
Curved shank for caddis pupae, floating nymphs, emergers, etc. 2x short. Black finish. Sizes 6-20.

TMC 900BL

Dry fly. Down-eye, 1x fine, 1x wide gape (short). Semi-dropped point. Forged. Black finish. Sizes 8-24.

TMC 902BL

Dry fly. Down-eye, wide gape, 2x fine wire. Standard length. Black finish. Sizes 12-20.

TMC 905BL

Steelhead or salmon dry fly. Down-eye, 1x fine wire. Forged. Black finish. Sizes 2-10.

TMC 947BL

Nymph and streamer. Down-eye, 2x-3x variable length shank. Forged standard wire. Bronzed. Sizes 4-20.

BASS FLY HOOKS

Mustad

80300BR BASS 'STINGER'

Very wide-gaped hooks used for bulky deer hair bass bugs. Forged, knife edge point, chemically sharpened, austempered, micro barb, ring eyed. Bronze. Sizes 2-10.

37189 STINGER HOOK

3x stout wire and stronger than 37187.

Daiichi

2720 WIDE-GAPE BASS 'STINGER'

Light wire, wide-gaped 'stinger' hook, for bass bugs, deer hair 'mice', 'frogs', etc. Straight (ring) eye. Bronze. Sizes 5/0-2.

Partridge

CS41 BASS 'FLASHPOINT'

Wide-gape 'Redditch' bend, to accommodate spun deer hair bass flies. Medium length shank, chemically sharpened ('flash pointed'). Straight ball eye. Bronze. Sizes 3/0-6.

Tiemco

TMC 8089

Wide gape, straight eye hook for deer hair bass bugs. Forged fine wire. Bronze. Sizes 2, 6,10.

TMC 511S

Popper and skipping bug hook. Straight eye, 4x long, 2x wide gape. Single hump on shank to prevent twisting of glued on popper body. Forged. Stainless steel. Sizes 2/0, 1/0, 2 and 6.

DRY FLY HOOKS

Daiichi

1100 WIDE GAPE

Standard shank length. Model Perfect bend, oversized down-eye, mini barb. Bronze. Sizes 16-24.

1110 WIDE GAPE

Standard length. Model Perfect bend, oversized straight eye, mini barb. Bronze. Sizes 16-24.

1170 STANDARD DRY

Round bend with standard shank length, down-eye, forged. Bronze. Sizes 8-16.

1180 STANDARD DRY FLY MINI BARB

As 1170 but with a mini barb. Sizes 6-24.

1280 2x LONG DRY FLY

Round bend down-eye dry fly hooks. 2x long, fine wire, mini barb. Used for Mayflies and Daddies. Bronze. Sizes 6-16.

1310 SHORT SHANK DRY FLY

Round bend down-eye, 1x short shank. Used for dry flies where a wide gape is needed (deer hair bodies,etc.) and for short bodied dry flies. Sizes 8-22.

1330 Up eye version of 1310. Sizes 8-24.

1480 SPECIAL PURPOSE DRY FLY

Limerick bend, straight eye, 1x fine, 2x short, mini barb. Bronze. For midges, spiders and variants. Sizes 12-24.

1640 MULTI USE DRY FLY

Round bend, straight eye, 2x short, reversed, forged. Used for caddis flies, spiders, 'eggs' and extended body dry flies. Bronze. Sizes 2-20.

Eagle Claw/Wright & McGill

DO58 STANDARD

Round bend, light wire, down eye. Wright & McGill 'Diamond Point'. Used for dries and light nymph patterns. Bronze. Sizes 4-18.

Kamasan

B400 DRY/EMERGER

A first class medium wire hook for dry flies and emerger patterns. Round bend. Bronze. Sizes 10-16.

B410 SMUT/MIDGE

Light wire, whisker barb 1x short, 'Crystal' bend. High carbon steel. Ideal for small dry flies. Bronze. Sizes 12-22.

B420 SEDGE/CADDIS

Special loop bend, high carbon steel. Light wire, with a slight turned up eye. Used for midge and caddis pupa imitations. Bronze. Sizes 8-16.

B440 TRADITIONAL

Up eye, 1x short shank. Lightly forged. Bronze. Sizes 10-20.

B401 WHISKER BARB

A standard shank dry fly hook, similar to the B400, but with a fine 'whisker' barb. Bronze. Sizes 8-20.

Mustad

94831 Forged, round bend, down eye, 2x fine wire, 2x long. A popular hook for adult stone and caddis flies. Bronzed. Sizes 4-16.

94833 Forged, round bend, down eye, 3x fine wire, standard length. A light wire hook for spinners, 'no hackles', thorax flies, etc. Bronzed. Sizes 12-18.

94840 Forged, round bend, down eye, standard weight wire, standard length. Considered the 'standard' hook for dry flies. Bronzed. Sizes 10-18.

94842 Forged, Round bend, up eye, standard weight wire, standard length. Up eye version of the 94840.

Bronzed. Sizes 12-24.

94859 Forged, round bend, straight eye, 1x fine wire, standard length. Used for 'midges' and other small patterns. The straight eye allows full exposure of the gape: important in very small hook sizes. Bronzed. Sizes 18-28.

80000BR Forged, knife edge point; chemically sharpened; austempered; micro- barb; turned down 30 degree ball eye. Bronzed. Sizes 10-24.

80100BR Forged, knife edge point; chemically sharpened; austempered; micro-barb; reversed 10 degree turned down ball eye. Bronzed. Sizes 20-26.

80250BR Forged, knife edged point, chemically sharpened, austempered, micro-barb, reversed 15 degrees; turned down 30 degree ball eye. Bronze. Sizes 10-22.

Partridge

L3A CAPTAIN HAMILTON
The 'ideal' dry fly hook. Almost round, forged Hamilton bend. Down-eye, wide gape. Bronze. Sizes 6-22.

GRS 3A
This an L3A (above) in Partridge's Grey Shadow ('Niflor') finish. Sizes 12-18.

K14ST VINCE MARINARO MIDGE
Designed with the late Vincent Marinaro, for small dry flies. Offset, wide gape bend. Down-eye. Bronze. Sizes 20-28.

L3B CAPTAIN HAMILTON
Up eye version of L3A. Sizes 10-18.

E4A RITZ DRY FLY
Offset bend dry fly hooks that have always been popular in France. 4x fine wire, forged. Bronze. Sizes 10-18.

A. ALBERT PARTRIDGE WIDE GAPE D/E
Normally used for wet and nymph patterns, but recommended by some experts as a strong dry fly hook. Offset bend. Bronze. Sizes 8-16.

E6A HOOPER DRY FLY Short shank, 4x fine wire. Forged Redditch bend. Bronze. Sizes 8-18.

K3A SWEDISH DRY FLY
Specially shaped hook shank, 'cranked' behind the eye. Used for 'upside down' and 'parachute' styles. Favoured by Gary LaFontaine for dry caddis imitations. Bronze. Sizes 10-18.

K10 YORKSHIRE FLY BODY
Extended body dry fly hook, originally developed with Peter Mackenzie-Philps in the 1970s. An improved design was re-introduced in the early 1990s. Bronzed. Sizes 10-16.

Tiemco

TMC 100 Down-eye, 1x fine. Forged, wide gape. Bronze. Sizes 8-26.

TMC 101 Straight eye, 1x fine. Forged, wide gape. Bronze. Sizes 8-26.

TMC 102Y Down-eye, 1x fine. Forged, wide gape. Black finish. Sizes 9-19.

TMC 531 Down-eye, 2x fine, 2x short. 'Perfect' bend.

Used for 'parachute' and 'thorax' patterns. Black finish. Sizes 10-20.

TMC 9300 Dry and wet fly hook. Down-eye, 1x fine. Forged 'Perfect' bend. Bronzed. Sizes 10-20.

TMC 5210 Down-eye, 1x fine wire. Forged 'Perfect' bend. Bronzed. Sizes 10-20.

TMC 5230 Down-eye, 3x fine wire. Forged 'Perfect' bend. Bronze. Sizes 10-18.

TMC 5212 Hopper and other 'terrestrial' hook. Down-eye, 2x long, 1x fine wire. Forged 'Perfect' bend. Bronze. Sizes 6-16.

TMC 921 Down-eye, 2x short, 1x fine. Forged. Bronze. Sizes 8-20.

TMC 500U Midge hook. Up eye, 2x short, standard wire. Forged, straight point. Bronze. Sizes 16-22.

TMC 501 Straight eye, 1x short, standard wire. Forged, straight point. Bronze. Sizes 20-24.

NYMPH HOOKS

Daiichi

1130 SPECIAL WIDE-GAPE
Continuous bend, down-eye, 1x-short, forged, reversed. Used for scuds, shrimp, grubs, pupae and San Juan worms. Bronzed. Sizes 10-16.

1140 SPECIAL WIDE-GAPE
Continuous bend, up-eye, 1x-fine, 1x-short, forged, reversed. Used for Midge, Pupae and Micro-Caddis. Bronzed. Sizes 18-22.

1150 HEAVY WIDE-GAPE
Continuous bend, up-eye, 1x strong, forged, reversed. Used for shrimps, grubs, pupae and San Juan worms. Bronzed. Sizes 8-16.

1155 GOLDEN WIDE-GAPE
Continuous bend, up-eye, heavy forged wire. Reversed. Gold-plated finish. Sizes 8-16.

1270 MULTI-USE CURVED
York bend, straight eye, 3x long. For hoppers, terrestrials and stonefly nymphs. Bronzed. Sizes 4-22.

1273 CURVED SHANK NYMPH (RED)
York bend, straight eye, 3x long, heavy wire. Red finish. Sizes 8-22.

1560 TRADITIONAL NYMPH
Sproat bend, down-eye, strong wire, 1x long. Bronzed. Sizes 6-18.

1710 STANDARD NYMPH
Round bend, down-eye, 2x long, 1x strong, forged. Bronzed. Sizes 2-18.

1720 LONG-BODIED NYMPH
3x long version of the 1710. Forged round bend, down-eye, 1x strong wire. Bronzed. Sizes 4-18.

1730 BENT-SHANK LONG NYMPH
Humped-shank version of 1720, for stonefly nymphs and crab patterns. Bronze finish. Sizes 4-14.

1740 UP-EYE NYMPH
Round bend, up-eye, 2x heavy wire. Bronzed. 6-16.

1770 SWIMMING NYMPH Sproat bend, straight eye, 1x fine wire, 3x long forged double curved shank. Used for leeches, San Juan worms, etc. Bronze. Sizes 6-16.

J220 EMERGER HOOK

Wide gape, down-eye, medium wire, offset bend. Used for emergers, shrimps and small nymphs. Bronzed. Sizes 20-24.

Eagle Claw/Wright & McGill

D052 CURVED NYMPH

Light wire, ring eye hook for stonefly nymphs, etc. Bronzed. Diamond point. Sizes 6-16.

Kamasan

B160 TROUT MEDIUM SHORT SHANK

A 3x short shank hook suitable for midge and sedge pupae, 'spiders' and even as a wide gape dry fly hook. Bronzed. Sizes 6-16.

B170 TROUT MEDIUM TRADITIONAL

Popular, standard wire Sproat bend wet fly hook. Bronzed. Sizes 2-16.

B175 TROUT HEAVY TRADITIONAL

Widely used, strong wire, Sproat bend wet fly hook. Characterised by Kamasan's fairly long conical point and slim barb, this heavy hook is very sharp. The thicker gauge wire also has less tendency to tear out of soft-mouthed fish, such as seatrout. Bronzed. Sizes 2-16.

B200 DEEPWATER NYMPH

Strong heavy gauge, high carbon steel wire. 2x long forged bend. A useful hook for steelhead and large trout nymphs. The gape is quite narrow in the smallest sizes. Bronzed. Sizes 6-16.

Mustad

80050BR Forged, knife edge point, chemically sharpened, austempered, micro barb, ball eye, bronzed.Sizes 6-22.

80150BR Swimming Nymph Forged, knife edge point, chemically sharpened, austempered, micro barb, shank bent up 45 degrees, ringed, bronzed. 8-16.

80200BR Forged, knife edge point, chemically sharpened, austempered, micro barb, reversed, 2x strong, turned down 30 degree ball eye, bronzed. Sizes 6-18.

37160 Wide gape, offset point, ball eye, slightly reversed, standard wire, standard length. A popular Caddis hook. Bronzed. Sizes 1/0-20.

9671 Forged, round bend, down eye, standard wire, 2x long. Standard light nymph hook. Bronzed 2-16.

9672 Forged, round bend, down eye, standard weight wire, 3x long. (3x long version of 9671). Bronzed. Sizes 2-16.

Partridge

HA1 CAPTAIN HAMILTON NYMPH

Basic 2x long nymph hook (also suitable for shorter streamers, dry sedges and mayflies). Forged bend. Bronzed. Sizes 2-18.

K12ST LONG SHANK SEDGE/CADDIS

Curved shank sedge pupa/emerger hook. Straight eye.

Bronzed. Sizes 8-22. Also in Grey Shadow finish, code GRS 12ST.

GRS 7MMB JARDINE LIVING SEDGE/CADDIS

A graceful curved shank hook, similar to GRS 12T, but with gentle up eye,in Grey Shadow finish. Sizes 10-20.

SH2 STRONGHOLD NYMPH

Strong wire nymph hooks. Grey Shadow finish. Sizes 8-16.

K4A JOHN VENIARD GRUB/SHRIMP

Curved shank, offset bend hook for 'grubs' and shrimp patterns. Bronzed. Sizes 8-18.

K14ST OLIVER EDWARDS NYMPH/EMERGER

Specially designed for small nymphs and emergers. Straight eye. Silver finish. Sizes 6-20.

H3ST DRAPER FLAT BODIED NYMPH

A special hook, with the shank doubled back on itself and brazed, to form an exaggerated shaped 'loop'. The design permits imitations of markedly wide, dorso-ventrally compressed creatures, notably large stonefly nymphs. Bronzed. Sizes 6-16.

K6ST TAFF PRICE SWIMMING NYMPH HOOK

Similar to the Tiemco 'swimming nymph' design, with a long double curved shank, used to impart a swimming movement to leeches, damselfly nymphs, etc. Straight eye. Bronzed. Sizes 8-14.

Tiemco

TMC 2487 For shrimp and caddis pupae. Down-eye. 2x wide, 2x short. Fine wire. Bronze finish. Sizes 10-22.

TMC 2457 Heavy wire shrimp and caddis pupa hook. Down-eye, 2x wide, 2x short, 2x heavy. Bronzed. Sizes 6-18.

TMC 200R Nymph and dry fly. Straight eye, 3x long, standard wire. Semi-dropped point. Forged. Bronzed. Sizes 4-22.

TMC 2312 Hopper and terrestrial hook. Straight eye. 2x long, slightly humped shank. Forged fine wire. Bronzed. Sizes 6-16.

TMC 2302 Terrestrial hook, with slightly humped shank. Down-eye, 2x long. Forged standard wire. Bronzed. Sizes 6-16.

TMC 400T Swimming nymph design, with wavy shank. Straight eye, forged fine wire. Bronzed. Sizes 8-14.

TMC 5262

Extra strong, 2x long hook for nymphs and short streamers. Down-eye. Forged 'Perfect' bend. Bronzed. Sizes 2-18.

TMC 5263

3x long version of previous hook, for nymphs and streamers. Down-eye. Forged 'Perfect' bend. Bronzed. Sizes 2-18.

SALMON, SEATROUT & STEELHEAD HOOKS

Daiichi

2050 ALEC JACKSON SPEY
Elegant 'Spey' bend fly hooks, designed by Alec Jackson. Curved shank and tapered loop up-eye. Forged. Colours: bronze, blue, black, nickel and gold. Sizes 11/2-7. Black only in size 7.

2131 BOB VEVERKA CLASSIC SALMON
Slightly curved shank with tapered looped up-eye. Round wire (un-forged). Colours: black, gold and blue. Sizes 2-12.

2151 CURVED SHANK SALMON
Tapered loop straight eye. Forged. Used for salmon and steelhead flies. Black finish. Sizes 2-10.

2161 CURVED SHANK SALMON
As 2151 but with up-eye. Sizes 1-2.

2421 MULTI USE SALMON/STEELHEAD
Tapered loop up-eye, forged fly hooks for salmon and steelhead low water and dry fly patterns. Black. Sizes 2-12.

2441 TRADITIONAL SALMON/STEELHEAD
Tapered loop up-eye, 1x strong, forged. Black finish. Sizes 2/0-8.

2451 SHORT SHANK SALMON/STEELHEAD
O'Shaughnessy bend, straight eye hooks. Used for salmon and steelhead flies; salmon 'trailer' flies; bass and tube flies. Black finish. Sizes 4/0-8.

2550 OCTOPUS SALMON HOOK
Beak bend, up-eye, short shank, reversed. Used for 'egg' flies, etc. Available in colours: bronze, nickel, red and stainless steel. Sizes 2-6.

4250 SALMON EGG HOOK
Up-eye, short shank, forged. Reversed bend. Available in colours: red, bronze or gold. 4-14.

7131 DOUBLE SALMON HOOK
Forged, Limerick bend, up-eye double salmon hooks. Black finish. Sizes 4-12.

Eagle Claw/Wright & McGill

D1197 SALMON/STEELHEAD FLY HOOK
Extra strong, down-eye salmon/steelhead hook. Used for both wet and dry patterns. 'Diamond' pointed. Sizes 1-8. Available in colours: D1197B - bronze; D1197N - nickel; D1197G - gold.

Kamasan

B380 LOW WATER SALMON TREBLE
A low water, treble fly hook, excellent in the smaller sizes for seatrout patterns. Forged turned up-eye. Black Japanned finish. Sizes 4-16.

B990 SALMON TUBE FLY TREBLE
Traditional round bend treble hook, with a neat eye designed specifically for use with tube flies. Bronze Sizes 2-14.

B290 DEEP WATER SALMON DOUBLE
An extra strong, heavy wire double hook for salmon or steelhead. Tapered looped up-eye. Black finish. Sizes 2/0-2.

B208 LOW WATER SALMON DOUBLE
A 'low water' salmon or steelhead double fly hook. Tapered, looped up-eye. Forged. Black finish. Sizes 4-10.

B180 LOW WATER SALMON SINGLE
Traditional single 'low water' hook. Tapered, looped up-eye. Forged. Black finish. Sizes 4-10.

B190 DEEP WATER SALMON SINGLE
An extra strong, heavy wire salmon hook for deep water. Tapered, looped up-eye. Forged. Black finish. Sizes 2/0-2.

Mustad

80500BL Salmon fly hook, knife edge point, chemically sharpened, austempered, forged, turned up tapered looped eye. Black finish. Sizes 3/0-10.

80501BL Salmon fly hook, knife edge point, chemically sharpened, austempered, forged, turned down tapered looped eye. Black finish. Sizes 3/0-10.

80525BL Double salmon fly hook, chemically sharpened, austempered, forged, brazed turned up-eye. Black. Sizes 2-10.

80526BL Double salmon fly hook. Like 80525BL (above), but down-eye. Sizes 2-10.

80550BL Treble salmon fly hook, chemically sharpened, austempered, forged, micro barb, turned down-eye. Black. Sizes 1/0-4.

Partridge

M SINGLE SALMON
Heavyweight forged salmon irons for traditional salmon, steelhead and seatrout flies. Looped up-eye. Black finish. Sizes 5/0-10.

N SINGLE LOW WATER
Medium/light wire, longer shanked 'low water' hook for salmon, steelhead and seatrout patterns. Looped up-eye. Black finish. Sizes 8/0-10.

01 SINGLE WILSON
Famous lightweight hook for salmon and seatrout extreme 'low water' and dry patterns. Looped upeye. Black finish. Sizes 2-16.

02 DOUBLE WILSON HOOK
Double version of the Single Wilson (01).

CS10/2 BARTLEET SUPREME
A shorter and heavier version of the traditional Bartleet hooks, used for salmon and steelhead. Looped up-eye, with elegant curved shank and 'out point'. Black finish. Sizes 1/0-10.

CS10/1 BARTLEET TRADITIONAL
A graceful and effective hook for salmon and steelhead. Elegant curved shank, with Dublin 'out point'. Looped up-eye. Black finish. Sizes 3/0-10.

P DOUBLE SALMON HOOK
A double version of the single salmon iron (Code M). For heavyweight salmon and steelhead flies. Up-eyed. Black finish. Sizes 2-12.

CS6 ADLINGTON & HUTCHINSON CLASSIC SALMON

Blind eye (eyeless) hooks of traditional patterns for tying 'authentic' reproductions of traditional, gut-eye salmon patterns. Dublin point, tapered 'blind eye'. Black finish. Sizes 3/0-2/0.

CS 42 MW BOMBER
Designed for Bomber flies with a bronzed finish. Really a down-eye version of the Single Low Water. Sizes 2.6,4.

Q1 DOUBLE LOW WATER
Double version of the single low water hooks (code N), for medium weight salmon and steelhead flies. Sizes 3/0-12.

X2B LONG SHANK SALMON FLY TREBLE HOOK
Long shank, out point treble hooks. Black finish. Sizes 2-16.

X3BL NEEDLE EYE TUBE FLY TREBLE HOOK
Out point treble hooks with an oval 'needle' eye to fit snugly into the flexible link tube of a tube fly. Black finish. Sizes 2-12.

X3S1 As X3BL but silvered finish.

Tiemco

TMC 7999 Salmon/steelhead wet fly hook. Tapered, looped up-eye. Forged heavy wire. Black finish. Sizes 2/0-12.

TMC 7989 Salmon/steelhead dry fly hook. Tapered, looped up-eye. Forged light wire. Black finish. Sizes 2-8.

TMC 105 Egg fly hook. Straight eye, 7x short, 2x strong wire, reversed bend. Bronze. Sizes 4-10.

TMC 800B Steelhead/salmon hook. Straight eye, forged heavy wire. Semi-dropped point. Black finish. Sizes 1/0-8.

SALTWATER FLY HOOKS

Daiichi

2546 SALTWATER FLY
Stainless steel, forged O'Shaughnessy bend. Straight eye, ground needle point. Popular for bonefish and tarpon flies. Sizes 8/0-6.

Eagle Claw/Wright & McGill

O'SHAUGHNESSY SALTWATER HOOKS Ringed eye, forged hooks for all saltwater applications. Available in sizes 14/0-6, in the following variations:

Standard Eye
254 Sea Guard
254N Nickel
L254N Nickel 'Lazer'
254SS Stainless steel

Small Eye
250 Sea Guard,long shank
253 Nickel, long shank
L253 Nickel, long shank 'Lazer'
255 Nickel, 2x long
L255 Nickel, 2x long, 'Lazer'

Large Eye
354SS Stainless Steel

354Z Zinc plated

Open Eye
252 Sea Guard

DO67 BILLY PATE TARPON FLY HOOK
Regular wire, ring eye, straight point saltwater fly hooks. 'Sea Guard' finish. Sizes 5/0-6.

Gamakatsu

SP11-3L3H
Tin plated with a perfect bend,straight eye and a fine long cone point. Sizes 6/0-8.

Kamasan

B840 SALTWATER
Long shank Aberdeen hooks for bucktails and larger saltwater patterns (also popular for pike flies). Straight eye, medium wire. Black finish. Sizes 6/0-6.

Mustad

3407 O'Shaughnessy bend, forged ringed cadmium plated and tinned hook for improved corrosion protection,in sizes 8/0-8.

34007 O'Shaughnessy bend forged ringed stainless steel sizes 8/0 -8.

34039SS O'Shaughnessy bend, stainless steel hook with chemically sharpened needle point, and a slightly longer than standard shank. Sizes 2/0-4.

34005 O'Shaughnessy hook in stainless steel with shank bent up for 'bend back' flies. Forged, austempered stainless steel. Knife edge point. Sizes 5/0-1.

77660SS Extra strong tarpon hook, forged, stain-less steel, needle point, chemically sharpened, austempered. Sizes 4/0-1/0.

79666S Saltwater 'keel' fly hook, designed to swim bend up. Forged, stainless steel, knife edge. Sizes 1/0-6.

90233S Stainless steel popper hook, with kinked shank to prevent bodies from twisting. Knife edge. 2/0.

Partridge

CS51 HOMOSASSA TARPON
High carbon steel with bright tinned-silver finish. Sizes 5/0, 4/0 and 2/0 have been added to the popular original 3/0.

CS52 SEA PRINCE SALTWATER
Extra strong shiny silver stainless steel hook, with slight outpoint and straight tightly closed ball eye. Sizes 6/0, 4/0, 3/0, 2/0, 1/0, 2 and 4.

CS53 SEA LORD SALTWATER
A longer shank (about 3x) version of CS52. Sizes 4/0, 3/0, 2/0, 1/0, 1, 2, 4, 6.

CS 54 SALTWATER SHRIMP
Grey shadow finish with curved profile, which can also be used for shorter streamer patterns. Sizes 2-10.

CS11/1 GRS JS SEA STREAMER
Grey Shadow finished in sizes 2-10. Also has variants CS11/2 in stainless steel and CS11/3 also in stainless steel but extra strong, slightly longer and with a looped down eye.

Tiemco

TMC 511S 4x long shank, stainless steel hook for poppers and skipping bugs. The single 'kink' in the shank prevents glued on popper bodies from twisting round. Straight eye, 2x wide. Sizes 2/0, 1/0, 2, 6.

TMC 800S Strong stainless steel saltwater fly hook. Straight eye, heavy wire, semi-dropped point. Forged. Sizes 4/0-8.

TMC 811S Standard length, extra strong saltwater fly hook. Straight eye. Forged stainless steel. Sizes 4/0-8.

TMC 411S Straight eye, extra strong saltwater fly hook. Bend back design for 'upside down' patterns. Forged. Stainless steel. Sizes 3/0, 1/0, 4-8.

STREAMER AND LONG SHANK HOOKS.

Daiichi

1750 STRAIGHT-EYE STREAMER
Forged round bend, 4x long, 1x strong. For muddlers, Streamers, Zonkers. Bronze. Sizes 4-14.

1850 FLAT-EYE STREAMER
Forged round bend, 4x long, 1x strong. Used for 'free swimming' patterns. Bronze. Sizes 6-12.

2370 7x LONG STREAMER
Modified Limerick bend, tapered loop eye, 7x long shank, 3x heavy wire. Designed by Dick Talleur for classic streamer patterns (Grey Ghost, etc). Bronze. Sizes 6-10.

2461 MULTI-USE ABERDEEN
Straight eye, Aberdeen (round) bend, 3x long. Used for muddlers, zonkers, matuka patterns, bass flies, etc. Black finish. Sizes 6/0-6.

J101 STREAMER
Improved Limerick bend, tapered loop eye, 4x heavy wire. Black finish. Size 6.

J141 STREAMER
Improved Limerick bend, tapered loop eye. Black finish. Sizes 1-6.

J171 STREAMER
Improved Limerick bend, tapered loop, turned-down eye. 6x long, 1x heavy wire. Black finish. Sizes 1-2.

2220 DOWN-EYE STREAMER
Round bend, forged, 4x long, standard wire hook. For Muddlers, Zonkers, Woolly Buggers, etc. Bronze. Sizes 1-14.

2340 TRADITIONAL STREAMER
Limerick bend, down eye, 6x long, 1x strong. Used for traditional bucktail and streamer patterns. Bronze. Sizes 4-12.

Eagle Claw/Wright & McGill

DO58 STREAMER
Round bend, 3x long, regular wire, forged streamer hooks with 'Diamond point'. Bronze. Sizes 4-14

Kamasan

B830 STREAMER
A 2x long version of the popular B800. Forged strong wire, for medium streamers and large nymphs. Bronze. Sizes 2-16.

B820 LURE, NYMPH, MUDDLER HOOK
A straight eye, 4x long, forged hook, for streamers and wet flies. Bronze. Sizes 4-12.

B800 EXTRA LONG STREAMER HOOK
A general purpose hook for streamers and long bodied nymphs. 4x long, heavy wire, forged high carbon hook. Bronze. Sizes 4-14.

B810 EXTRA LONG LURE HOOK
A 4x long shank hook with a special 'cranked' shank, for tying upside down 'keel' type, weedless streamers. Useful for bass and pike patterns for use in weedy locations. Bronze. Sizes 6-14.

Mustad

38941 Sproat bend, tapered down eye, standard wire, 3x long. This is an excellent long nymph hook, and regarded as the standard for Muddler and Matuka patterns. Bronze. Sizes 2-16.

3665A Limerick bend, tapered down eye, standard wire. Standard shank length for size plus one half inch. Regarded as a standard among streamer hooks. Bronze. Sizes 2-12.

9575 Limerick bend, tapered looped down eye, standard wire. Standard length for hook size, plus one half inch. The same as the 3665A except for loop eye. Bronze. Sizes 2-12.

79580 Round bend, tapered down eye, standard wire, 4x long. Bronze. Sizes 2-14.

94720 Round bend, tapered down-eye, standard wire, 8x long. A very long shank hook suited to trolling streamer patterns. Bronze. Sizes 2-8.

Partridge

D4A BUCKTAIL/STREAMER
Long shank hook for general streamer and bucktail patterns. Down-eye. Bronze. Sizes 2-14.

GRS4A
The same patterns as D4A, but in Partridge's Grey Shadow 'Niflor' finish.

D3ST STRAIGHT EYE STREAMER
A general streamer hook (in smaller sizes also good for nymphs). Forged flat, wide gape bend. Bronze. Sizes 4-14.

D7A FINNISH STREAMER
Special hooks designed for large streamers for big brown trout in Finland. Very strong wire, with a special long point to give 'increased' holding area. Slightly turned down eye. Bronze. Sizes 2-8.

CS5 KEITH FULSHER THUNDER CREEK
Very strong long shank hooks, originally designed for the Thunder Creek series of flies. Straight ball eyed, heavy

RIGHT (clockwise from top left):Brown Partridge, Kiwi, Grey Partridge, Golden Pheasant (red body), Golden Pheasant (dyed blue), Golden Pheasant (natural), Cul de Canard, Golden Pheasant (yellow body). Centre top: French Partridge. Centre bottom: Jay.

wire. Dark blue finish. Sizes 4-6.

CS15 CARRIE STEVENS' STREAMER A very long (10x) shank, heavy wire hook for big trout and pike streamer patterns. Looped down-eye. Bronze. Sizes 2/0-4.

Tiemco

TMC 300 Streamer hook. Down-eye, 6x long, heavy wire. Forged. Bronze. Sizes 2-14.

TMC 700 Streamer and wet fly hook. Down-eye, heavy wire. Forged Limerick bend. Semi-dropped point. Black finish. Sizes 1/0-10.

TMC 9394 Streamer hook. Straight eye, 4x long, 3x heavy wire. Nickel plated finish. Sizes 2-10.

TMC 9395 Same as TMC 9394, but bronze finish.

TAG HOOKS

A hook with another loop where the point would be, to 'touch and go' causing no penetration to the fish. Available from dealers in Partridge Hooks under the name of Bramley/Betts Tag Hook.

CS2001 Dry Fly
CS2002 Long Shank
CS2003 Nymph

WET FLY HOOKS

Daiichi

1510 GLO BUG

Sproat bend, down-eye, 3x short. Used for 'Glo-bug egg' patterns and spiders. Bronze. Sizes 6-18.

1530 HEAVY WET FLY

Sproat bend, down-eye, 1x short. For short bodied wet flies, nymphs and steelhead patterns. Bronze. Sizes 4-16.

1550 STANDARD WET FLY

Sproat bend, down-eye. For traditional wet fly patterns. Bronze. Sizes 2-18.

Kamasan

B405 WET/NYMPH

1x short shank hook for traditional wet flies (also a useful strong dry fly hook). Lightly forged medium wire. Bronze. Sizes 8-20.

B270 TROUT DOUBLE

A strong wire double hook for large trout and seatrout. The extra weight of the double bend makes this hook ideal for anchor point flies in blustery conditions. Bronze. Sizes 6-14.

B100 SHRIMP & BUZZER

1x short shank, special loop bend, for realistically curved shrimp and 'buzzer' patterns, when dressed round the bend. Forged, offset bend. Bronze. 10-16.

B100G

Gilt finish version of model B100.

Partridge

L2A CAPTAIN HAMILTON

The ideal hook for all types of wet fly and nymph. Forged 'Hamilton' bend. Bronze. Sizes 6-16.

GRS 2A is L2A in Partridge's Grey Shadow ('Niflor') finish. Sizes 6-16.

G3A SPROAT FORGED WET FLY

Traditional strong, wet fly and nymph hooks. Forged 'Sproat' bend. Bronze. Sizes 6-16.

J1A LIMERICK

Traditional strong wet fly hook with Limerick bend. Bronze. Sizes 4-16.

MM1B McHAFFIE MASTER'S WET FLY

For traditional trout wet flies. Up-eye, with special 'Dublin' point. This is a particularly elegant hook that is perfect for display flies. Black finish. Sizes 2-12.

R3A OUTPOINT DOUBLE

The correct hook for 'wee doubles'. Down-eye, out-point. For trout and small sea trout flies. Bronze. Sizes 10-18.

Tiemco

TMC 3769

Wet fly and nymph hook. Down-eye, 2x heavy wire. Sproat bend. Bronze. Sizes 6-18.

TMC 3761

Wet fly and nymph hook. Down-eye, 1x long shank, 2x heavy wire. Sproat bend. Bronze. Sizes 2-20.

Directories of Suppliers

Suppliers listed in text

The following suppliers have been mentioned in the preceding pages of this book. They all provide a direct mail service, many have detailed catalogues listing the various products they can supply. Orvis have a number of company shops as well as full dealerships in various countries. For this reason, we have referred to them under a distinct international heading (*INT*). The Directory contains details of these Orvis outlets, listed by country. For information on the international dialing codes for all these suppliers see page 171.

For reasons of space some suppliers' names featured in the text have had to be given in abbreviated form. Here are the acronyms used and the corresponding names of the companies. Full details can be found in the following pages.
AA - AA Pro Shop, BT - BT's Fly Fishing Products, BR - Blue Ribbon, EAT - English Angling Trappings, MM - Montana's Master Angler, RE - River's Edge.

ARGENTINA

Hector D. Trape Fly Fishing Supplies
Corrientes 216, 2000 Rosario.
Tel 54-41-482220
Fax 54-41-214075
Orvis dealer

AUSTRALIA

Alpine Angler
Snowy Mountains Highway,
Cooma West,
NSW 2360.
Tel 64-525538
Fax 64-525539

CANADA

Artista Custom Frame Shoppe
132 Adrianno Crescent, Woodbridge,
Ontario L4L 5R5
Tel 905-850-7129
Fax 905-264-0355

Country Pleasures
Bow River Shop 570,
10816 MacLeod Trail Street,
Calgary, Alberta T2J 5N8.
Tel 403-271-1016
Orvis dealer

Grand River Troutfitters Ltd
790 Tower Street S.Fergus,
Ontario N1M 2RE.
Tel 519-787-4359
Orvis dealer

Howard's Super-Natural Hackle
Box 1, Site 5, R.R.2, Didsbury AB T0M 0W0.
Tel 403-335-9155
Fax 403-335-9155

L'Ami du Moucheur Inc.
7390 Rue Notre-Dame,
Trois-Rivières-Quest, Quebec G9B 1L8.
Tel 819-377-4367
Fax 819-377-4367

La Boutique Salmo
Nature Ltee,110 McGill Street, Local 101,
Montreal, Quebec HY2Y 2EF
Tel 514-871-8447
Orvis dealer

La Maison du Moucheur
1515 Boulevard Hamel, Quest,
Quebec QC G1N 3Y7.
Tel 418-681-6100
Orvis dealer

Ruddick's Fly Shop Ltd
3726 Canada Way, Burnaby, Vancouver,
British Columbia V5G 1G5.
Tel 604-434-2420
604-681-3747
Orvis dealer

CHILE

Gray Fly Fishing Supplies
Roberto Gray, San Francisco 447,
PO Box 474, Puerto Varas.
Tel 65-232496
Fax 65-232496
Orvis dealer

CZECH REPUBLIC

Fishing Sport / Siman Ltd
Jan Siman, Kpt. Jarose 1,
307 07 Plzen.
Tel 019-72-42207
Fax 019-72-42207

FINLAND

Perhokellari
Minna Canthin katu 3 C,
33230 Tampere.
Tel 358-31-7080
Fax 358-31-222-7089
Orvis dealer

GERMANY

Fly Fishing Brinkhoff
Auf der Liet 1,
D-59519 Mohnesee-Delecke.
Tel 02924-637
Fax 02924-332

and at:
Maienbeeck 42, 24576 Bad Bramstedt.
Tel 04192-4702
Fax 04192-85377

and at:
Hirblinger Strasse 6, 86154 Augsberg.
Tel 0821-425511
Fax 0821-426227

ITALY

Orvis Shop of Italy
Via Saccarelli 16,10144 Torino.
Tel 011-480023
Fax 011-480023

LUXEMBOURG

Articles de Peche
16 Rue de la Montagne, BP 143,
L-6470 Echternach.
Tel 352-72356
Fax 352-726085

JAPAN

Sawada's Inc. / Pro-Shop Sawada
3-13-4 Minamicho, Kokubunji, Tokyo 185.
Tel 423-21-0836
Fax 423-21-0983

NETHERLANDS

Kelson Collection
Rijksweg Zuid 142, 6161 BT Geleen.
Tel 046-4749197
Fax 046-4757774

NORWAY

Rakkelhanen Jagt Fiske
Og Zoo Senter, Lietorvet, 3717 Skien, Norge.
Tel 35 52 1064
Fax 35 52 1064

Lennart Bergqvist Flugfiske
Sorumsgate 28, N-2000 Lillestrom, Norge.
Tel 63 80 11 60
Fax 63 80 11 61

SWEDEN

Lennart Bergvist Flugfiske
Box 2014, S-433 02 Partille.
Tel 31-26-9890
Fax 31-26-98-70

Fiske & Fiskar
Box 5194, 200 70 Malmo.
Tel 040-260677
Orvis dealer

SWITZERLAND

A&H Hebeisen
Schaffauserstrasse 514, CH-8052 Zurich.
Tel 1-301-22-21
Fax 1-302-06-38

UNITED KINGDOM

Anglian Water Tackle Shops
Rutland Water Fishing Lodge, Edith Weston,
Oakham, Leices LE15 8HD.
Tel 01780 - 721999
Fax 01780-720993

Angling Pursuits
Peter Scott, 315 Keel Avenue,
Old Drumchapel, Glasgow G15 6PB.
Tel 0141-941-2322
Fax 0141-941-2322

Beadworks / The Bead Shop
43 Neal Street, Covent Garden,
London WC2H 9PJ.
Tel 0171-240-0931

D.J. Hackle
Manbys Farm,
Oaksey, Malmesbury,
Wiltshire SN16 9TG.
Tel 01666-577399
Fax 01666-577399

Hobby Horse
15-17 Langton Street,
London SW10 OJL.
Tel 0171-351-6951
Fax 0171-352-6193

Lathkill Tackle
Unity Complex, Dale Road North,
Darley Dale, Matlock,
Derbyshire, DE4 2HX.
Tel. 01629 735101
Fax 01629 735101

McHardys of Carlisle
South Henry Street, Carlisle,
Cumbria, CA1 1SF.
Tel 01228-23988
Fax 01228-514711

Peter Masters
12 Werdale Road, Chandlers Ford,
Eastleigh, Hampshire SO53 3BH.
Tel 01703 254249

Niche Products
1 White Mead,
Broomfield, Chelmsford,
Essex CM1 7YB.
Tel 01245 442041
Fax 01245-442041

John Norris
21 Victoria Road, Penrith,
Cumbria, CA11 8HP.
Tel 01768-864211
Fax 01768-890476

K.F. Odehames Precision Engineers
Crow Mill, Countesthorpe Road,
South Wigston, Leicester LE18 LPG.
Tel 0116-2774231

Orvis (Harrogate)
17 Parliament Street, Harrogate, North Yorkshire
HG1 2QU.
Tel 01423-561354

Orvis (London)
27 Sackville Street, London W1X 1DA.
Tel 0171-494-2660

Orvis (Stockbridge)
The Mill, Nether Wallop, Stockbridge,

Hampshire, SO20 8ES.
Tel 01264-781-212 or 01264-810-017
Fax 01264 781882

Rooksbury Mill
Rooksbury Road, Andover,
Hampshire SP10 2LR.
Tel 01264-352921

Tom C. Saville Ltd
Unit 7, Salisbury Square, Middleton Street,
off Ilkeston Road, Radford,
Nottingham NG7 2AB.
Tel 0115-978-4248
Fax 0115-942-0004

Ellis Slater
47 Bridgecross Road, Chase Terrace,
Burntwood, Staffs WS7 8BU.
Tel 01543-671377

Scotia Complete
136 Victoria Street, Dyce,
Aberdeen AD2 0BE.
Tel 01224 722253
Fax 01224 722253

Sparton Fishing Tackle
Unit 2, Fields Farm Road, Long Eaton,
Notts NG10 3FZ.
Tel 0115-946-3572
Fax 0115-946-3571

Sportfish
Winforton, Nr. Hereford, HR3 6EB.
Tel. 01544 327111
Fax. 01544 327093
Mail order catalogue

Walkers of Trowell
Nottingham Road, Trowell Nottingham NG9 3PA.
Tel 0115-930-1816
0115-930-7798
Fax 0115-944-0898

Watercraft Products
899 Harrogate Road, Greengates,
Bradford BD10 0QY.
Tel 01274-620173
Fax 01484-421559

Davy Wotton
Heron House, Station Road,
Griffithstown, Pontypool, Gwent NP4 5ES.
Tel 01495-762911
Fax 01495-762911

UNITED STATES

AA Pro Shop
RD 1, Whitehaven, PA 18661.
Tel 800-443-8119
Fax 717-443-9996

Angler's Choice
PO Box 466, Custer, WA 98240.
Tel 360-366-5894
Fax 360-366-5894

Dan Bailey's Fly Shop
PO Box 1019, Livingstone, MT 59047.
Tel 406-222-1673
Fax 406 222 8450

Beadworks
139 Washington Street,
South Norwalk, CT 06854.
Tel 203-852-9194
Fax 203-852-9034

349 Newbury Street
Boston MA 02115.
Tel 617-247-7227
Fax 617-247-2322

Harvard Square, 23 Church Street,
Cambridge MA 02138.
Tel 617-868-9777
Fax 617-868-9229

225 South Street, Philadelphia, PA 19147.
Tel 215-413-2323
Fax 215-413-2211

290 Thayer Street, Providence, RI 02906.
Tel 401-861-4540
Fax 401-861-6670

Brick Market
227 Goddard Row, Newport, RI 02840.
Tel 401-846-1440
Fax 401-849-0110

7632 Campbell Road 309, Dallas TX 75248.
Tel 214-931-1899
Fax 214-931-1883

Stockyards Station, 140 East Exchange Avenue,
Fort Worth, TX 76106.
Tel 817-625-2323
Fax 817-232-4331

Blue Ribbon Flies
PO Box 1037, West Yellowstone, MT 59758.
Tel. 406 646 7642
Fax 406-646-9045

Brandt, Dave
R.D.4, Box 444, Oneonta NY 13820
Tel 607-433-2924

BT's Fly Fishing Products
Al & Gretchen Beatty, 3020 Secor Avenue,
Bozeman, MT 59715-6150.
Tel 406-585-0745
Fax 406-585-6150

Cabela's
812 13th Avenue, Sidney, Nebraska 69160.
Toll Free 800 237 4444
Fax 308 254 2200

Collins Hackle Farm
436 Kinner Hill Road, Dept FT,
Pine City NY 14871.
Tel 607-734-1765

Custom Aquatics
1542 Youngfield Street,
Contract Station No.27, PO Box 312,
Lakewood, CO 80215.
Tel 303 238 3612

D&T Enterprises
20518 Meadow Lake Road, Dept. FT,
Snohomish, WA 98290.
Tel 360-805-9231

E.A.T. (English Angling Trappings)
PO Box 8885, New Fairfield, CT 06812.
Tel 203 746 4121
Fax 203 746 1348

Enrico's
Enrico Puglisi Ltd, 249-17 37th Avenue,
New York 11363.
Tel 718-631-7869

Evets & Co
5825 Dover Street, Oakland CA 94609.
Tel 510-652-9387

Fishing for Ideas
Thomas Potter, 9 Woodland Road,
Sewickley, PA 15143.
Tel 412-741-7622
Fax 412-741-7713

Fly & Field
560 Crescent Boulevard,
Glen Ellyn, IL 60137.
Tel 800-328-9753

Fly Dye
PO Box 14258, E. Providence, RI 02914.
Tel 401-434-3300

Fly-Rite Inc.
7421 S. Beyer, Dept. FT,
Frankenmuth, MI 48734.
Tel 517-652-9869
Fax 517-652-2996

George Roberts Inc.
4335 Beck, St Louis MO 63116.
Tel 314-773-4949
Fax 314-752-2114

H. Gerstner & Sons
20 Cincinnati Street, Dayton
OH 45407.
Tel 513-228-1662

Goodwin Manufacturing Co
PO Box 378, Luck, WI 54853.
Tel 715-472-2800 or 800-282-5267
Fax 715-472-2810

Gorilla & Sons
PO Box 2309, Bellingham WA 98227.
Tel 360-738-1761 or 800-246-7455
Fax 800-647-8801

Hook & Hackle Co
7 Kaycee Loop Road, Plattsburgh, NY 12901.
Tel 518-561-5893
Fax 518-561-0336

ABOVE Some natural materials from Norway, including Grouse tail, Capercaillie (female tail), Reindeer hair, Moose mane, Roe deer, Ptarmigan wing.

Hunter's Angling Supplies Inc
Central Square, Box 300, New Boston,
NH 03070.
Tel 603-487-3388
Fax 603-487-3939

JW Outfitters
169 Balboa Street, San Marcos,
CA 92069.
Tel 619-471-2171
Fax 619-471-1719

Kaufmann's Streamborn Inc
PO Box 23032, Portland,
OR 97281-3032.
Tel 503-639-6400
Fax 503-684-7025

King Tool
5350 Love Lane, Bozeman
MT 59715.
Tel 406-586-1541
Fax 406-585-9028

Longhorn Flies & Supplies
Jeff Mack, Route 4, Box 139A,
Mckinney TX 75070.
Tel 214-562-9542
Fax 214-542-4558

Magni Lite Manufacturing Inc
3741 NE 163rd Street, Suite 276,
Miami FL 33160.
Tel 305-682-0883 or 305-944-7565
Fax 305-944-8343

Bob Marriott's Flyfishing Store
2700 W. Orangethorpe, Fullerton, CA 92633.
Tel 714 525 1827
Fax 714 525 5783

Matthias
PO Box 673, Lansdale PA 19446
Tel 215-679-8988

MFD Enterprises
222 Sidney Baker South, Suite 205,
Kerrville, TX 98028.
Tel 800-210-6662

Montana's Master Angler
Tom Travis
PO Box 1320, 107 South Main Street,
Livingston, MT 59047.
Tel 406-222-9434
Fax 406-222-9433

Mountain Shadowbox Company
PO Box 339-A, Glide, OR 97443.
Tel 503-496-0343

Norlander Company
PO Box 926, Kelso, WA 98626.
Tel 360-636-2525
Fax 360 636 2558

Perry Design
7401 Zircon Drive SW, Tacoma, WA 98498.
Tel 206-582-1555

Pockit Sports Co
7235 Syracuse Drive, Dallas, Texas 75214.
Tel 214-553-1845
Fax 214-553-0347

Rainy's Flies and Supplies
690 North 100 East, Logan,
UT 84321.
Tel 801 753 6766
Fax 801 753 9155

River's Edge
Dave Corcoran, 2012 North 7th Avenue,
Bozeman, MT59715.
Tel 406-586-5373
Fax 406-586-5393

Sawdust & Stitches
Dept FT, 9 Timber Lane,
New Cumberland, PA 17070.
Tel 717-774-3893
Fax 717-774-5280

Sespe Supplies
925 A Calle Puerto Vallarta, Santa Barbara,
California 93103.
Tel 805-966-7263

Shadowcraft Limited
14 Whichita Road, Medfield, MA 02052-2931.
Tel 508-359-4333

Small Fry Materials and Accessories
Mike Martinek,
3 Florence Street, Franklin, MA 02038.
Tel 508-528-6640

Temple Fork Outfitters
435 East Boulevard, Logan, UT 84321.
Tel 801-753-1823
Fax 801-752-4074

Whitetail Fly Tieing Supplies
6179 Barnstable Drive, Toledo, OH 43613.
Tel 419-474-2348
Fax 419-474-2348

Worrywood Fishing Products
PO Box 91943, Tucson, AZ 85752-1943.
Tel 520-744-0011
Fax 520-744-0011

Davy Wotton
1098 Randville Drive,
Palatine, Illinois 60067.
Tel 847-359-0297
Fax 847-359-0297

Other Retail Suppliers

ARGENTINA

Federico Prato Fly Shop
Ob. Pozo y Silva 1979, Bo. Villa Cabrera,
Cordoba 5009.
Tel 51-805810

S.A. Angel Baraldo C.I.A.
Tacuari 32, Buenos Aires 1071.
Tel 342-7744
342-3786
342-4233
Fax 334-7631

AUSTRALIA

Aus Fly
182 Crawford Street, Queanbeyan NSW 2620.
Tel 6-299-4846

Australian Fly Fisherman
583 Lygon Street, Carlton North, Victoria 3054.
Tel 3-9388-1942
Fax 3-9388-2009

Australian Fly Fisherman
148 Bayswater Road, Rushcutters Bay
NSW 2011.
Tel 2-360-2830
Fax 2-331-2149

Cairns Fly Fishing Supplies
PO Box 431 Gordonvale, Queensland 4865.
Tel 70-562-094
Fax 70-563-595

Compleat Angler
19 McKillop Street, Melbourne.
Tel 3-9670-2518

702 Station Street, Box Hill.
Tel 3-9890-7439-

132 Walker Street, Dandenong.
Tel 3-9794-9397

92a Maroondah Highway, Ringwood.
Tel. 3-9870-7792

915 Nepean Highway, Moorabin.
Tel 3-9557-8011

Dymock's Bld, 3rd Floor, 428 George Street,
Sydney.
Tel 2-241-2080

938 Woodville Road, Villawood.
Tel 2-724-7474

Bridge Bros, 142-146 Elizabeth Street, Hobart.
Tel 02-343-791

Compleat Flyfisher
Tavistock House,
381 Flinders Lane, Melbourne 3000.
Tel 3-9621-1246
Fax 3-9621-1247

Harbord Tackle Supply
16c Lawrence Street, Harbord NSW.
Tel 2-939-1991

JV Fly Shack (JV Marine Motors)
1347 North Road, South Oakleigh, Victoria 3167.
Tel 3-95-441377
Fax 3-95-440942

Man from Tumut River
(Ron Bowden)
58 Wynyard Street, Tumut NSW 2720.
Tel 69-471100

Frank O'Reilly's Gun & Rod Shop
869-871 High Street, Thornbury, Victoria 3071.
Tel 3-480-3366
Fax 3-480-3186

Tas Fly & Tackle
131 Gilbert Street, Latrobe , Tasmania 7307.
Tel 04-261188
Fax 04-261188

Trout on the Wildside
103 River Road, Ambleside, East Devonport, 7310
Tasmania.
Tel 04-270997
Fax 04-248833

AUSTRIA

Roman Moser
Kuferzeile 19, A-4810 Gmunden.
Tel 07612-5686
Fax 07612-5633

Holler
A-4810 Gmunden,
Kammerhof.
Tel 07612-3308

BELGIUM

Hero-Jacht & Vliegvisshop
Leuvensestraat 134, 3300 Tienen.
Tel 168-14581

N.V. Janssen Sport
Oude Bevelsesteenweg 10, 2508 Kessel (bij Lier).
Tel 34801254
Fax 34893259

CANADA

Atelier de Peche
(Richard Verret), 104 Proulx Avenue, Vanier,
Quebec G1M 1W4
Tel 418-688-7590
Fax 418-527-5565

Cowichan Fly & Tackle
211-1531 Cedar Hill X Road, Victoria,
British Columbia V8P 2P3.
Tel 604-721-4665

W.W. Doak
331 Main Street
PO Box 95,
Doaktown, New Brunswick, EOC 1GO.
Tel 506 365 7828
Fax 506 365 7762

Hook & Hackle
Box 6, Lethbridge,
Alberta T1J 3Y3.
Tel 403 328 7400
Fax: 403 328 7577

Learning to Fly
407-A Ogilvie Street, Whitehorse, Yukon
Territories YIA 2S5.
Tel 403-668-3597

Michael & Young Flyshop
10484 137 Street, Surrey BC V3T 4H5.
Tel 604-588-2833

Pollack Sporting Goods
337 Queen Street E,
Toronto, Ontario M5A 1S9
Tel 416-363-1095
Fax 416-363-1096

Russell Sporting Goods
8228 MacCleod Trail, Calgary, Alberta T2H 2B5.
Tel 403-258-0545

Serge Boulard Inc.
302 Rivard, Joliette, Quebec, J6E 6T8.

Smallman's Fly Shop
220 First Street, Cochrane, Alberta T0L 0W0.
Tel 403-932-2122

Streamside Fly & Tackle
20270 Industrial Avenue 106, Langley,
British Columbia V3A 4K7.
Tel 604-532-0405

Macaw feathers (from left): centre tail sections (red), wing quill, side tail, main wing quill. See Feathers, pages 11-25.

CHILE

Andean Trout Angler
AV. Alonso de Cordova, 406 Vitacura, Santiago
Tel 2-207-0447

DENMARK

Fiskegrij, J.F.
Saksen C2 2nd Th MI, Taastrup, DK2 630

Go Fishing
Brogade 6-8, DK-5000 Odense C.
Tel 66-12 1500
Fax 66-14 0026

Steff's Fluebinding
Skjolevaenget 14, 83100 Tranbjerg

Korsholm
Ostergade 36-42, 6900 Skjern,
Tel 97-35 0999

Fiskeri & Fritide
Rungstedvej 77, 2980 Rungsted kyst.
Tel 45-76 1012

Ostjsk Vabenhandel
Constantiavej 1, 8722 Hedensted.
Tel 75 89 05 00
Fax 75 89 07 00

FINLAND

Tampereen Kalastusvaline Oy
Hatanpaanualtatie 17, 33100 Tampere

Kalastin Oy
Et Hesperiakatu 12, 00100 Helsinki, Finland
Tel 4540 805 Fax 4540 855

FRANCE

Guy Plas
19320 Marcillac-La-Croisille

GERMANY

Angelcenter Karlsruhe
Gunther Fleckenstein, Sophienstrasse 232,
76185 Karlsruhe.
Tel 0721-553406

Angelsport-Center
Ostertor 7, 31134 Hildesheim.
Tel 05121-35477
Fax 05121-37737

Angler Shop Bruggen
Mundsburger Damm 44.
Tel 2-29-62-53

Angler Steg
Peter Hemmann,
Blumlage 85, 29221 Celle.
Tel 05141-21-4726
Fax 05141-21-4726

Ash Angel-Shop Hamm
Am Biegen 17,
35094 Lahntal-Gossfelden bei Marburg.
Tel 06423-7696
Fax 06423-4692

Flypoint by AKM
Hermann-Lingg Strasse 11, 80336 Munchen.
Tel 089-53-2480
Fax 089-53-28860

F. Gees Angelsport
Buttermarkt 5-7, 50667 Koln-Altstadt.
Tel 0221-258-1383
Fax 0221-258-1371

Rolfe Grimme
Postfach 1366, 37503 Osterode/Harz.
Tel 5522-2674
Fax 5522-2674

Nordwest-Flyfishing
M.Korth, Kanalstrasse Sud 62, 26629 Grobefehn.
Tel 04943-4129

Uwe Schwald-Flyfishing International
Heidelberger Strasse 30, D-68723 Schwetzingen
Tel 06202-10679

Steinsdorfer
Regensburger Strasse 38, 93333 Neustadt/Donau.
Tel 09445-1789
Fax 09445-7303

V.A.S. Angelgerate
Max-Eyth Strasse 2, D 71141 Steinenbronn.
Tel 07157-72766
Fax 07157-9654

ICELAND

Vesturrost Ltd
Box 8563, 128 Reykjavik.
Tel 116-770
Fax 181-3761

Litla Flugan
Laugarnesv. 74A, Reykjavik, Island.
Tel 553 1460
Fax 553 2642

ITALY

Francesco Palu
33030 Campoformido,
Via Silvio Pellico 44, Udine.

LUXEMBOURG

Fly Fishers Tackle Shop
Weiswampach 30 A, L-9990.
Tel 97225   Fax 979382

JAPAN

Anglers's Paradise
46-1 Nishiharashin-machi, Numata-shi,
Gunma 378.   Tel 278-23-0986

Blue Dun
YM Bldg 3F, 208-1 Tomuro, Atsugi-Shi,
Kanagawa Ken 243.
Tel 462-95-1315

Eastwood Fly Shop
29 Daikumachi, Hachinohe-Shi, Aomori-Ken 031.
Tel 178-22-0241

Jock Scott
142 Urisimamachi, Shizuoka Pref.
Tel 0545-53-3650

Thames
Nishi 11 choume, Kita 4 jou, chuuouku,
Sapporo City.
Tel 011-271-6070

Grasshopper
2-3-4 Kyomatibori, nishiku, Osaka City
Tel 06-441-7275

NETHERLANDS

Hengelsport Arnhem,
Broerenstraat 18, 6811 EB Arnhem.
Tel 026-3515615
Fax 026-4439800

Hengelsport Handy Fish
Kennemerstraatweg 127, 1851 BC Heiloo
Tel 072-5336961
Hengelsport Martin
Burg. Baumanniaan 95-97,
3043 AG Rotterdam-Overscshie.
Tel 010-437-1615

Otter Hengelsport
Hagelstraat 9, 8011 RN Zwolle.
Tel 038-4216825

P&S Hengelsport
Spaarnwouderstraat 134, 2011 AH Haarlem.
Tel 023-5333768
Fax 023-5354133

Rien Rothfusz Hengelsport
Beestenmarkt 11, 2611 GA Delft.
Tel 015-125898
Fax 015-143996

NEW ZEALAND

Composite Developments (NZ Ltd)
PO Box 100063, North Shore Mail Centre,
Auckland 10.

Tel 9-4159915
Fax 9-4159965

Just Fishin'
25 Teed Street, Newmarket, Auckland
Tel 9-52-49427
Fax 9-52-40227

Raised Hackle
123 Taupehi Road, Turangi
Tel 7-386-0374
Fax 7-386-7917

Smart Marine
123 Beaumont Street,
Westhaven, Auckland
Tel 9-358-2850
Fax 9-358-1742

61 Chapel Street, Tauranga
Tel 7-578-8088
Fax 7-578-8087

Sporting Life
Town Centre, Turangi
Tel 7-386-8996
Fax 7-386-6559

Tisdalls
Queen Street, Auckland.
Tel 9-379-0254
Fax 9-303-4321

Broadway, Palmerston North.
Tel 6-358-6377

Main Street, Upper Hutt.
Tel 4-528-5244

Willis Street, Wellington.
Tel 4-472-0485

NORWAY

Classic Country Sports
Verkseir Furulunds,
Vei 47, Postboks 12, Alnabru, N-0614, Oslo.
Tel 2230461

Streamside Service
Postboks 2092, Hasle 3202 Sandefjord.
Tel 33-453445
Fax 33-453344

Harris & Harris A/s
Marken 33, 5017 Bergen, Norge.
Tel 55 23 26 33
Fax 55 23 26 30

SOUTH AFRICA

Anglers Corner
18 Marshall Street, Johannesburg.
Tel 11-832-1188/9 or 11-838-5488
Fax 11-838-2758

4 Hand Strydom Drive, Fountainbleau, Randburg.
Tel 11-793-3321 or 11-793-2414

43 Howard Avenue, Benoni.
Tel 11-422-2995
Fax 11-422-2996

Elands River Fly Shop
Station Street, Waterval Boven,
PO Box 50 Waterval Boven 1195.
Tel 013262-193

Fishy Pete's Fly Shop
PO Box 122
Lydenburg 1120.
Tel 01323-51693
Fax 01323-51693

Fly Anglers
Shop 14, Berea Centre, 4007 Berea Road,
Durban, Natal.
Tel 31-21-3522
Fax 31-21-3527

Flyfisherman
24 Deane Street, 3200 Pietermaritzburg
Tel 331-42-1855
Fax 331-94-4008

and in Johannesburg:
Tel 11-463-4281
Fax 11-706-4926

and Cape Town:
Tel 21-794-4314
Fax 21-794-3799

Fly Fishing Adventures
44 Norfolk Road, Carlswald, Midrand,
PO Box 1160, Halfway House - 1685
Tel 11-702-1041
Fax 11-468-2045

Hastie Sports,
345 Main Street,
6001 Port Elizabeth
Tel 41-524138
Fax 41-525-138

SPAIN

Julius Sport
Caunedo 32, 28037 Madrid
Tel 91-304-22-57
Fax 91-327-26-96

Salmo
Apartado De Correreos
53206 Madrid

SWITZERLAND

Flugestobe
Buchenstrasse 30
CH-9042 Speicher, Marryat Interfly, Postfach
8031, Gasometererstrase 23, CH-8005 Zurich

Fischerei 7 Sportartikel AG,
Stadthausquai 1, 8022 Zurich 1
Tel 01-2115540

UNITED KINGDOM

Datam Products Ltd
Unit 7, Salisbury Square, Radford,
Nottingham NG7 2AB
Tel 0115-978-4248
Fax 0115-942-0004

Farlows of Pall Mall
5 Pall Mall, London SW1
Tel 0171-839-2423
Fax 01285-643743

Fly Box
95 Burren Road, Ballynahinch, Co.Down,
N.Ireland 8T24 8LF
Tel 01238-533311

Graham's
494-496 Chorley Old Road, Bolton, Lancs BL1
6AB
Tel 01204-841337

House of Hardy
61 Pall Mall, London SW 1Y 5JA
Tel 0171-839-5515
Fax 0171-930-9128

J.Weaver & Son
Deetech House, 411 B Alexandra Avenue,
Rayners Lane, Harrow, Middlesex HA3 9XG
Tel 0181-429-4894
Fax 0181-426-8970

UNITED STATES

American Angling Supplies & Services
23 Main Street, Salem NH 03079
Tel 603-893-3333
Fax 603-898-8141

Angler's Workshop
PO Box 1010, Woodland, Washington 98674
Tel 360-225-9445
Fax 360-225-8641

Angling Surgeon
12515 SE 74th Street,
Newcastle WA98056-1313
Tel 206-255-8009
Fax 206-682-3309

Arrick's Fishing Flies
Arrick Swanson, PO Box 1290, 125 Madison
Avenue, West Yellowstone, MT 59758.
Tel 406-646-7290
Fax 406-646-4748

Bass Pond
PO Box 82, Littleton, Colorado 80160-0082.
Tel 800-327-5014
Fax 303-730-8932

Bastian's Anglian Specialities
RD 2 Box 104-A, Cogan Station PA 17728.
Tel 717-998-2481

Clouser's Fly Shop
101 Ulrich Street, Middle Town, PA 17057.
Tel 717 944 6541

Cote's Fly Shop
115 Manville Street, Leicester MA 01524.
Tel 508-892-3765

Donegal Inc
(Paul Filippone)
6 Stewart Avenue, PO Box 106,
Roscoe, NY 12776-0106.
Tel 607-498-5911
Fax 607-498-5912

Duranglers Flies and Suppplies
801 B Main Street, Durango CO 81301.
Tel 970-385-4081

Duranglers Flies and Supplies
San Juan River, New Mexico.
Tel 505-632-5952

Eagle River Fly Shop
PO Box 12859, Drawer 12,
Rochester, NY 14612-0859.
Tel 716-265-3593

Egger's
PO Box 1344, Cumming, Georgia 30128

Feather Craft
8307 Manchester Road, PO Box 19904,
St Louis, MO 63144.
Tel 1-800-659-1707

Fish Hair Enterprises Inc
1484 W.County Road C., St.Paul MN 55113
Tel 612-636-3083
Fax 612-636-3083

Fly Shop
4140 Churn Creek Road, Redding CA96002
Tel 916-222-3555
Fax 916-222-3572

Flyfisher's Paradise
2603 East College Avenue,
State College PA 16801
Tel 814-234-4189
Fax 814-238-3686

Frontier Anglers
680 N. Montana St, PO Box 11
Dillon MT 59725
Tel 406-683-5276
Fax 406 683 6736

Foust's Fly Fishing
PO Box 583, Dept. A, Hamilton MT 59840

Golden Hackle Fly Shop
329 Crescent Place, Flushing MI 48433
Tel 810-659-0018
Fax 810-659-0018

Home Waters Fly Fishing
444 W 3rd Avenue, Eugene, OR 97401.
Tel 541 342 6691

House of Harrop
PO Box 491, Dept. RK, St.Anthony, Idaho 83445.
Tel 208-624-3537
Fax 208-624-3455

Hunter Banks Co.
29 Montford Avenue, Asheville NC 28801
Tel 704-252-3005 or 800-227-6732

Hyde Fly Shop
1520 Pancheri, Idaho Falls, ID 83402
Tel 208 529 4343
Fax 208 529 4397

Jacklin's
Box 310, 105 Yellowstone Avenue,
West Yellowstone, MT 59758.
Tel 406-646-7336
Fax 406-646-9729

K&K Flyfishers' Supply
8643 Grant, Overland Park KS 66212.
Tel 800-795-8118

Little Dixie Flies
3801 Eminence, Berkeley, MO 63134.

Bud Lilley's Trout Shop
39 Madison Avenue, West Yellowstone,
Montana 59758.
Tel 406-646-7801
Fax 406-646-9370

Manhattan Custom Tackle Ltd
913 Broadway, New York, NY 10010.
Tel 212-505-6690

Montana Troutfitters Shop
1716 West Main,
Bozeman, MT 59715.
Tel 406-587-4707
Fax 406-586-0724

Morning Dew Anglers
2100 W. Front Street, Berwick PA 18603.
Tel 717-759-1260

New England Angler
Dave Klausmeyer, PO Box 105,
Steuben, ME 04680-0105.
Tel 207-546-2018

On the Fly
3628 Sage Drive, Dept WFT, Rockford, IL 61114.
Tel 815-877-0090
Fax 815-877-4682

Patrick's Fly Shop
2237 Eastlake Avenue E, Seattle, WA 98102.
Tel 206-323-3302
Fax 206-328-FISH

Rainbow Run Fly Shop
2244 Grand Avenue, Billings, Montana 59102.
Tel 406-656-3455

The Rod & Reel
701 West 36th Avenue, Anchorage, Alaska.
Tel 907-561-0662
Fax 907-561-1475

Round Rocks Fly Fishing
PO Box 4059
Logan, UT 82323-4059.
Tel 801-755-3349
Fax 801-755-3311

Tackle-Craft
PO Box 280, Dept.A,
Chippewa Falls, WI 54729.
Tel 715-723-3645

Urban Angler
118 East 25th Street, New York Ny 10010.
Tel 212-979-7600
Fax 212-473-4020

Waters West
PO Box 3241, Port Angeles, WA 98362.
Tel 360-417-0937

Westbank Anglers
PO Box 523, Teton Village WY 83025
Tel 307-733-6483
Fax 307-733-9382

Yellowstone Angler
George Anderson, Highway 89 South, PO Box 660,
Livingston MT59047
Tel 406-222-7130

'Behind the Scenes' Companies

The following list comprises names of companies
you may well have noticed on products but which
do not normally sell direct to the public.
Nevertheless they will usually be happy to answer
questions about their products and advise as to the
nearest stockists or local distributors.

AUSTRALIA

Advanced Angling Supplies
PO Box 1629, Hobart, Tasmania 7001.
Tel 02-730930
Fax 02-730930

Tiewell
PO Box 720 Newport Beach, NSW 2106.
Tel 2-9973-1107
Fax 2-9973-1953

AUSTRIA

Roman Moser
Kuferzeile 19, A- 4810 Gmunden.
Tel. 07612-5686
Fax. 07612-5633

CANADA

Uni Products Inc
561 Rue Principale, Ste-Melanie,
Quebec, JOK 3AO.
Tel 514 889 2195
Fax 514 889 8506

DENMARK

Swan Products
Jyllandsgade 16 A, DK-6700 Esbjerg.
Tel 75-454630 or 43-719313
Fax 75-124785

GERMANY

Traun River Products
Haupstrasse 4
D-83313 Siegsdorf.
Tel 8662 7079
Fax 8662 2711

INDIA

Bhagwati FlyMaster
PO Box 16052, 27 Circus Avenue, Calcutta 17.
Tel 33-2472334
Fax 33-401165 or 33-406482

Burima Industry
P-17, Tagore Park, Calcutta 700056.
Tel 33-5531215
Fax 33-5531215 or 33-2429806

Jindal International
10/A Shakespeare, Sarani, Calcutta 700071.
Tel 33-242-8616
Fax 33-242-9044

Suiza Exports
PO Box 816, 89 Netaji Subhas Road, 2nd Floor,
Calcutta A 700 001.
Tel 33-243-2237 or 33-242-1256
Fax 33-243-3120 or 33-238-4802

Sunrise International
71 Lake Road, Calcutta 700029.
Tel 33-466-5860 or 33-464-3750
Fax 33-466-6987

Vijender International
PO Box 8432, Delhi 110052.
Tel 11-7427888
Fax 11-7252857

ITALY

Giorgio Benecchi's Products
Via Giotto 279, 41100 Modena.

Tel 059-34-11-90
Fax 059-34-26-27

SOUTH AFRICA

David Levene Agencies
98, 17th Street, Parkhurst, Johannesburg 2193, PO
Box 589, Parklands 2121
Tel 11-442-6480
Fax 11-788-7995

Purglas Marketing (Pty) Ltd
PO Box 4, Durban 4000.
Fax 31-307-2019

UNITED KINGDOM

Fishermen's Feathers
Hillend Farm, Bransford, Worcester WR6 5JJ.
Tel 1905-830548
Fax 1905-831810

Gordon Griffiths
8 Lifford Way, Binley Industrial Estate,
Willenhall Lane, Coventry CV3 2RN.
Tel 01203-440859
Fax 01203-635694

John Hunt
59 Tawelfan, Nelson, Treharris,
Mid Glamorgan CF46 6EH.
Tel 01443-451861

Lureflash
Victoria Buildings, Victoria Street, Kilnhurst,
Rotherham, South Yorkshire S62 5SQ
Tel 01709-580081 or 01709-580238
Fax 01709-586194

Ken Newton Tools
302 Oldfield Road, Altrincham,
Cheshire, WA14 4JA.
Tel 0161- 928-1836
Fax 0161-928-1836

Pearsalls Sutures
Tancred Street,
Taunton, Somerset TA1 1RY
Tel. 01823-253198
Fax. 01823-336824

H. Turrall & Co
Dolton, Winkleigh, Devon EX19 8QJ.
Tel 01805-804352
Fax 01805-804572

E. Veniard Ltd
Paramount Warehouses, 138 Northwood Road,
Thornton Heath, Surrey CR7 8YG.
Tel 0181 653 3565
Fax 0181 771 4805

Weaver Tackle Engineers
12 Beechwood Gardens,
South Harrow, Middlesex HA2 8BU.
Tel 0181-429-4894

UNITED STATES

A.K.'s Fly Tying Tools
PO Box 6250, Annapolis, MD 21401.
Tel 410-573-0287
Fax 410-573-0993

John Betts
1452 South Elizabeth, Denver, CO 80210
Tel 303-722-7052

Black Canyon Flies & Supplies
91 Market Street, Wappingers Falls, NY 12590.
Tel 914-297-0098
Fax 914-297-0142

Cascade Fly Supply / Crest Tool
13290 Table Rock Road, Central Point OR 97502.
Tel 541-826-4030
Fax 541-826-4698

Castle Arms
Box 30070, Springfield, MA 01103.
Tel 413-567-8268
Fax 413-731-1292

Corsair Products
33 Carroll Road, Woburn MA 01801.
Tel 617-932-0558

Danville Chenille Co Inc
PO Box 1000, Route 111A, Danville, NH 03819.
Tel 603-382-5553

D's Flyes
Darrel Sickmon, Colorado.
Tel 303-934-7066

Dyna King
Abby Precision Manufacturing
70 Industrial Drive, Cloverdale, CA 95425.
Tel 707 894 5566
Fax 707 894 5990

Edgin Manufacturing
1321-L W. Airport Way, North Bend, OR 97459.
Tel 541-756-1269
Fax 541-756-1694

Flycraft
PO Box 582, Greendale Station,
Worcester, MA 01606.
Tel 508-853-3676

Fly Dye
PO Box 14258, East Providence,
Rhode Island 02914-0258.
Tel. 401 434 3300

Chuck Furimsky
615 Broadway, Rockwood, PA 15557.
Tel 814-926-2676
Fax 814-926-2650

Gordon Griffiths
1190 Genella, Waterford, MI 48328.
Tel 810-673-7701
Fax 810-673-7701

Griffin Enterprises Inc
PO Box 754, Bonner,
MT 59823.
Tel 406-244-5407
Fax 406-244-5444

Gudebrod
PO Box 357, Pottstown, PA 19464.
Tel 610 327 4050
Fax 610 327 4588

Hareline Dubbin
24712 Territorial Road, Monroe, OR 97456.
Tel 541-847-5310
Fax 541-847-6064

Hedron Inc
402 North Main Street, Stillwater,
Minnesota 55082.
Tel. 621 430 9606
Fax.612 430 9607

Hobbs Feather Co Inc
PO Box 187, West Liberty, Iowa 52776.
Tel 319-627-4258
Fax 319-627-6529

Henry E.Hoffman Fly Tying Innovations
Route 1 Box 695, Warrenton, OR 97146.
Tel 503-861-2627

InterTac (Larva Lace)
PO Box 4031
110 W. Midland Ave., Woodland Park CO 80866.
Tel 719 687 2272
Fax 719 687 9820

JS Marketing Inc
8200 E. Pacific Pl., 202 Denver, CO 80231.
Tel 303-369-8839
Fax 303-369-8938

Kennebec River Fly & Tackle Co
39 Milliken Road, North Yarmouth, ME 04097.
Tel 207-829-4290
Fax 207-829-6002

Kreinik Manufacturing Company Inc
3106 Timanus Lane, Suite 101, Baltimore, MD
21244.
Tel 410-281-0040
Fax 410-281-0987

L&L Products
12 Raemar Court, Bethpage, NY 11714.
Tel 516-931-6714

Largatun
16741 S. Old Sonoita Highway, Vail, AZ 85641.
Tel 520-762-5900
Fax 520-762-5959

Loon Outdoors
7737 West Mossycup, Boise, Idaho 83709.
Tel 208-362 4437
Fax 208-362 4497

Mad River Dubbing Co Inc
207 Clark Street, Canastota, NY 13032.
Tel 800-231-9314
Fax 315-697-9314 or 315-697-5313

Franco Matarelli
4426 Irving Street, San Francisco, CA 94122.

McKenzie Fly Tackle Company
1075-A Shelley Street,
Springfield, OR 97477.
Tel 541-741-8161
Fax 541-741-7565

Merco
1525 Norland Drive, Sunnyvale CA 94087.
Tel 408-245-7803
Fax 408-245-7803

Metz Hatchery
(*see also* Umpqua Feather Merchants)
PO Box 5666, Belleville, PA 17004.
Tel 717 935 2124
Fax 717 935 5474

Nature's Spirit
7552 E. Greenlake Drive N., Seattle, WA 98103
Tel 206-527-1600
Fax 206 527 2702

Oregon Upstream
Red Soils Business Park, 406 Beaver Creek Road,
Oregon City, OR 97045.
Tel 503-557-3022
Fax 503-557-3022

Orvis Company Inc
Distribution Centre:
1711 Blue Hills Drive, PO Box 12000,
Roanake, VA 24022-8001.
Tel 800-541-3541
Fax 540-343-7053

Head Office:
Manchester, Vermont.
Tel 802 362 3622
Fax 802 362 3525

Palsa Outdoor Products
PO Box 81336, Lincoln NE 68501-1336, 4300
Cooper Avenue, Lincoln, NE 68506.
Tel 402-488-5288
Fax 402-488-2321

Pamola Fly Tool Co
Box 435, Upton ,MA 01568.
Tel 508-529-6086

Regal Engineering Inc
RFD 2, Tully Road, Orange, MA 01364.
Tel 508 575 0488

Renzetti Inc
6080 Grissom Parkway, Titusville FL 32780.
Tel 407-267-7705
Fax 407-264-5929

Riverborn Fly Co Inc
Box 65 Wendell, ID 83355.
Tel 208-536-2355
Fax 208-536-6103

Rocky Mountain Dubbing
PO Box 1255, 115 Poppy Street,
Lander, WY 82520.
Tel 307 332 2989
Fax 307 332 2697

Raymond C. Rumpf & Son
PO Box 319, Sellersville, PA 18960.
Tel 215-257-0141
Fax 215-453-9758

Scintilla
Kenn M. Ligas
615 MacGregor Road,
Belgrade, MT 59714.
Tel 406 388 7169
Fax 406 388 7169

Scherer Designs
1309 Arch Street, Berkeley, CA 94708.
Tel 510-849-1703
Fax 510-849-1703

Shannon's Fancy Hackle
Rt. 2, Box 236, Lamar, Arkansas 72846.
Tel 501 885 3598

Dr Slick
114 S.Pacific, Dillon, MT 59725.
Tel 406-683-6489
Fax 406-683-5123

Sierra Pacific Products
PO Box 276833, 10087-1 Mills Station Road
Sacramento, CA 95827.
Tel 916-369-1146
Fax 916-369-1564

Spirit River Inc
423 Winchester Street, Roseburg, OR 97470.
Tel 541-440-6916
Fax 541-672-4309

Swaffarco Feather 'N Trading
5083 Dearing Road, Springdale, AR 72762.
Tel 501-756-8898
Fax 501-756-8828

Tiemco (*see* Umpqua Feather Merchants)

D.H. Thompson Inc
11 North Union Street, Elgin, IL 60123.
Tel 708-741-7719
Fax 708-741-0470

H. Turrall & Co USA
45 Knobhill Street, Sharon, MA 02067.
Tel 617-784-3732
Fax 617-784-3732

Universal Vise Corp
16 Union Avenue, Westfield, MA 01085.
Tel 413-568-0964 or 800-456-4665
Fax 413-562-7328

Umpqua Feather Merchants
17537 N. Umpqua Highway, PO Box 700,
Glide, OR 97443.
Tel 503-496-3512
Fax 503-496-0150

Fritz Von Schlegell
1135B Westminster, Alhambra, CA 91803.
Tel 818-282-3173
Wapsi Fly Inc
27 CR 458, Mountain Home AR 72653.
Tel 501-425-9500
Fax 800-425-9599

Whiting Farms Inc (Hoffman Hackle)
PO Box 100, Delta C0 81416.
Tel 970-874-0999
Fax 970-874-7117

Witchcraft Tape Products
PO Box 937, Coloma, MI 49038.
Tel 616-468-3399
Fax 616-468-3391

List of Hookmakers

FRANCE

VMC Peche
12 Rue du General de Gaulle
90120 Morvillars
Tel 84-27-89-10
Fax 84-23-50-90

ITALY

Mustad Pesca (Otalia) Srl
Via Como 14, 20020 Lainate (MI).
Tel 293 570 390
Fax 239 570 885

JAPAN

Hayabusa Fishing Hook Co Ltd
Watase, Yokawa-Cho, Mino-Gun, Hyogo 673-11.
Tel 7947-30212
Fax 7947-30200

NORWAY

Mustad
PO Box 41, N-2801 Gjovik.
Tel 61 137700
Fax 61 137952

UNITED KINGDOM

Airflo Distribution Ltd
Unit 6 Industrial Estate
Brecon, Powys LD3 8LA
Tel 01874 624448
Fax 01874 625889

Ashima Hook Co.
Hook House
40 Buckhurdt Road, Frimley Green
Camberley, Surrey GU16 6LJ
Tel 01252 838264
Fax 01252 836474

Aiken Ltd, Henry W.
139/147 Kirkdale, Sydenham, London SE26 4QW
Tel 0181 699 1141
Fax 0181 291 5759

Drennan International Ltd
Bacardo Court, Temple Road, Cowley
Oxford OX4 2EX.
Tel 01865-748989
Fax 01865-748989

Kamasan
(formerly Kamatsu, a division of Drennan International), Unit 1, Sandford Lane Industrial Estate
Kennington, Oxford, OX1 5RW.
Tel 01865 326655
Fax 01865 326650

Mustad UK
2 Brindley Road, SW Industrial Estate,
Peterlee, Co. Durham, SR8 2LT.
Tel 0191 5869553
Fax 0191 5180901

Partridge of Redditch Ltd
Mount Pleasant, Redditch,
Worcestershire, B97 4JE.
Tel 01527 541380 or 01527 543555
Fax 01527 546956

Sprite
Unit 4, Arrow Road North, Lakeside, Redditch,
Warwichshire B98 8NT
Tel 01527 65164
Fax 01527 65164

Scorpion
FMF Tackle Ltd
5/46 Croydon Road, Reigate, Surrey RH2 0NH
Tel 01737 243991
Fax 01737 221594

UNITED STATES

Daiichi Hooks
c/o Anglers Sports Group
6619 Oak Orchard Road, Elba, NY 14058.
Tel 716 757 9958
Fax 716 757 9066

Dai-Riki Fly Hooks
c/o Dan Bailey
PO Box 1019
Livingston, MT 59047
Tel 406 222 1673
Fax 406 222 8450

Eagle Claw
Wright & McGill Co.
PO Box 16011, 4245 East 46 Avenue,
Denver, Colorado 80216.
Tel 303 321 1481
Fax 303 321 4750

Fenwick Corporation
5242 Argosy Drive
Huntington Beach, CA 92649
Tel 714 897 1066
Fax 714 891 9610

Gamakatsu USA Inc
PO Box 1797, Tacoma WA 98401
Tel 206-922-8373
Fax 206-922-8447

Mustad (USA) Inc
PO Box 838, 247-253 Grant Avenue,
Auburn, NY 13021.
Tel 315 253 2793
Fax 315 253 0157

Owner American Corporation
17165 Von Karman
Suite 111, Irvine, CA 92714
Tel 714-261-7922
Fax 714 261-9399

Tiemco
PO Box 700
Glide, OR 97443
Tel 541 496 0150
Fax 541 496 0151

ABOVE Grey Partridge skin: this one is from Hungary.

INTERNATIONAL TELE-PHONE DIALLING CODES

Argentina 54	Italy 39
Australia 61	Japan 81
Austria 43	Luxembourg 352
Belgium 32	Netherlands 31
Canada 1	New Zealand 64
Chile 56	Norway 47
Czech Republic 42	Peru 51
Denmark 45	Poland 48
Finland 358	South Africa 27
France 33	Spain 34
Germany 49	Sweden 46
Iceland 354	United Kingdom 44
India 91	USA 1
Irish Republic 353	

0800 NUMBERS

These only operate free to the caller in the local country. Generally, these can be accessed when, for example, telephoning into the United States but the caller will first be given the option of hanging up or paying for the call at the International Call Rate. The outcome of trying 0800 numbers in other countries from outside the country in question is often not successful.

FIRST 0 IN LOCAL CODES

When calling from overseas this 0 should be omitted.

There have recently been some Code changes in in the states of Colorado and Oregon in the US. Whilst we hope that we have tracked down recent changes, directory enquiries should be consulted in the event of there being any difficulty in reaching numbers in these two states.

Magazines

Magazines with a flytying focus

UK

Fly-Fishing & Fly-Tying
Rolling River Publications Ltd, 3 Aberfeldy Road,Kenmore, Perthshire PH15 2HF
Tel 01887-830526
Tel 01887-830526

The Flydresser
Dewhurst Lodge, Dewhurst Lane,
Wadhurst, East Sussex TN5 6QB
Tel o1892-784498
Magazine of the Fly Dressers Guild

US

Anglers Journal
Box 1427, Livingston, MT 59047
Tel 406 222 9602
Fax 406 222 7767
A quarterly with one edition each year fly tying focused

Fly Tyer
126 North Street, PO Box 4100, Bennington VT 05201-4100
Tel 802-447-1518
Fax 802-442-2471

Roundtable
PO Box 2478, Woburn, MA 01888
Magazine of United Fly Tyers

Western Fly Tying
4040 SE Wister Street, Milwaukie, Oregon 97222
Tel 503-653-8108

Fishing magazines with some flyting

AUSTRALIA

FlyLife
St.Johns Circle, Richmond, Tasmania,
Australia 7025
Tel 002-602409
Fax 002-602751

BELGIUM

Beet
Mottantstraat 52, bus 2, 9308 Hofstade
Tel 053-710604
Fax 053-710604

GERMANY

Der Fliegenfischer
Verlag Von Joachim Schuck, Lohhofer Strasse 11, D-90453, Nurnberg
Tel 0911-63-50-55
Fax 0911-6-32-43-48

Fliegenfischen
Jahr Verlag GmbH & Co, 22754 Hamburg, Jessenstrasse 1
Tel 040-38-90-60

NETHERLANDS

Beet
Willemstraat 14, 4811 AK Breda
Tel 076-530-1729
Fax 076-520-5235

De Nederlandse Vliegvisser
R.Van Duijnhaven, Hollands Klooster 18, 6562 JE Groesbeek
Tel 0124-397-4417
Fax 0124-397-4417
Magazine of the V.N.V. (Vereniging Nederlandse Vliegvissers)

NEW ZEALAND

Fish & Game
604 Great South Road, PO Box 1746,Auckland
Tel 09-579-3000
Fax 09-579-3993

SOUTH AFRICA

Flyfishing
PO Box 20545, Durban North 4016
Tel 031-52-2289
Fax 031-52-7891
Official Journal of the Federation of South African Flyfishers

UK

Stillwater Trout Angler
Kings Reach Tower, Stamford Street,
London SE1 9LS
Tel 0171 261 5000

Trout Fisherman
EMAP Pursuit Publishing Ltd, Bretton Court, Bretton
Centre, Peterborough PE3 8DZ
Tel 01733-264666
Fax 01733-263294

Trout & Salmon
EMAP Pursuit Publishing Ltd, Bretton Court, Bretton
Centre, Peterborough PE3 8DZ
Tel 01733-264666
Fax 01733-263294

US

American Angler
126 North Street, PO Box 4100, Bennington VT 05201-
4100
Tel 802-447-1518
Fax 802-447-2471

Fly Fisherman
PO Box 8200
6405 Flank Drive,Harrisburg PA 17105-8200
Tel 717-657-9555
Fax 717-657-9526

Fly Rod & Reel
PO Box 370
Camden ME 04843
Tel 207-594-9544
Fax 207-594-5144

Western Flyfishing (formerly Flyfishing)
PO Box 82112, Portland OR 97282
Tel 503-653-8108

Trade Magazines

UK

Tackle Talk International
Pendragon Publishing
The Red House
High Street
Bushey
Watford
WD2 3DE
Tel 0181 950 6360
Fax 0181 420 4163
(Also publish *Who's Who in the Tackle Trade*)

US

Fly Tackle Dealer
PO Box 370, Camden ME 04843
Tel 207-594-9544
Fax 207-594-5144

Select Bibliography

FLY-DRESSING MATERIALS
John Veniard ISBN 0-7136-1690-3 (Black 1977)

FLY TYING METHODS
Darrel Martin ISBN 0-7153-9132-1
(David & Charles 1987)

FLYTYING TOOLS AND MATERIALS
Jacqueline Wakeford ISBN0-7136-3398-0 (Black 1992)

FLY TYING WITH SYNTHETICS
Phil Camera ISBN 1-85310-338-1)
(Swan Hill/ Voyageur 1992)

FLUORESCENT FLIES
Joseph Keen (Herbert Jenkins 1964)

MICROPATTERNS
Darrel Martin ISBN 1-55821-260-4
(Lyons & Burford 1994)

MODERN FLY-TYING MATERIALS
Dick Talleur ISBN 1-55821-344-9
(Lyons & Burford 1995)

RARE & UNUSUAL FLY TYING MATERIALS   A
Natural History. Volume I: Birds. Paul Schmookler and
Ingrid V. Sells. ISBN 1-886961-01-8 (The Complete
Sportsman, 1994). Note: Volume II: Birds & Mammals
by the same authors will be published in 1996.

SYNTHETIC FLY TYING COLOUR GUIDE
John Gross ISBN 0-9515732-1-7 (Lureflash 1991)

THE BOOK OF FLY PATTERNS
Eric Leiser ISBN 0-394-54394-7 (Knopf 1987)

THE BOOK OF THE HACKLE
Frank Elder ISBN 7073-0223-4 (Scottish Academic
Press 1979)

THE TRUTH ABOUT FLUORESCENTS
Thomas Clegg (Booklet 1967)

THE HOOK BOOK
Dick Stewart ISBN 0-936644-02-8
(Northland Press 1986)

TYING FOAM FLIES
Skip Morris ISBN 1-878175-89-0 (Frank Amato 1994)

Acknowledgements

No book of this nature can be brought to fruition without immense help from many people. The numerous companies mentioned in the text are testimony alone to those who have given very generously of their time, advice and examples of materials.

Many individuals have also helped in the course of conversations or by answering our apparently idiosyncratic questions. Among them, we are especially grateful to Peter Veniard, Dr Thomas Whiting, Alan Bramley, Paul Hodson, Buck Metz Jnr, Paul Hodsman,, Runar Warhuus, Martin Booth, Ken Sawada, Christopher Helm, John and Stephen Cross, Michael Martinek Jnr, Rainy Riding, Jeff Mack, Gordon Griffiths, John Betts, Torill Kolbu, Chuck Furimsky, Marvin Nolte, Norm Norlander, Shim Hogan, Ray Treanor, Dave Corcoran, Davy Wotton, Kenn and Marcia Ligas, John Bailey, Al and Gretchen Beatty, Tom and Krys Travis, Jan Siman, Philip and Mary White, Bill Merg, Richard Wolfe, Robert Sloane, Karl Schmuecker, Brett Patterson, Graham Wyman, Jim Krul, Russell Conchie, Phil Castleman and to the Olympus Optical Company, Hamburg.

Thank you to all of you. Your collective knowledge and wisdom has given us an enormous amount of material to distil into this one volume. Any errors, mis-interpretations or misconceptions are ours alone - and we will be pleased to continue to receive advice about this immense and complex field, in the hope that future editions of the book may be as accurate as possible.

Barry Ord Clarke

Robert Spaight

Index

Abby-Dyna-King Tools 123
Accessories 133-136
Acrylic Paint 121
African Goat 27
Aire-Flow Cut Wings 93
A.K. Best's Series of Flytying Tools
  123,130
Angel Hair 93
Angler's Choice 103
Angler's Corner Head Cement 115
Angler's Corner Lure Coat 121
Angora Goat 27, 51
Antelope 39
Antron 81
Antron Bodywool 71
Antron, Clear 81
Antron Dubbing 52
Antron Dubbing Brush 63
Antron/Hare Blend 52
Antron Sparkle Dubbing 52
Antron Sparkle Yarn 81, 91
Antron Yarn 91
Ant Legs 85
Arizona Sparkle Yarn 72
Aron Alpha Glue 115
Artificial Raffia 68
Audible Eyes 79
Aunt Lydia's Sparkle Yarn 72
Australian Possum Dubbing 52
Australian Opossum 52
Awesome Possum 52

Badger 27
Ballan Rotary Vice 130

Bankside Vice 130
Barbless Hooks 140
Bassarisk 27
Bass Fly Hooks 141
Bass Hair 39
Bead Chain 78
Bead Head 69
Beads 69
Bear: Black; Black Bear Masks;
  Brown/Grizzly, Polar 27
Beaver 28
Beaver Blend Plus 52
Beaver Dubbing 52
Beetle Legs 85
Behind-the-Scenes Companies 164-168
Benecchi 103
Berlin Wool 72
Big Fly Fibre 93
Bill's Bodi-Braid 72
Blackbird 11
Blended Muskrat Dubbing 52
Blended Rabbit Dubbing 52
Blue Ribbon Dyes 120
Boar, Chinese 28
Bobcat 28
Bobbin holders 123
Bobbins 123
Bobbin threaders 124
Bodi-Stretch 72
Body-Brite 72
Body-Flex 72
Body Gills 72
Body Glass 72
Body Stretch 68, 72

Booby Eye Netting 79
Booby Eyes 83
Borealis Back 91
Borger Colour System 65
Brassie, The 125
Brazilian Velour 77
Brighton Flash 86
Brite Beads 69
Brite Eyes 79
BT's Ezy Beads 69
Bucktail 28, 38, 39
Buffalo 28
Bug Back 68
Bugskin; Naturals; Flash Naturals;
  Pearlized Naturals; Wild Naturals 72
Burlap 73
Bustard: Great, Florican 11

Cactus Chenille 77
Caddis Cases 70
Caddis Emerger Dubbing 52
Calf: Body Hair 28; Tail (Kip) 28; Red;
  Grey; Silver 28
Camel 28
Camel Dubbing 52
Canadian Series Mohair 73
Caribou 39
Capercaillie 11
Cellire 115
Celo-Z Wing 93
Cements 115-119
Ceramic Tipped Bobbin Holders 124
Ceramiscrape Dubbing Rake 124
Chamois 39
Chanticleer 46
Charles Jardine Signature Series 52
Chatterer, Blue 11
Chenilles 76-78
Chickabou 11
Chinchilla 29
Chinese capes 46
Clark's Tying Yarn 73
Clear Antron 81

Clouser Minnow 56
Coastal Deer Hair 40
Cock capes 43
Cock hackles 43
Collins 46
Colour Systems 65
Condor 12
Cone Heads 69
Coot 12
Cork Bodies 70
Corsair 89
Coyote 29
Coypu 33
Coq de Leon 12
Craft Hair 93
Crane 12
Crimped Nylon 81
Crow: Carrion, Indian 12
Crystal Chenille 77
Crystal Clear Epoxy 115
Crystal Eyes 79
Crystal Flash 93
Crystal Hair 93
Crystal Seal 53
Crystal Twist 93
Cul de Canard 12
Cul de Canard Dubbing Brushes 64
Cul de Cygne 13
Cyclops Eyes 69

Daddy Longlegs (Crane Fly): Pre-Tied
  Legs 85
Dall Sheep 34
Damsel & Dragon Fly Foam 83
Dan Bailey Body Fur 73
Dan Bailey Hi-VIS Floater 93
Dan Bailey Rainbow Thread 93
Dan Bailey Wing Fibre 93
Danville 103
Darlon 82
Datam Products 103
Dave's Bug Dub 53
Dave's Flexament 115

Davy Wotton's Series of Tools 124
Dazl Eyes 79
Dazl Hare's Ear 53
Dazl-Tron 53
Deer Mask 40
DeLeon Blue Dun Turkey Feathers 13
Delta Bond 115
Delta Flexi-Tails 91
Design II Permanent Markers 121
Detached Bodies: Mayfly; Daddy
  Longlegs 70
Devcon 2 Ton Epoxy 116
Devcon 5 Minute Epoxy 116
Diamond Braid 73, 91
DJ Hackle 47
Doll Eyes 79
Donkey: African, Spanish 29
Dotterel 13
Drew's Dubbing Brush 63
DRF Flourescent Materials 86
Dry Fly Hooks 141
Dubbing Aids 124
Dubbing Block 124
Dubbings 50-65
Dubbing Bristles 64
Dubbing Brushes 63
Dubbing Needle 124
Dubbing Threads 63
Dubbing Twisters 124
Dubbing Waxes 113
Dubbing Whirl 124
Duck 13: White 13; Casarca 13; Gadwall
  13; Lemon Wood 13; Mallard 13;
  Mandarin 13; Muscovey 13; Pygmy 13;
  Rouen 14; Teal 14; Tree 14; Wood Duck
  or Carolina 14
Dumbell Eyes 79
Dun Wing 93, 101
Duro Quick Gel No Run Super Glue 116
Dyed Rainbow Chenille 79
Dyes, Paints & Pens 120-122
Dynacord 103

Easy-Dubbing 64
Easy Dub Micro Chenille 77
Edge Bright 86
Edgewater Foam: Terrestrial Bodies;
  Pencil Poppers; Divers 83
Egg Heads 78
Elk: Bull Elk; Cow Elk; Elk Hock; Elk
  Mane; Yearling Elk 40
Elastic Necklace 133
Emu 14
Enrico's Squid Tentacles 85
Enrico's Super Set Epoxy; 1-Minute
  Epoxy 116
Epoxies 115-119
Epoxy Eyes 80
Epoxy Paint 116, 121
Ermine 29
Esmond Drury Hooks 139
Estaz 77
Ever-Float 53
Everglow Flash 87
Everglow Tubing 87
Evett's Wing Material 93
Ewing 47
Eyes, Black 79
E-Z Bobbin Threader 125
EZ Body Braid 89
EZ-Body Dubbing 64
E-Z Leg Tool 124

Fantastic Wing 94
Faux Seal 53
Feathers 11-26
Feather Glue 116
Feather Weld 116
Fibett Tails 91
Fibre Optic Eyes 80
Fibres 81-83
Fine and Dry 53
Fire Fly 94
Fire Fly Products: Double-sided Strip;
  Lumi Beads; Adhesive backed Sheet;
  Lumi Paints; Lights; Holographic Sheet;

Super Wings; Hot Tail 87-88
Fire Tip Sili Legs 85
Fishair 94
Fisher 29
Fishscale Body Tube 89
Fishscale Body Wrap 89
Fish Scale Powder 80
Fitch 29
Flamingo 14
Flashabou 95-96
Flashabou; Saltwater Flashabou; Glow-in-
  the-Dark Flashabou; Flashabou Accent
  95-96
Flashabou Dubbing 53
Flashabou Flakes Lacquer 116
Flashabou Minnow Body 89
Flashabou Tubing 89
Flashback 68
Flat Braid 73
Flexibody 68
Flexi Floss 73
Flex-Loc Head Cement 116
Float Foam 83
Floo Gloo 116
Floss Flex 73
Flosses 108-109
Fluorescent Twinkle Bodywrap 88
Fluorescent Wool 88
Fly Body Foam 83
Fly Dye dyes 120
Fly Film 96
Fly Foam 83
Fly Fur 96
Fly-Rite Claret Polypropylene Dubbing
  53
Fly-Rite Extra Fine Ply Dubbing 53
Fly-Rite Natural Dubbing 53
Fly-Rite Non-Toxic Head Cement 116
Flytyers Gauge 135
Fritz Glass 73
Fritz Von Schlegell Head Cement 116
Foam 83-85
Foam Ant Bodies 84

Foam Beetle Bodies 84
Foam Bodies 71, 84
Foam Frog Bodies 84
Foam Popper Bodies 84
Foam Spider & Ant Bodies 84
477 Killer Bug Yarn 73
Fox: Artic, Grey, Red, Silver 29
Fox Fur Dubbing 54
Frog's Hair Dubbin' 54
Frog Legs 85
Frost Bite 89
Fur Blender 133
Furry Foam 84
Furry Lead 73
Fuzzy Leech Yarn 73

Gallena 16
Gallows Parachute Tool 125
Genetic Hackle 47
Ghost Fibre 82
Glass Beads 69
Glass Eyes 80
Glimmer 96
Glissen Glass 73
Glitter Body 91
Glo-Brite Chenille 77
Glo-Brite Fluorescent Suede Chenille 77
Glo-Bug Yarn 78
Glo-in-the-Dark Pearl Piping 88
Glow Materials 88
Glue Gun 133
Goat: Snow Goat 29
Golden Plover 22
Goose: Shoulder feathers; Biot; Canada;
  Egyptian; Malaga; Maned; Zebra 15
Gold Heads 69
Golden Bullets 69
Gordon Griffiths 103
Gordon Griffiths' Wool Yarn 73
Griffin Cement 11
Groundhog 30
Grouse: Blue; Red; Ruffed; Sage;
  Sharptail 15-16

Gudebrod 103
Gudebrod Bobbin 125
Gudebrod Head Cement 116
Guinea Fowl: Common, Vulturine 16

Hackle Back 125
Hackle Colours: Classification of; single colours; white; cream; ginger; light ginger; red; red game; black; bi-colours; badger; yellow badger; furnace; coch-y-bonddu; barred; cuckoo; cree; grizzle; dun hackle; dun; blue dun; iron blue dun; rusty dun; honey dun; off-colours; white splashed; variant 44-46
Hackles 43-50
Hackle Gauge 135
Hackle Guards 125
Hackle Pliers 125
Hair Hackle 91
Hair Packers 125
Hair Packers, Stackers & Eveners 125
Hair Stackers 125
Half Hitch Tool 125
Hard As Nails 117
Hare 30-31
Hare Masks 34
Hare & Flash 64
Hareline Dubbin 54
Hareline Sheared Dubbing 54
Hare: Snowshoe 30-31
Hare's Ear Plus Dubbin 55
Hare-Tron Dubbin 55
Haretron Dubbing 55
Harrop Dubbing 55
Hebert, Ted 47
Helm, Christopher 37
Hen, Domestic 16
Hen Hackles 48
Heron 16
Hi-Vis 82,96
Hoffman hackles 48
Hologram Eyes 80
Holographic Fly Fibre 88

Holographic Flash 88
Holographic Sparkle 96
Holographic Tinsel 88, 104, 111
Holographic Tubing 74, 88
Hook and Hackle Gauge 135
Hook Hone 133
Hooks 137-148
Hooks, types of 140
Hopper Legs 85
Horse Hair 31
Hourglass Eyes 80
House of Harrop Fly Tying Cement 117
Howard's Hackle 48
Humbrol Superfast Clear Epoxy Resin 117
100 per cent Beaver 57
Ibis, Scarlet 16
Ice Chenille 77
Idaho Seal Dubbing 55
Imitation Jungle Cock Eyes 80
Impala 40
Indian Capes 46
Indio 12
Intertac 84. 103
Inter-Tac Dubbing 56
Iris Tweezers 126
Irise Dub 56
Italian Bead Eyes 80

Jackdaw 16
Jay 16
Japanese Silk Floss 103
Javelina 31
Jumbo Chenille 77
Jungle Cock, Grey 16

Kangaroo 31
Kapok 56
Kaufmann's Nymph Blends 56
Kaufmann's Rabbit Dubbing 56
K-Dub 56
Kennerk, Steve 37
Keough 48

Killer Caddis Glass Beads 69
Kingfisher 17
Kip Tail 31
Kits 125
Kiwi Rabbit Strips 31
Kreinik Manufacturing Co. Inc. 103
Krinkle Flash; Holographic 96
Krystal Dub 56
Krystal Eggs Chenille 77
Krystal Flash 78: Solid; Pearlescent;
  Fluorescent 96
Krystal Flash Chenille 77
Krystal Glo-Balls 78

Lace Wing 96
Lagartun 104
Lamb, Tuscana 35
Lance 126
Landrail 17
Lap Tray 133
Larva Lace 92
Larva Lace Foam Sheets 84
Larva Lace Midge 92
Latex 73
Lazer Light 56, 96
L&L Fly Foam 84
L&L Stretch Foam 84
Lead Dumbell Eyes 80
Lead Eyes 80
Leech Yarn 73
Legs 85-86
Life-Flex 74
Ligas Ultra Translucent Dubbing 56
Linx 32
List of Hookmakers 168
Lite Brite 56
Liqui Lace 92: Polymorphic Glitter 74;
  Midge Lace; Medium Lace;
  Woolybugger Lace; Iridescent Lace 92
Llama 31
Longhorn Necks 49
Longhorn Saddles 49
Loon Dubbing 56

Loon Hard Body Epoxy Kit 117
Loon Hard Head Fly Finish 117
Loon Head Cement System 117
Loon Head Finish System 117
Loon Hydrostop New Fly Treatment 117
Loon Soft Body Epoxy Kit 117
Loon Water Base Head Cement System
  117
Loon Water Base Head Finish 117
Louper Tubing 89
Luminous Body Wrap 88
Lureflash 64, 104
Lureflash Lifelike Dubbing 56
Lureflash Selfblend Dubbing 56
Lureflash Twister Tails 91
Lureflash Varnish 117
Lurexes 109-110

Macaw 17
Mad River Beaver Dubbing 57
Magazines (Flytying & Related Subjects)
  173
Mag Eyes 135
Magic Dub: Squirrel; Hare's Ear Plus;
  Antron; Marabou 64
Magic Glass 74
Magnifiers 135
Magpie 17
Magnum Lite Brite 57
Marabou 17
Marabou Chenille 77
Marabou Dubbing Brushes 64
Marbled Latex 74
Marmot 32
Marten 32
Material Clip 126
Materials, Manmade 67-102
Materials Spring 126
McGinty Quill 18
McFlyfoam Material 74, 84
McFlylon Fly Material 96
McMurray Ant Bodies 71
Meg-a-Egg 78

Metallics 111
Metallic Beetle Bodies 84
Metz hackles 49
Microfibetts 91
Microweb 97
Midge Metallics 91
Minah 17
Mink 32
Mix and Match 57
Mobile: Luminous Mobile; Twinkle
  Mobile; Translucent Mobile 97
Moe Blanks 71
Mohair 32
Mole 32
Mohlon Wool 75
Molded Eyes 80
Monga Ringtail 32
Mongoose 32
Monkey 32
Mono Nymph Eyes 80
Moorhen (Waterhen) 18
Moose 39, 40
Moose Body Hair 39, 40
Moose Mane 39,40
Mosaic Bristles 64
Moser 104
Moser Color-it Pens 121
Motion 97
Mottled Wing Material 97
Mule Deer 40
Multi-Bobbin 125
Muskrat 32
Muskrat Dubbing 57
Mylar Cord Tubing 74, 89
Mystic Winging Fibre 97

Napthalene Crystals 135
Natural Fibre Dubbing Brushes 64
Nature's Spirit Dubbing 57
Neer Hair 97
New Dub 64
Northern Whitetail 40
Nutria 33

Nymph Glass 75
Nymph Hooks 142
Nymph Rib Glass 75
Nymph Rib 75
Nymph Rope 71,75
Nymph Wrap 75

Ocean Hair 97
Oliver Edwards' Sparkle Yarn 75
One-Minute Epoxy 116
Opal-Life Body Braid 89
Opossum: American 27; New Zealand 33
Optic Eyes 80
Optics 86-89, 110
Optima Nymphbody 75
Organza 97
Organza Wing Material 97
Orvis 104
Orvis Deepwater Eyes 80
Orvis High Gloss Head Cement 117
Orvis Pre-Painted Eyes 80
Orvis Vise Lamp 134
Orvis Quick-Sight Ant Bodies 84
Ostrich 18
Otter 33
Owl; Barn; Tawny 19

PAC 104
Paints 121
Pamola fly lathe 132
Pantone Pens 121
Pardo 12
Partridge: Brown; Chukar; Cinnamon;
  French (Red-legged); Grey; Hungarian;
  Japanese 19-20
Parrot 17, 20
Paxton's Buggy Nymph 57
Peacock 20: White 25
Peahen 20
Pearsall 104
Pearl Chenille 77
Pearlescent Sheet 68
Pearlescent Bead Chain 81

Pearlescent Tubing 89
Pearl Plastic Eyes 81
Pearl Shell-Back 68
Pearls 110
Peccary 33
Pelican 20
Pens 121
Perfect Cut Wings 93
Permabond Adhesive 117
Permatron 82
Permatron Dubbing 57
Peter Master's Dub 57
Pheasant: Argus; Blue-eared; Copper;
  Elliot's; Golden; Hardwick; Impeyan
  Monal; Lady Amherst; Manchurian; Red
  Tragoran; Melanistic; Metallic; Red;
  Red Temminks; Red Tragopan; Reeves;
  Ring-necked; Satyr Tragopan;
Shepsters;
  Silver, Yellow Golden 20-23.
Pig Bristles 33
Pipings 89-90
Plastic Bead Chain Eyes 81
Pliers 126
Plover, Golden 22
Plushille 82
Polar 27
Polar Aire 71, 97
Polar Bear Dubbing 57
Poly Chenille 77
Polycelon 85
Poly Flash 75, 90
Polyethylene foam 85
Polyfluff 97
Polygarn 98
Polyarn 83
Polywing 98
Polythene Buzzer Tubing 92
Polypropylene Yarn 83
Polystyrene Balls 85
Poly-Seal Sparkle Fibre 57
Poly II 57
Poly-Wiggle 57

Poly Yarn 83
Porcupine 33
Prairie Chicken 22
Prisma Color Pens 121
Prismatic Film Back 68
Prism Lite 88
Pseudo Seal 58
Pukeko 22
Pumice Stone 135

Quail 22
Quick Gel Super Glue 117-118
Quill Body 75

Rabbit, Crosscut 29, 33
Rabbit Haretron 58
Racoon 33
Raffia 68
Raffene 68
Rainy's No Dub 64
Rainy's Round Rubber Legs 85
Rainy's Sparkle Dub 58
Rayon Straw 68
Razzle-Dazzle 75
Real Eyes 81
Red Coachman Tinsel 91
Re-Flash Tubing 88
Reflecta Foil 75
Reflections 98
Reindeer 39, 40
Rhea 23
Ripple Flash 88
Roe Deer 39, 40
Rosella 23
Rotary Vice 130-131
Rubber Legs (Rubber Hackle) 85

Salmon and Steelhead Dubbing 58
Salmon, Seatrout and Steelhead Hooks
  144
Salmo-Web Dubbing 58
Saltwater Eyes 81
Saltwater Fly Hooks 145

Schlappen 23

Scintilla Caliente 59

Scintilla Dubbing 59

Scintilla Fly Buoy Body Foam 85

Scintilla Wing Film 98

Scintillator Bubbles 69

Scissors 127

Scotia Complete Tartan Dubbing 59

Scud Back 69

Sea Fibres 71, 98

Sea Flash 98-99

Seal 33

Seal-Ex 59

Seal's Fur 59

Sealtron Dubbing 60

Second Skin 90

Serrated Edge Shears 127

Shadow Boxes 135

Shannon's Fancy Hackle 49

Sheared Beaver 60

Sheep 33-34: Icelandic; Tiewell Mara
  Wool; Dall Sheep 33-34

Shimmer Bristles 64

Shimmer Skin 75

Shimazaki Air Thru Wing 99

Shimazaki Fly Wing 99

Silk Dubbing 60

Silicone 118

Sili Legs 85

Siman Products; Marabou; Crystal
  Antron; Squirrel Plus; Mohair; Mohair
  & Reflex; CDC Plus; Fine Mylar 64-65

Sitka Whitetail 41

Skunk 34

SLF Twists 65

Snipe 23

Solid Eyes 81

Soft Dubbing Brushes 64

Soft Wing 99

Spandex 76

Sparkle Chenille 77

Sparkle Wing 100

Sparkle Yarn 74, 83

Sparton 104

Speckled Chenille 78

Speckle-Flake 76

Spectrablend 60

Spectra-Flash 69

Spectra Hair 100

Spencer's Hackle 49

Spey Hackle 24

Spinner Glass 100

Spinner Tails 92

Spinning Loop Tool 124

Sponge Bodies 71

Spooled Materials 91

Squirrel 34; Grey 58

Squirrel Blends 60

Squirrel Brite 60

Squirrel Dubbing 60

Squizzers 127

Star Fire 60

Star Flash 89

Starling 24

Steelhead/Salmon Dubbing 60

Stick-on Eyes 81

Stick-on Prismatic Eyes 81

Stoat 35

Streamer and Long Shank Hooks 146

Streamer Hair 100

Suede Chenille 78

Superbug Yarn 75

Super Chenille 78

Super Hair 100

Super Fine Dry Fly Dubbing 60

Super Fine Dubbing 60

Super Floss 76

Super-Possum 60

Super Soft Web Hackle 24

Super Thin Tails 92

Suppliers: listed in text 149; other
  retailers 156

Supreme Hair 100

Sussex 104

Sussex Meta-Flash 100

Swan 24

Swannundaze 76
Swift 24
Swiss Straw 68
Syn-Sham 76
Synthetic Living Fibre 60-61, 100
Synthetic Living Fibre (SLF) 60-61; SLF
  Standard; SLF Finesse; SLF Master
  Class; Oliver Edward series; Davy
  Wotton series; SLF Hanks; SLF Midge,
  SLF Supreme; SLF Poul Jorgensen
  series 60-61
Sythrapol 120

Tag Hooks 148
Tails 91-92
Tanuki Tail 35
Tape Eyes 81
Teal 24
Tear-Drop Wing Material 100
Texas Whitetail 41
Threads, Tinsels & Flosses 103-114
Thompson 104
3-D Hologram Eyes 80
Tiewell 104
Tiewell Sparkle Flash 100
Tin Heads 70
Tinsel Chenille 78
Tiny Mohair Yarn 76
Tools 123-128
Tool Caddies 136
Tool Carousel 136
Toucan 24
Touch Dubbing 61
Trashabou 100
Travel Tying Kits 136
Travel Vice 132
Tube Vice 131
Tubings 92
Tuff-Film 118
Tungston Beads 70
Turkey 24-25; Oak, Mottled, Biots, Flats
  24-25
Tuscana Lamb 35

Tweezers 127
Twinkle 100
Twisted Threads 104
Twister Tails 92

Ultra Chenille 78
Ultra Deer Hair Dubbing 61
Ultra-Dub 61
Ultra Fine Easy Dub Microchenille 78
Ultra Hair 101
Ultra Lace Tubing 92
Umpqua Sparkle Blends Dubbing 62
Upstream Dubbings: Dry Fly, Caddis,
  Dubbing; Antron Fibre; Nymph,
  Big Bug 62-63
Under Body Foam 85
Uni-Products 104
Uni Wool Yarn 76
Uni-Yarn Mohair 65

Varnish Applicators 127
Varnishes 115-119
Velvet Tubing 90
Veniard 104
Veniard Dyes 120
Veniard Dubbing Brushes 65
Venpol 121
Vernille 78
Vernille Suede Chenille extra fine 78
Vices 129-132
V-Rib 76
Vinyl Rib 76
Vinyl Round Rib 76

Waddington Shanks 140
Waggle 192
Wallaby 35
Wapsi 104
Wapsi Celluloid Lacquer 118
Wasp Wing 101
Waterhen 18
Waterproof Marking Pens 121
Weasel 35

Weaver Bird 25
Wet Fly Hooks 148
Western Black-Tailed Mule Deer 41
Whip Finish Tool 128
Widgeon 25
Widow's Web 101
Wing Burners 128
Wing Cutters 128
Winging 101
Wings 93-101
Wing-It 101
Woodchuck 36
Woodcock 25
Wolverine 35
Woolly Bugger 56
Wrap-a-Dub 65, 91
Wyandotte Hen 25
Wyngs 101

Yak 36

Zap-A-Gap 118
Zing 101
Z-Lon 71, 83
Zonker Strips 36